Paradata

To make sense of data and use it effectively, it is essential to know where it comes from and how it has been processed and used. This is the domain of paradata, an emerging interdisciplinary field with wide applications. As digital data rapidly accumulates in repositories worldwide, this comprehensive introductory book, the first of its kind, shows how to make that data accessible and reusable.

In addition to covering basic concepts of paradata, the book supports practice with coverage of methods for generating, documenting, identifying and managing paradata, including formal metadata, narrative descriptions and qualitative and quantitative backtracking. The book also develops a unifying reference model to help readers contextualise the role of paradata within a wider system of knowledge, practices and processes, and provides a vision for the future of the field.

This guide to general principles and practice is ideal for researchers, students and data managers.

This title is also available as Open Access on Cambridge Core.

ISTO HUVILA is Professor in Information Studies at the Department of ALM at Uppsala University.

LISA ANDERSSON is a researcher at the Department of ALM at Uppsala University.

ZANNA FRIBERG is a PhD candidate in Information Studies at the Department of ALM at Uppsala University.

YING-HSANG LIU is a researcher at the Department of ALM at Uppsala University.

OLLE SKÖLD is Senior Lecturer at the Department of ALM and the director of the Master's Programme in Digital Humanities at Uppsala University.

Paradata

Documenting Data Creation, Curation and Use

ISTO HUVILA

LISA ANDERSSON

ZANNA FRIBERG

YING-HSANG LIU

OLLE SKÖLD

CAMBRIDGE UNIVERSITY PRESS

Shaftesbury Road, Cambridge CB2 8EA, United Kingdom

One Liberty Plaza, 20th Floor, New York, NY 10006, USA

477 Williamstown Road, Port Melbourne, VIC 3207, Australia

314–321, 3rd Floor, Plot 3, Splendor Forum, Jasola District Centre, New Delhi – 110025, India

103 Penang Road, #05-06/07, Visioncrest Commercial, Singapore 238467

Cambridge University Press is part of Cambridge University Press & Assessment,
a department of the University of Cambridge.

We share the University's mission to contribute to society through the pursuit of
education, learning and research at the highest international levels of excellence.

www.cambridge.org
Information on this title: www.cambridge.org/9781009366588

DOI: 10.1017/9781009366564

First published 2025

Cover image: MediaNews Group/Reading Eagle via Getty Images / Contributor

A catalogue record for this publication is available from the British Library

*A Cataloging-in-Publication data record for this book is available from the Library of
Congress*

ISBN 978-1-009-36658-8 Hardback
ISBN 978-1-009-36661-8 Paperback

Contents

Contents

Preface

The story of this book goes back either a couple of years, half a decade or a quarter of a century depending on where the starting point of this particular process is set. The bulk of the text was written in 2023 and during the first half of 2024. The preparations for writing started sometime in 2021 or 2022, when the book proposal was submitted or accepted. Another reasonable point of time could be the time when Isto started drafting a research proposal for the European Research Council in 2017, or a few years earlier when the question of paradata – to put it simply, information on diverse practices and processes – started to reemerge in previous projects as a crucial question in archaeologists' information work. Going back in time, yet another starting point could be the time when Isto's interest in studying the documentation of archaeological 3D visualisations started in the late 1990s, a process that is partly documented and reported in his doctoral thesis from 2006. Some of the work in the middle can be found in the list of references of this volume and the lists of references of the cited references. At the same time, this volume is also a collaborative effort that builds in different ways on the studies we have done and the lengthy discussions we have had on the nature and practice of paradata since mid-2019.

You might wonder why we go into this much detail in outlining where this particular book process started. It is after all conventional in a preface to set a starting point whether it is the somehow real starting point or something that is convenient to mark as the beginning of a believable origin story without turning it into a research problem. For our book, however, this is important as it is what this volume and our work in the CApturing Paradata for documenTing data creation and Use for the REsearch of the future (CAPTURE) project between 2019 and 2024 has been all about: to understand how processes and practices are understood, described and documented, and preserved.

Tracking the process (or practice – depending on perspective and theoretical framing) of writing this book provides an illustrative example of how difficult it can be to figure out when a process starts and ends not to mention how to trace them back in time and how to document them in such detail that is useful and makes sense for future use. However, it is also fair to note that even if writing this book was far from straightforward, it is not exemplary of a spectacularly complicated undertaking. The practices and processes we have been investigating in the CAPTURE project that this book builds on, have been often much more convoluted in terms of how they unfold, and how many actors, material and conceptual things are engaged.

In spite of the diversity of their nature, scale and complexity, a common denominator for both writing this book and the instances of data work we have studied as a part of our empirical work is that understanding practices and processes matters when trying to make sense and utilise their outputs and underpinnings. Paradata obviously plays a key role in conveying such an understanding. However, similarly to the practices and processes themselves, the paradata itself is complex and diverse, multimodal, deeply ingrained and relational to practices and processes and their constituting elements. The cover of the book is here to remind us of how it is itself a part of what it conveys. Without being able to identify, keep and convey relevant paradata – in all of its complexity, which we venture to exemplify in this volume – there would hardly be any use or reuse of data or, for that matter, anything that comes out of it.

Acknowledgements

Like all books, this volume on paradata is a group effort. All of the chapter authors have been working in the CApturing Paradata for documenTing data creation and Use for the REsearch of the future (CAPTURE) research project, which has provided a productive, intellectually inspiring and thoroughly enjoyable environment for our work. Even those of our colleagues who have not participated in the writing of the chapters have not escaped discussions on the book and its different chapters. We are all grateful, for productive discussions on paradata, feedback and insights during the process, to Stefan Ekman, Amalia Juneström, Jessica Kaiser and Michael Olsson. Michael also undertook the daunting task of acting as a commentator of an almost final manuscript providing relentless critique and suggestions for improving both the context and language throughout the manuscript. We also thank Dr Maureen Henninger for helpful comments on Chapter 4. We further thank the advisory board of the project, Costis Dallas, Melanie Feinberg, Jeremy Huggett, Eric Kansa, Costas Papadopoulos and Sally Wyatt, for enlightening and intellectually rewarding discussions on paradata, documentation and 'things appropriable as informative' of practices and processes. In particular, the development of the theory of paradata and framing its contexts outside of the domain of archaeology have also benefited from the work of the paradata working group of the InterPARES Trust AI working group under the firm and friendly leadership of Professor Emerita Patricia Franks. Finally, even though we are unable to list everyone, we are also grateful to all the colleagues who have presented at CAPTURE Talks, our online and onsite seminars, workshops and panel discussions, listened and commented on our work so far, and engaged in lively discussions on practice and process documentation, and paradata. All of these longer and shorter exchanges of ideas have had an impact on our thinking and writing.

This volume is part of a project that has received funding from the European Research Council (ERC) under the European Union's Horizon 2020 research and innovation programme (Grant agreement No. 818210) for the research project CApturing Paradata for documenTing data creation and Use for the REsearch of the future (CAPTURE).

1

Introduction

Paradata – Documenting Data Creation,
Management and Use

Isto Huvila

1.1 Introduction

The datafication of social life and economy dominates the contemporary experience. It has been claimed, not without reason, to concern 'everything' from the personal self to working life, freetime, scientific and scholarly knowledge-making and civic life (Mascheroni 2020; Millington and Millington 2015). Similarly it has been portrayed both as an opportunity (Mayer-Schönberger et al. 2013) and a potential threat underpinned by a particular ideology that Van Dijck (2014) aptly terms dataism. Data is to an increasing extent used both as a substitute and augmentation of physical things when making decisions and creating new knowledge. Even if repeatedly criticised, more data is routinely equated with better. As a consequence, the quantity of data in circulation has burgeoned and the demands to extract more value out of data through effective reuse have increased. For many, data has become a commodity and resource beyond anything else. Its potential to contribute to economic gain, cementing political power, is difficult to underestimate.

Symptomatic of the surge of data and dataism in contemporary existence, there is no one generally accepted definition of what it entails. The observation that a major obstacle to research data management is the multiplicity of understandings of what counts as 'data' is illustrative of the difficulty in finding a consensus. Data can be many things. In this volume that delves into data and its practical underpinnings, our working definition is purposefully broad. For us, data is all kinds of material – or colloquially, 'the stuff' – used in knowledge production. Different scientific and scholarly disciplines and practical everyday contexts understand it often in more specific, both implicit and explicit, terms. The purpose of our working definition is to be inclusive of them all.

The rapidly growing reliance on data across society has made it increasingly apparent that just having data or information might not be enough to manage or utilise it. Data can neither be trusted by default nor is it intelligible in and of itself. Even if there are tendencies to frame data as raw, there is nothing raw or neutral about it. Making sense of data, and making it useful and manageable, requires understanding of what the data is all about. Otherwise the vast repositories of data become, as Parisi (2021) fears, a 'purposeless purpose' of the colossal enterprise of contemporary data making. In addition to knowing what data is *about*, it is equally vital to know where it comes from and how it has been processed, manipulated and used. The importance of understanding data-related practices and processes for successful data management and reuse has propelled researchers and professionals in different disciplines across science and scholarship from information and computer sciences to knowledge management and organisational learning to inquire into how to describe, document and communicate processes of how data – and in relation to data, information and knowledge – have come about and been processed, managed and used (e.g., Amairia 2023; Edwards et al. 2017; Faniel et al. 2019). As Barrowman argues, 'the very production of data is . . . always relevant to its interpretation' (Barrowman 2018 p. 133). Understanding how data is produced and reproduced in different phases of its lifespan is crucial for its reuse independent of the purpose of using data to create new knowledge, reproduce and validate earlier knowledge-making efforts, or to create trust. In parallel to developing a comprehensive understanding of data-related practices and processes and practical means to document and describe them for conveying the understanding to others, there is a critical need for theorising the phenomenon, for empirical research, identifying existing and forming of new methods and tools, technologies and infrastructures, standards and practices, and for developing novel concepts on practice and process information.

Paradata, one of the key concepts used to describe information about practices and processes, surfaced independently in multiple disciplinary contexts (Davet et al. 2023; Edwards et al. 2017; Huvila 2022a; Sköld et al. 2022). The aim of this book is to provide a first comprehensive overview of the concept and phenomenon of paradata from data management and knowledge organisation perspectives and an introduction to its practical and theoretical implications for research and practice.

The volume introduces the notion of paradata, how and why it can be a useful concept to consider and use to describe data about data creation, curation and use. It also expands the conceptual discussion to inquire into practical aspects of how better understanding of the practices and processes creation, management and use of data can contribute to knowledge creation and data, information and knowledge management within and across disciplines to support data sharing and (re)use, and understanding of data practices and their consequences and implications. To support paradata practice, the volume also provides an overview of a selection of methods for capturing and documenting, for managing, and for extracting and employing paradata for data creators and (re)users, and data managers. Finally, the volume develops and synthesises the current state of the art of theory and practice in a paradata reference model to inform understanding of the paradata phenomenon and outlines directions for future research and practice in paradata, and future empirical research into scientific and scholarly information work.

The principal focus of our exposé is on research-related paradata, that is, paradata that is generated and/or used in research. Our understanding of research is broad and goes beyond academic knowledge-making covering corresponding professional and non-academic practices (Börjesson and Huvila 2019). However, even if our main interest is research, many of the insights in what paradata can be and how it works are relevant in a much broader array of contexts that operate with diverse types of data. Especially in a theoretical sense, their ambition and pertinence extends even beyond data to how paradata as a concept and lens can contribute to understanding the workings of knowledge extracted from and incorporated in practices and processes.

To exemplify the importance of understanding data-related practices and processes, consider having a simple spreadsheet filled with several thousands of rows of numbers (Figure 1.1). They are all decimals and a closer look reveals that they vary between 1.3 and 4.43. The filename SmithJ_appendix3 might suggest that they form an appendix to something, and someone called J. Smith had something to do with either the appendix or main product. However, this does not get you very far. Having descriptive metadata that explains that the file contains measurements of the volume of pottery vessels in litres helps a little and knowing what types of vessels and where they were found might help you a lot more. But without paradata including, for instance, explanation of how the volume was measured, whether the vessels were (unlikely) whole or if the measurements were done on the basis of retrieved or preserved sherds, how experienced the measurer was, and how carefully and for what purpose the measurements were taken, the spreadsheet or 'dataset', might not be that useful at all. In the worst and not especially hypothetical case, to have a (re)usable dataset, it might be necessary to try to find the original pottery vessels if they still exist, and measure them again using a

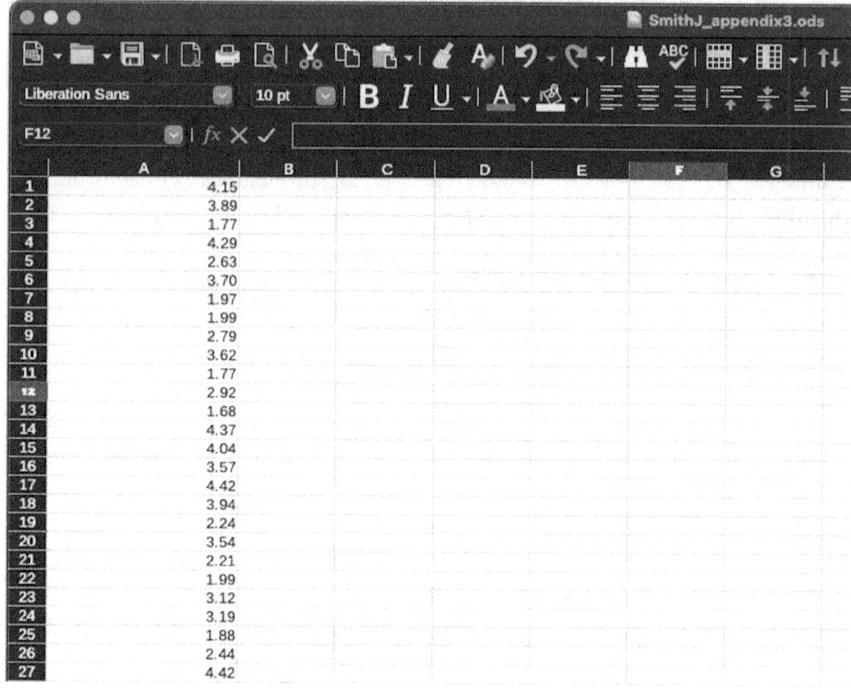

Figure 1.1 A spreadsheet with little explicit paradata.

method and level of accuracy adequate for the purpose. Remaking data takes a lot of time and effort. When this endeavour is multiplied with the escalating number of datasets and other potentially (re)usable assets produced and preserved in the contemporary datafied world, it becomes untenable.

1.2 The Concept of Paradata

As per defining paradata, we start with a working definition of paradata as information about the practices and processes of data making, management and use. It is worth noting that the definition is broader than the first conceptualisation of paradata in survey research that focused on automatically generated metainformation (Couper 1998, 2017) and even broader than such later definitions that have focused on decisions rather than practices and processes relating to data generation as a whole (Rabinowitz 2019). We distinguish information and data from knowledge in an analytical sense as its building blocks, respectively as matters used to inform (information) and typically construct information (data), while referring to knowledge as being held by human-beings. However, unlike the popular data-information-knowledge-wisdom pyramid, we are not suggesting that information or knowledge would be directly reducible to data (or paradata) (cf. Fricke 2009; Huvila 2022b). By referring to making, management and use this volume aims to capture the full temporal and contextual continuum of data incorporating all types of moves, makings and changes data might end up facing.

Before proceeding to Chapter 2 with a comprehensive overview of paradata and central related concepts, it is useful to point out that neither previous perspectives on paradata nor the one offered in this volume are singular. Rather than trying to force paradata into one form, we have focused on identifying what different things function as paradata, how they do so and when. Paradata from a standards or systems perspective differs from a policy or principle-driven data management perspective. Also, the theorising of data making, management and use has an impact on what makes paradata and when. Paradata on a practice – as conceptualised from the perspective of practice theory – is not necessarily the same as paradata would be for someone approaching it from the perspective of activity theory. To emphasise that paradata is an applicable term across multiple conceptual framings of data-related doings, we write about information relating to data making, management and use the (admittedly somewhat clumsy) notion of 'practices and processes' instead of only one term. We do this in an attempt to capture two of the most prominent conceptualisations used in the literature, namely data practices and processes. Even more importantly, we do this to underline how paradata has relevance across the entire conceptual landscape.

1.3 Perspectives on Paradata

In parallel to approaching paradata as an a priori multifaceted concept, this volume also combines several analytical perspectives. The overall perspective is ours, that is, of the group of authors with background in a spectrum of scholarly disciplines, from information and archival studies to archaeology and cultural research, with an interest in understanding paradata from an information perspective as a form of information relating to informational doings. Paradata is approached from a knowledge organisation perspective as a means for 'describing, representing, filing and organizing documents, document representations, subjects and concepts both by humans and by computer programs' (Hjørland 2016 p. 475). As a form of information on making, managing and using data, paradata unfolds from the perspective of information behaviour research (Bates 2015) as a referent to (informational) undertakings. This opens up to an inquiry on what paradata is and should be about (Chapter 2), and how paradata is dealt with in different contexts and situations (Chapters 3, 4, 5). We are also interested, from an information retrieval perspective, in how paradata ultimately makes data creation, management and use processes more accessible and intelligible (Chapter 7). From an archival studies viewpoint, we discuss the longevity and preservation of paradata for use and re-use not only in the present but in the near and long-term future (Chapter 6; Edquist 2014). Finally, a fifth complementary perspective draws from professional and personal (research) data management and its interest in storing and managing data for use and re-use as an asset in research and work practices (Chapters 6, 7, 8).

The background of this volume is the research project (funded by the European Research Council) CApturing Paradata for documenTing data creation and Use for the REsearch of the future (CAPTURE). The empirical focus of the project has been archaeology, chosen as an appropriate multi-disciplinary context with a plethora of parallel epistemic perspectives and knowledge interests and where utilising diverse and fragmented data is a commonplace. This focus, even if the curiosity of CAPTURE was not limited to archaeology and archaeological paradata alone, explains why also this volume contains multiple examples from that domain, however, together with others from a wide range of scientific, scholarly and professional contexts from archives, records and knowledge management to survey research and public administration.

We have endeavoured to make this work relevant for both researchers and practitioners across scholarly and professional disciplines: from researchers of paradata to those interested in documenting their data, making sense of others' data, developers of data management systems, data managers, experts and learners alike. However, while venturing in this direction, it is important to acknowledge that the differences in the perspectives of those who work with paradata are not merely a matter of adapting the tone of writing. The baseline we have been confronted with throughout this volume is that the perspectives of data creators, users and managers are not necessarily reconcilable. Borgman (2016) pointed to this direction in her 'Not fade away' paper referring to three perspectives with mutually competing ideals of research data reuse. A social scientist emphasises innovation and novel findings. A data librarian is concerned with optimising the production of well-documented reusable data. At the same time, a policymaker is concerned with timely release of traceable and discoverable datasets for other actors to use for societal benefit. The incompatibility of ideals means in practice that when pondering what is preferable, good or bad, throughout the following chapters, there is always more than one perspective to consider and a fair chance that, for example, pursuing for manageability or timeliness narrows the usability of data for truly novel discoveries but also that prioritising comprehensive documentation takes time and resources perhaps beyond what is reasonable.

The practical interest in paradata does apparently also vary from the context and field of data practices and processes to another. Paradata has obvious resonance in explicitly data intensive research and work from sciences and technology to medicine and humanities, big data, and even more so in disciplines like data science and digital humanities and social sciences with an episteme that forthrightly builds on 'data'. However, with an intentionally broad take on paradata, the relevance of this book and paradata extends to fields where data is conventionally conceptualised as, for example, material, sources, evidence or documents.

1.4 How to Read This Book

We address different target groups in the different chapters. Some chapters are specifically targeted towards repository managers (Chapter 6), others data creators (Chapter 4), data reusers (Chapter 5), researchers interested in para-data theory (Chapter 2) and practice (Chapter 3). For this reason, the chapters differ in character and style but are hopefully readable both individually or as a part of the book-long narrative.

After this introduction, Chapter 2 provides an overview of the concept of paradata and selected related concepts as discussed in the existing research literature. It delves into the complexity and diversity of the notion to show its broad applicability in both research and practice. Chapter 3 continues to explore the manifestations of paradata by providing an overview of where it can be found. The chapter draws from empirical research conducted in the CAPTURE project focusing on archaeological documentation but also makes ample reference to other disciplinary contexts to exemplify how paradata can be context-specific but also how there can be structures that are technically and epistemically pervasive across domains. Such archetypes function as markers and help to identify commonplace documentation types and 'genres' of how paradata is recorded and embedded in data and data documentation.

In comparison to the beginning of the volume, Chapters 4 to 6 focus on providing practical and conceptual advice for readers considering how to tackle paradata in their work. Chapter 4 showcases a set of methods and approaches for researchers and other data makers on how to plan for creating and capturing paradata in advance before data making takes place and how to generate and document paradata when datasets are in the making. Chapter 5 presents a similar selection of methods for data reusers, which can be used for finding and identifying implicit and explicit paradata in already existing datasets and data documentation where such information is not necessarily clearly marked as being paradata. In Chapter 6, the focus is on data managers. Rather than presenting a comparable set of methods to Chapters 4 and 5, it sets forth a framework of strategies for managing paradata on a scale from standardised, structured descriptors to material with varying degrees of potential to inform users of data-related practices and processes.

The final two chapters of this volume embark on comprehensive theorisation and reflection of what paradata is and how it works. Chapter 7 presents a paradata reference model with an aim of providing a framework for conceptualising paradata and how it links to practices and processes, and the human working knowledge used to engage with them. Rather than providing an objectivist account of paradata as a thing, the model emphasises the processual nature of paradata as being made and being in the making on a continuum of data being constantly produced and reproduced. At the closing of the volume, Chapter 8 discusses the premise of making paradata matter, paths for future research, and emphasises the need for ethical commitment when pursuing the documentation of data making.

1.5 Conclusion: Paradata Matters

As a final introductory note, it is fair to disclose already at the outset that the general premise of this volume is that paradata matters. Put simply, we posit that without paradata it is questionable if there can be meaningful data reuse. Having said that, we also want to underline at the very beginning that paradata takes many forms that are difficult to find and identify. Also, as the following chapters demonstrate, people still do a lot without knowing what 'needs' to be known, circumventing paradata, and without knowing what they know that they 'need' to know. People also adapt their data reuse to what is possible, changing their behaviour to match what they find doable with the available paradata. Paradata is also quite obviously difficult. Paradata, the work required to make paradata and to make it useful is a part of the invisible work of rendering (Ellingsen and Monteiro 2003) that often remains under the radar and is genuinely demanding to support. What this implies though is not that paradata does not matter but rather that its complexity makes it both challenging and crucial to understand.

References

Amairia, A. (2023). De la donnée à la connaissance, de l'intelligibilité à l'action [From data to knowledge, from intelligibility to action]. *Communication & Organisation*, **64**(2), 147–160.

Barrowman, N. (2018). Why data is never raw. *The New Atlantis*, (56), 129–135.

Bates, M. J. (2015). Information behavior. In *Encyclopedia of Library and Information Sciences, 3rd ed.*, CRC Press.

Borgman, C. L. (2016). Not Fade Away: Social Science Research Data in the Digital Era, Presented at the Knowledge Rules: Curating Knowledge in the Social SciencesSocial Sciences Research Council Meeting, 2 May 2016, New York Public Library, New York. Retrieved from https://escholarship.org/uc/item/3ps9p9rc

Börjesson, L. and Huvila, I. (2019). Introduction. In Börjesson L. and Huvila, I. (eds.), *Research outside the Academy: Professional Knowledge-Making in the Digital Age*, Cham: Springer International Publishing, 1–19.

Couper, M. (1998). Measuring survey quality in a CASIC environment. In *Proceedings of the section on survey research methods of the American Statistical Association*.

Couper, M. (2017). Para deta gainen no tanjo to fukyu / Birth and diffusion of the concept of paradata. *Shakai To Chosa (Advances in Social Research)*, **18**, 14–26.

Davet, J., Hamidzadeh, B. and Franks, P. (2023). Archivist in the machine: Paradata for AI-based automation in the archives. *Archival Science*, **23**(2), 275–295.

Edwards, R., Goodwin, J., O'Connor, H. and Phoenix, A. (2017). *Working with Paradata, Marginalia and Fieldnotes*, Cheltenham: Edward Elgar.

Faniel, I. M., Frank, R. D. and Yakel, E. (2019). Context from the data reuser's point of view. *Journal of Documentation*, **75**(6), 1274–1297.

Fricke, M. (2009). The knowledge pyramid: A critique of the DIKW hierarchy. *Journal of Information Science*, **35**(2), 131–142.

Hjørland, B. (2016). Knowledge organization (KO). *Knowledge Organization*, **43**(4), 475–484.

Huvila, I. (2022a). Improving the usefulness of research data with better paradata. *Open Information Science*, **6**(1), 28–48.

Huvila, I. (2022b). Making and taking information. *JASIST*, **73**(4), 528–541.

Mascheroni, G. (2020). Datafied childhoods: Contextualising datafication in everyday life. *Current Sociology*, **68**(6), 798–813.

Mayer-Schönberger, V. and Cukier, K. (2013). *Big Data: A Revolution That Will Transform How We Live, Work and Think*, London: John Murray.

Millington, B. and Millington, R. (2015). 'The datafication of everything': Toward a sociology of sport and big data. *Sociology of Sport Journal*, **32**(2), 140–160.

Parisi, L. (2021). Instrumentality. In Thylstrup, N. B. Agostinho, D. Ring, A. D'Ignazio, C. and Veel, K. (eds.), *Uncertain Archives: Critical Keywords for Big Data*, Cambridge, MA: MIT Press, 289–298.

Rabinowitz, A. (2019). Communicating in three dimensions: Questions of audience and reuse in 3D excavation documentation practice. *Studies in Digital Heritage*, **3**(1), 100–116.

Sköld, O., Börjesson, L. and Huvila, I. (2022). Interrogating paradata. *Information Research*, **27**(special issue). https://urn.kb.se/resolve?urn = urn:nbn:se:uu:diva-490374

Van Dijck, J. (2014). Datafication, dataism and dataveillance: Big data between scientific paradigm and ideology. *Surveillance & Society*, **12**(2), 197–208.

2

The Concept of Paradata

Olle Sköld

2.1 Introduction

Paradata belongs to a family of concepts – together with, for example, meta-data and provenance data – that in different ways express the characteristics of, and the relationships between, forms of information and information about them. Metadata is a term that is often used to denote the informational hierarchy of more complex forms of information (books, journals, datasets) and higher-level or more general descriptions thereof (titles, creators, file formats) (Mayernik, 2020). Paradata, drawing on the provisional definition provided in Chapter 1, is information describing the practices and processes involved in how forms of information are created, curated and used. This very wide characterisation branches in multiple directions and can serve to illustrate some of the complexity appended to the concept of paradata and how it has been put to work in multiple domains of research and in service of a broad range of objectives.

Paradata is at its core information that tells the user about how and possibly why something, or a facet of something, emerges in the way that they do (Andersson et al., 2025; Sköld et al., 2022). This 'something' becoming paradata might offer information about a great many things, but is commonly made by humans, machines or humans and machines together. Paradata can be information about how data and datasets were collected or aggregated (Börjesson et al., 2022a), how a method of analysis was put to use (Huvila et al., 2021b), or the automatically recorded information describing how a piece of equipment carried out its task – like the digital camera embedding camera settings and image metrics in photographs (Kreuter, 2013) or evidence of AI processes (Franks, 2024). In addition to techniques of creation and use, paradata can explicate underpinning intellectual processes (choices, deliberations, interpretations) and horizons (disciplinary perspectives and approaches, theoretical resources) (Bentkowska-Kafel et al., 2012; Huvila and Sköld, 2021). Paradata also, as stressed by InterPARES Trust AI's (forthcoming; cf. Chapter 3 of this volume and Franks, 2024) definition of the term, crucially involves information about the persons involved in the documented data procedures and not only the procedures themselves. There is no specific informational scope associated with paradata, rather paradata can offer either comprehensive and full-range information about the events and processes and shape forms of information, or reflect the same chain of happenings in an incomplete and fragmentary manner (Geiger and Ribes, 2011; Huvila et al., 2023). There is little consensus regarding how to object-agnostically describe paradata. Connecting to the same core theme of paradata being about the factors impacting the creation or re-fashioning of the things being created or re-fashioned, paradata is differently construed to be information about 'processes' (Couper, 2000), 'practices' (Huvila et al., 2021a), 'behaviours' (Stieger and Reips, 2010) 'events' (Sendelbah et al., 2016), 'provenance' (Dahlström and Hansson, 2019), 'traces' (Huvila et al., 2023) or other expressions of chained and to some extent coordinated action (see e.g., Huvila and Sköld, 2021; Rösch, 2021).

The users and uses of the concept of paradata are just as intricate as its empirical characteristics and frameworks. The notion of paradata is present in many fields of research, including extensive use in survey research, archaeology, heritage research, and information studies. In these fields, paradata has garnered both academic and professional interest by parties invested in how paradata can be used, how it can be created and how it can be curated and theorised. In relation to paradata making, it has been suggested that paradata can be captured by structured approaches like workflows and conceptual models (Börjesson et al., 2020; Post and Chassanoff, 2021; Siqueira and Martins, 2022), reflective journals and other narrative means of documentation (Matei and Hunter, 2021; Phillips and Smit, 2021), and video- and photo documentation (Chrysanthi et al., 2016). Paradata use by reading, following or otherwise tracing paradata is seen to facilitate a range of ends all differently connected to paradata being informative about processes that shape scholarly outputs – data, visualisations, conclusions etc. (e.g., Arshia et al., 2021; Fear and Donaldson, 2012). Paradata can, for instance, push algorithmic accountability by facilitating the tracking of operations (Cameron et al., 2023; Davet et al., 2023). It can also be used as an explorative device in grasping how and where provenance is recorded in archival holdings, and how it can be mobilised to underpin archival credibility and trustworthiness (Andresen, 2020). A key paradata use case is cross-stakeholder data reuse, where paradata can be seen to be a part of the core resources required to enable shared research data to be purposefully put to work in support of research tasks other than those originally intended when the data was collected or created by allowing insight into how the data came into being, how it has been processed, and used (Borgman, 2012; Faniel and Yakel, 2017).

This chapter seeks to delve into the concept of paradata and to offer the tools required to link paradata's notable complexity to broad usefulness. As illustrated, paradata can be used as a conceptual explorative device to interrogate how activities of the past intersect with present ends and means via modes of documentation and recording across a wide variety of settings (Reilly et al., 2021; Sköld et al., 2022). Paradata can also be used to refer to specific types of data that can be collected or consulted to find information about processes of becoming (cf. Chapter 3), and to denote corresponding methods of (para)data collection and use. Following Moore's (2004) call to investigate scholarly concepts by approaching them in both theory and academic practice, the present chapter will consider the conceptual dimensions of paradata alongside its prominent empirical examples and scenarios of application. In doing so the chapter will provide the groundwork for subsequent exploration in this volume of how paradata can be be found and harnessed in research documentation (Chapter 3), in methods for documenting and generating (Chapter 4) and identifying (Chapter 5) paradata, and approaches to managing paradata in data repository contexts (Chapter 6). The review of paradata will be done by first investigating the etymology of the concept. Then, paradata definitions in survey research, archaeology and heritage visualisation research will be reviewed. Subsequently, the chapter will move on to discuss metadata and provenance data, two key related terms that will be used to discuss and further interrogate the concept of paradata. The chapter concludes with a discussion of the concept of paradata drawing on the different strands of analysis and exploration previously presented.

2.2 The Etymology of Paradata

The building blocks of the composite term paradata are *para-* and *-data*. Delving into the etymology of these component words specifically as they pertain to scholarship and research settings, it can be observed that *data* is derived from the Latin word with the same spelling (plural of *datum*) signifying '(thing[s]) given' (Online Etymology Dictionary, 2024, no pagination). The classical use of *data* denotes a premise of mathematical calculations

(Online Etymology Dictionary, 2024). Current and colloquial uses of the term include data being a collection, thematisation, or grouping of qualitative or quantitative information (or datum) often in the framework of science, computing and epistemology (Oxford English Dictionary, 2024). While seeing widespread use in scholarship and ancillary fields as a prefix to designate a broad range of activities, skill sets, tools and platforms as having to do with data (data management, data literacy, data repositories), it is difficult to precisely define data because of its epistemic variability (Borgman, 2012; Gitelman, 2013). As shown in Chapter 3, where contextual and practice-led approaches to understanding and identifying data and paradata are discussed and put to work, it can be argued that data is something that ultimately emerges (differently) depending on for what purposes it is being sought and by what methods it is being read, created or curated. Chapter 3 also follows Hjørland (2018) in operationalising recorded data, that is, data manifested in such a way that it can be interacted with, as documents and documentation – for instance: datasets, scholarly papers and monographs, notes and correspondence.

Like 'data-', *para-* is a prefix that sees considerable academic and, to some extent, everyday use. The *para-* prefix has both Latin and Greek roots and its significance varies depending on which origin is being considered. Words like parachute and parasol stem from the Latin prefix meaning 'defense, protection against; that which protects from' (Online Etymology Dictionary, 2023). The *para-* prefix in 'paradata' however relates more closely to the Greek provenance, where it designates 'alongside' and 'beyond' as also seen in the concept of 'paratext' (Genette and Maclean, 1991). The prefix has an array of other meanings in Greek (cf. Online Etymology Dictionary, 2023), which might be a part of the explanation of its wide and varied use in English. The Oxford English Dictionary (2023) notes that the most general application of *para-* is to form terms that are closely related to but distinct from the root word. More specific applications exist in biology and the medical sciences, where the prefix is used to express co-location, proximity, and dysfunction. The use of *para-* to form words and terms in chemistry, which has been said to stem from Berzelius' work in the 1830s (Crosland, 1962 as cited in Oxford English Dictionary, 2023), is notably close to what is manifested in paradata: There, *para-* denotes substances that are varieties or modifications of the root substance and, for paradata most importantly, substances that have been produced or occur alongside the root substance (Oxford English Dictionary, 2023; cf. 'para-archives' in Wall and Hale, 2021). This highlights a discussion continued in Chapters 3, 6, and 7 relating to paradata making: Paradata emerges in related but varied ways – before (prospective paradata), during (in situ paradata) or after (retrospective paradata) – to the enactment or creation of the data, process or practice that the paradata informs about. It is also interesting to note that Efthymiou et al. (2015) stress that the meaning of *para-* in present-day Greek, beyond locational and non-evaluative significances (including resemblances and parallelity), also has a presence in the semantic space of evaluation of divergences and errors. This use of the *para-* prefix corresponds to a certain segment of paradata scholarship use cases, most notably those in survey research (see e.g., Kreuter, 2013, Nicolaas, 2011, and below).

Although the etymology of paradata and its component words is many times more complex than is expressed here, it is possible to note that the *data-* component can be considered to determine its basic significance of the term: Paradata is, crucially, anchored in the semantic space of data and data-related phenomena even though it may vary quite considerably across settings of use what this data is and how it is manifested. The prefix *para-* on the other hand is possibly the main operational force of the two composite parts of the concept of paradata, expressing that paradata is data that has a close relationship to another set of data in the sense of having epistemological utility, but existing beyond and in parallel to it.

2.3 Paradata Definitions

As shown in the beginning of this chapter, paradata is a concept that has seen diverse uses in a broad range of tasks, settings and disciplines; from research to data management and data theorising. Even though paradata might not have received as much attention in theoretical and empirical research as, for example, data and metadata, there have been far-reaching attempts to define paradata in several of the research studies preceding this volume (see e.g., Börjesson et al., 2020; Huvila et al., 2022; Sköld et al., 2022), especially in survey research, archaeology, and heritage visualisation research. These research areas are linked in being interdisciplinary and by their relatively long and established use of the concept of paradata, but they are also distinct in many ways. Survey research and heritage visualisation research can be characterised by being focused on the development, application and interpretation of the range of methods that are the focus of the research area – for instance, photogrammetry and other techniques to build visualisations (3D models, maps) on the basis of heritage and archaeological data (e.g., Niccolucci et al., 2013), and different kinds of survey methodologies (e.g., Edwards et al., 2017; Kreuter, 2013). Archaeology is an academic discipline with a long history that is hallmarked by a diverse array of sub-disciplines where data types, methods of data collection, and modes of work and epistemic horizons, including data curation and use, vary to a notable degree (Huvila, 2014; Khazraee, 2019). Descriptions of data-related practices and processes have been produced in survey research, archaeology, and heritage visualisation research using many other terms (see e.g., Huvila et al., 2021a) than paradata and since before the notion emerged. The review of paradata below, however, is based on literature that employs precisely the 'paradata' concept.

2.3.1 Paradata in Survey Research

There are indications that the earliest academic use of the concept of paradata took place in survey research, although the roots of the concept and particularly the data frame of mind it encapsulates are unclear – see for instance Huvila (2012) referencing Adkins and Adkins (1989) as an early example of paradata-related discussions of how to record past data processes in analogue settings. While Lyberg (2009) has traced the origins of the term paradata even further back to the 1920s, studies that seek to find a core paradata definition commonly reference two papers by Couper from the turn of the millennium (Couper, 1998 and 2000, the former as cited in Kreuter and Casas-Cordero, 2010). Working with the issue of how to improve the usability of computer-assisted survey methods, Couper defines paradata as 'auxiliary data describing the [survey] process' (Couper, 2000, p. 393). Paradata here is described as data that can provide insight into the work of enacting surveys, manifesting for instance in (para)data telling about the survey procedure (the no. of interviewer calls per response, response rates, keystroke logs showing how the interviewer managed the survey system) and the survey results (e.g., interview length per average). Couper (2000) also suggests that useful paradata can trace data from web surveys that would allow evaluation of different parameters that together show how the respondents interacted with the survey website or tool.

Couper's conceptualisation of paradata has seen widespread use both in survey research (e.g., Nicolaas, 2011; Olson, 2013) and in other domains (e.g., Huvila et al., 2021a; Reilly et al., 2021), and it has three key characteristics that are recurrent in a large portion of academic paradata use cases. One such characteristic is that paradata has an 'auxiliary' or supporting role in relation to another dataset that is the principal outcome of the practices or processes described by the paradata, like the survey results in Couper (2000). Another characteristic is that paradata is quite intimately tied to the wide-ranging documentation affordances of technology, where large amounts of data of different granularities can be recorded that describes system interactions almost in parallel to the interactions taking place. A third characteristic is the multimodal temporality of paradata. Paradata is directed towards the past in the sense that it informs about past events and processes. Paradata is, however, also tied to the present and future in its strong utilitarian connotations – paradata is sought because it informs about past events and processes in a way that facilitates present or future actions, evaluations or interpretations in connection to the main product or principal outcome that the paradata describes.

Subsequent survey methodology research has continued to develop the concept of paradata and associated methodologies in several directions, emphasising different facets of the concept and its applications and uses (Nicolaas, 2011). One significant development is that paradata began to shift into something not solely a 'by-product' (Kreuter and Casas-Cordero, 2010, p. 2) of the survey process recorded by the survey software, but also as a type of data collected using multiple means in service of a broader range of goals and intentions. Beyond offering information about the processes underpinning collected data, paradata was seen to be relevant for understanding missing data and data not collected, like survey non-responses, and gauging respondent interest and involvement in the survey instruments (Couper and Kreuter, 2013; Olson, 2013). This more comprehensive definition of paradata further included different types of qualitative data generated both by the data creators them-selves and the technologies involved in the research work. Paradata became inclusive of observations by the interviewers about, depending on the present research objective, not only the survey process itself and how the respondent approached answering questions, but also pertaining to the appearance of the respondents and impressions and observations stemming from the broader circumstances of the interview (e.g., state of the respondent's domicile or neighbourhood) (Durrant et al., 2011; Edwards et al., 2017). This type of paradata, manifested commonly in field notes and audio recordings, could include estimations of the respondents' intellectual process, like the extent to which they were certain about their answers and what, and if so how, docu-mentation was consulted by the respondent when providing responses to queries (Nicolaas, 2011).

The concept of paradata was also refined in how it connects to paradata use, driven in part by technological innovation which provided additional and more intricate approaches to creating paradata. For example, eye-tracking method-ologies were implemented to record paradata of respondent-computer survey interactions (West, 2011). As available trace paradata in computer-driven survey systems began to increase qualitatively and diversify quantitatively, procedures around how to interpret the resulting data developed. Stieger and Reips (2010) and Sharma (2019) point to the many challenges involved in knowing how log files from systems with different functions in the infrastruc-tures underpinning digital survey systems can be used to capture respondent's often dynamic and idiosyncratic modes of survey-response behaviours. Further expanding the boundaries of the concept of paradata and its use in the survey settings, there have also been calls to delve into existing datasets in search of paradata that can usefully inform researchers about data-related processes. This paradata, what is termed 'retrospective paradata' in Chapter 7, may originally have been recorded for other purposes but can in the current contexts of use provide valuable insights into past data procedures of data creation, curation, and use (Edwards et al., 2017; cf. Börjesson et al., 2022a).

2.3.2 Paradata in Archaeology and Heritage Visualisation Research

The concept of paradata as it emerges in both archaeology and heritage visualisation research is somewhat similar across the two fields, although differences exist. An important point of common reference is The London Charter, a collection of six principles seeking to promote modes of work in computer-driven visualisation efforts that ensures methodological robustness and transparency, and also advance computer-based visualisations as a means to manage and inquire into heritage and archaeological data (The London Charter Organization, 2009b). Principle 4 in the charter outlines how visualisation methods and the resulting visualisations should be documented. Sub-principle 4.6 is titled 'Documentation of process (paradata)' and reads as follows:

> Documentation of the evaluative, analytical, deductive, interpretative and creative decisions made in the course of computer-based visualisation should be disseminated in such a way that the relationship between research sources, implicit knowledge, explicit reasoning, and visualization-based outcomes can be understood. (The London Charter Organization, 2009a)

Writing about the processes and discussions leading up to the establishment of The London Charter, Beacham et al. (2006) characterise the issue of documentation as being among the most difficult challenges addressed in the charter. The difficulties stemmed not principally from attaining a sufficient degree of methodological transparency via documenting the steps and decision-making involved in visualising heritage and archaeological data, but rather to greatly varying methodological expectations rooted in the methodological traditions of the many disciplines and fields of research that engaged in the production and use of computer-based visualisations. Paradata was suggested by Denard (see Denard, 2016) as a way of denoting descriptions of the mental and physical activities   involved   in   creating   the   visualisations,   complemented   by articulations of the intellectual context and implicit assumptions and principles, that might serve to bridge methodological frameworks (Beacham et al., 2006). Beacham (Beacham 2011, p. 51 see also Beacham et al., 2006) stresses that paradata are descriptions of 'intellectual capital' being operationalised in the making of computer-based visualisations, further broadening the scope of paradata to possibly include representations ranging from discrete tasks and strategies of action to epistemic horizons.

The London Charter is widely referenced in archaeology and heritage visualisation research discussing paradata (e.g., Huggett, 2012; Morgan and Winters, 2015; Niccolucci et al., 2013), although it has been noted that paradata in the archaeological context is not well defined (Huggett, 2020), and that the principles of the charter require adaptation to the specific circumstances and objectives of archaeological heritage, as done in the Seville Charter (Lopez-Menchero and Grande, 2011). Other and complementary conceptualisations of paradata have been suggested that, for example, also highlight that paradata should include descriptions of the evidence (literary sources, image resources, archival data) involved in creating, curating and using archaeological data and heritage visualisations beyond activities and decisions (Barratt, 2016; D'Andrea and Fernie, 2013). Barratt (2016), referencing Dell'Unto et al. (2013) further expands upon the concept of paradata by categorising different types of evidence (testimonial sources, sources based on current measurements and analyses) and intellectual processes (deduction, comparison, hypotheses) that are useful to include when describing past processes of scholarly work. Exploring paradata from a data management perspective, Kansa et al. (2020; cf. InterPARES Trust AI, forthcoming) determine that information about the data authors and their areas of expertise and training are paradata that can be employed to better understand the data or scholarly product created. Kansa et al. (2020) also underline that it is important to also think about paradata that is more closely associated with the data itself to be of wider scope than the data and include, for example, sampling biases and information about missing data (cf. Ullah, 2015) that can help explain why the data appears in the way it does.

Paradata as it is defined and used in archaeology and heritage visualisation research has several similarities to how paradata is approached in survey research, but there are also other conceptual trajectories emerging. The characterisation of paradata as an auxiliary data type vis-à-vis the 'principal' data or visualisation scholarly outcomes remains, however, with a slight difference in framing. The general understanding of scholarly work as it is represented in this literature resembles a network of interacting research practices, methodologies and varying kinds of data and epistemic circumstances, where the specific relationships between these network components become important due to how they impact each other and ultimately the nature of the scholarly work as a whole (e.g., Denard, 2016; Richards-Rissetto and Landau, 2019). Paradata, in reflecting how research is enacted and data is produced in practice, emerges as a data type that encompasses a wide range of key elements and their interplay (see Reilly et al., 2021), from qualitative paradata describing how understanding and interpretation has happened (D'Andrea and Fernie, 2013) to operational trace data and data detailing machine settings (Reilly et al., 2021). While the concept of paradata remains closely associated with technology and technology's capacity to record representations of how it is used and calibrated (Niccolucci et al., 2010), it is in archaeology and heritage visualisation research to a notably higher degree associated with descriptions of the practices and processes engaged in by the makers of scholarly data and their epistemic attributes. Here, the principal paradata stakeholder group is made up of researchers or other parties seeking to gain insight into data processes by consulting paradata representing the original setting of data creation in a broad-spectrum way, while paradata in survey research commonly reflects the activities of the respondent stakeholder group and how they impact the survey data outputs (Ballin et al., 2006; Nicolaas, 2011).

2.4 Paradata's Conceptual Siblings

There are many concepts that relate to paradata. Among these concepts, metadata and provenance – or provenance data – are arguably most closely connected to paradata in terms of conceptual significance and how they are used in research practice. Metadata, provenance data, and paradata are all concepts that signify 'data about data' in both different and related ways. A working definition of metadata is that it is data about data in the sense that metadata describes data, for example titles, author names and information about standards and tools used in organising and processing the data (Pomerantz, 2015). Provenance data is also data about data, signifying instead data providing information about the actors, activities and resources that have been involved in shaping and maintaining the data (Lemieux, 2016). The close semantic links between metadata and provenance data, and between these terms and paradata, is reflected in their intertwined and diverse uses. As observed by Mudge (2016), metadata and provenance data are frequently used interchangeably in scholarly settings. It is also not uncommon to see the term 'provenance metadata' denoting provenance data (see e.g., Doerr et al., 2016; Reilly et al., 2021) or paradata (Gant and Reilly, 2018). Dahlström and

Hansson (2019, p. 6) write that paradata is 'an interesting form of metadata' that is connected to digital provenance while Beacham (2011, p. 49) likens paradata with 'contextual metadata', noting, however, slight differences in emphasis between the terms. The term 'provenance paradata' is, for instance, used in Chapter 6 of this volume and in Börjesson et al. (2022b, no pagination). The closeness between paradata and provenance data is also repeatedly underlined in the literature (see e.g., D'Andrea and Fernie, 2013; Huggett, 2012; Niccolucci et al., 2013).

Below, metadata and provenance will be explored definitionally and by delving into prominent use cases in a series of domains including e-science, computer science, archival studies, archaeology, heritage visualisation research and the information disciplines. Particular interest is given to how the terms connect to each other and, crucially, how they can also offer a useful window into the concept of paradata.

2.4.1 Metadata

The term 'metadata' is said to have originated in the 1960s within the field of computer science (Furner, 2020) and has since gained widespread recognition, being utilised in numerous and varied contexts. Metadata is firmly established in the LAM (libraries, archives, museums) sector and associated disciplines (information studies, archival studies, museum studies), where it principally refers to the resources used to describe the attributes of physical and digital collections and holdings so their items can be made searchable, findable, and possible to use and manage and preserve (Mayernik, 2020; Ronzino et al., 2012). Gilliland (2008) and Pomerantz (2015) argue, however, that metadata in actuality predates the coining of the term, and that its manifestations have been in existence since the earliest attempts at organising information. The increasing pervasiveness of digital technology in all domains of leisure and labour has been a driver in metadata becoming a colloquial term and a ubiquitous and impactful phenomenon, indispensable in the operation and handling of digital data and digital communications, including social media and other digital platforms and infrastructures (Pomerantz, 2015; Zeng and Qin, 2016).

The literature offers several conceptualisations of metadata that illustrate the purposes that metadata is envisioned to fulfil. Metadata's fundamental function is to in varying ways enrich the form or forms of information it is appended to by facilitating a range of actions. Some of these actions have to do with knowledge organisation and the work of ordering and describing items, data, books and records according to certain principles and systems that support information search (Mayernik, 2020) and required administrative and managerial tasks (Kalová, 2020; Tompkins et al., 2021), including repository storage and long-term preservation (Day, 2002). Metadata also enables both reuse, that is, use by a party external to an item's context of creation) and use of the item described by offering insight into its features and attributes (Gilliland, 2008) and relationships to related items (Force and Smith, 2021). Metadata supports the usability and reusability of forms of information by being a resource that users can employ to validate and contextualise the items, and as evidence in efforts to determine their authenticity, integrity and trustworthiness (Tennis, 2008). Conversely, metadata is also an essential tool in the successful sharing of data, documentation and other forms of information (Chao, 2014). Metadata is, however, no silver bullet in facilitating sharing and reuse. It is necessary that the metadata shared is the metadata needed by the stakeholders set to reuse what is shared (Kim, 2021), and there might be infrastructural and epistemic challenges that impact their ability to apply the metadata (Hansson and Dahlgren, 2021).

Instances and Definitions of Metadata

The literature shows that there are many types of metadata across the diverse domains where it is used. Further, while there are many metadata standards available, metadata is often differently standardised and defined in the contexts of its use (Furner, 2020). In more domain-agnostic writings about metadata, commonly mentioned metadata types are administrative metadata (for managing information), descriptive metadata (for making information findable and identifiable), technical metadata (for managing the systems underpinning information search and repositories), and paradata- and provenance-like use metadata (for describing the use and use-limitations of information) (Gilliland, 2008; Mayernik, 2020; Zeng and Qin, 2016). Metadata types and their naming also vary between applications. For example, projects invested in online interactions can use social metadata describing comments and ratios of positive and negative ratings (Drachsler et al., 2012), while archival metadata applications can include metadata typologies including records creation, record keeping and preservation (Tennis, 2008).

Metadata definitions are similarly diverse and can be found in an array of standards (see Furner, 2020 for an overview of metadata standards), charters, glossaries and scholarly outputs. Zeng and Qin (2016, p. 11) identify the most basic metadata definitions in use as 'information about information' or 'data about data'. Pomerantz (2015, p. 26) remains on a similar level of abstraction, and ties into what is akin to a sociomaterial understanding of information, where information is something that emerges out of human practices rather than being simply encoded into informative objects (see Chapter 3 for a discussion of the sociomateriality of information, documentation and data), by positing that metadata is 'a potentially informative object that describes another potentially informative object'. Gilliland (2008, no pagination) offers an alternate approach to describing metadata by conceptualising it as potentially everything that can be said about different forms of information, while saying that metadata should reflect the content, context and structure of the item it describes. Other definitions point to metadata having more specific characteristics. Greenberg (2003) and Smiraglia (2005) propose that metadata is structured and Zeng and Qin (2016) underline that metadata in addition to being structured also is encoded, that is, in some way involved in a system of description. Tennis (2008) says that metadata is readable by humans and machines, and that it is always artificial and derived on the basis of an analysis of the forms of information being described. Some definitions furthermore tie metadata to certain purposes. Mayernik (2020) understands metadata as something that is always intended to help solve an issue or to be otherwise useful. Greenberg (2003, p. 1876) writes that metadata is supposed to facilitate 'functions' tied to the item in focus of the metadata descriptions. Smiraglia (2005) stresses that metadata should underpin information retrieval, and Zeng and Qin (2016) regard metadata as resources holistically supporting interactions with different forms of information, from identification to evaluation, use, preservation and management.

2.4.2 Provenance and Provenance Data

Like metadata, the concept of provenance is employed in an extensive array of domains and contexts – from computer science to archival science and beyond. Its modes of use and the connotations it carries, including the significance of provenance and the utilities of provenance data, also varies. Provenance has strong connections to the archival field, where it is operationalised in, among other things, the principle of provenance. The principle of provenance is a key tenet of archival theory that describes how archival holdings should be organised by keeping the records from one record creator together and separate from records from other record creators, in this way preserving the meaning and context of the records (Michetti, 2016; Sweeney, 2008). Provenance also sees use in other fields and disciplines concerned with tracking and documenting data trajectories, and using information about past interactions with forms of information (again, data, records, books, manuscripts) to further present analytical or interpretative efforts (see e.g., Lemieux, 2016). Provenance is an important term in the field of computer science, in particular in scholarly efforts to better model and describe data workflows and the management of scientific data (Curcin, 2017; Doerr and Theodoridou, 2011). Additional examples of settings where provenance and provenance data is a concern includes archaeology (Huggett, 2012), information studies (Fear and Donaldson, 2012), museum studies (White, 2017), geology and palaeontology (Reilly et al., 2021), and art history and cinema studies (Bernardi et al., 2021).

While being used in many settings for a range of purposes, provenance data is broadly conceptualised as a resource principally for making visible how forms of information travel between stakeholders and repositories, and to describe the impacts that these travel pathways have had on the forms of information themselves (Gehani et al., 2021; Lemieux, 2016; MacNeil, 2008). The literature shows that the information about the 'histories' of different forms of information provided by provenance data is understood to be useful for a range of more specific reasons. In settings of use more closely affiliated with the data-centric understandings of the concept, provenance data is seen to facilitate examinations of different kinds, including data audits and validations (Davidson and Freire, 2008). Curcin (2017) and Ludäscher (2016) outline how provenance data also can be used to assess results and outcomes by facilitating replicability and reproducibility of data tasks and processes, including both analytic and data management operations. Provenance in the data sciences commonly represent very fine-grained representations of data interactions. Provenance graphs and other provenance accounts can provide detailed insight into the discrete steps involved in data creation, curation and use (Davidson and Freire, 2008; Doerr and Theodoridou, 2011).

The use of provenance in disciplines and contexts more aligned with the archival discourse shows many similarities, but also some differences in emphasis and in how the provenance data is manifested. Similarities include using provenance data to drive data exploration (Davidson and Freire, 2008) and the determination of authenticity and other qualities, including accuracy and relevance (Fear and Donaldson, 2012; cf. Davet et al., 2023). Provenance data is also used to better understand the origins of the data or record at hand, inclusive of both actors involved and the broader contexts in which the materials emerged or were created (Buchanan, 2016; Michetti, 2016), together with impactful epistemic and theoretical circumstances (Huggett, 2012). However, provenance data in the archival setting less often pertains to the objects or records it describes on the item-level, instead existing predominantly at the collection-level. This makes it difficult, often impossible, to base estimations of authenticity and trustworthiness on detailed documentation of data interactions. Instead, an important function of provenance data is to show chains of custody and ownership that can be used to assess relevance and task-related value (Lemieux, 2016). It is also often highlighted that provenance data underpins all basic categories of archival work and functionality (arrangement, description, acquisition, retrieval, appraisal, Lemieux, 2016; Michetti, 2016; Sweeney, 2008), including preservation (Li and Sugimoto, 2014).

Instances and Definitions of Provenance Data

Instances of provenance data discussed in the literature mirror the diverse applications of the concept across its domains of use. There is, for example, data provenance (Asuncion, 2013), archival provenance (Bearman and Lytle, 1985), network provenance (Gehani et al., 2021), digital provenance (Dahlström and Hansson, 2019), and many other types of provenance used to describe the custody trajectories and modes of creation and use of the forms of information they relate to, including provenance detailing field-agnostic occurrences like processes (Cuevas-Vincenttin et al., 2016) and events (Doerr and Theodoridou, 2011). The W3C Working Group (2013) identifies three types of provenance in their PROV Data Model: provenance tied to the agents (people, organisations) involved in creating or manipulating forms of information; provenance tied to the forms of information themselves, describing their origins and connections to other items; and provenance tied to the processes of creating the forms of information. This categorisation connects to the where-provenance, why-provenance, and how-provenance discussed by Huggett (2012), which contains provenance reporting modes of creation (how) and origins of the data or items (where), but to greater extent emphasises the reasons for creating the data and the underpinning choices and deliberations (why). CRMdig, a data model for scientific observations, additionally contains what-provenance and when-provenance, offering information about resources and tools involved in the events described and temporal details respectively (Doerr and Theodoridou, 2011). There are also provenance typologies that are organised wholly on a temporal basis (see Cuevas-Vincenttin et al., 2016; Davidson and Freire, 2008; Ludäscher, 2016). Prospective provenance is used in both the archival and computer science domains. Common examples include 'records management plans' in the former field and 'workflows' in the latter. Prospective provenance is documentation that covers the workflows and procedures involved in creating information. Retrospective provenance, on the other hand, describes how forms of information have been created, comprising – like prospective provenance – of data inputs and other resources and tools employed in their creation.

Definitions of provenance data abound, but share many of the same elements. Sweeney (2008, p. 193) observes that a recurring common denominator is that provenance is information that describes 'the origins of an information-bearing entity or artifact'. Beyond this point, definitions diverge depending on the field. In archival settings, many definitions stress that provenance data ties the record to the individuals or organisations who during the course of their activities created or modified it (see e.g, the archival ISAD(G) standard, International Council on Archives, 2000), sometimes covering also the specific organisational functions or processes involved in shaping or making the record (Lemieux, 2016, see also Sundberg, 2013). Some definitions limit the chronology of relevance for provenance data to the activities prior to inclusion into the holdings of an archive or records centre (International Council on Archives, 2004), while others include custodial and post-custodial provenance (Cook, 1993). Information about the chain of custody and ownership is, however, ubiquitous in the archival understanding of provenance (Lemieux, 2016; Michetti, 2016; Sweeney, 2008).

Definitions of provenance in more data-centred domains commonly stress that the data interactions detailed in the provenance data can be carried out by both human and technological actors (Missier, 2017) – as do several archival definitions, see for instance MacNeil, 2008 – and can have a notably comprehensive scope. The PROV Data Model defines provenance as 'descriptions of the entities and activities involved in producing and delivering or otherwise influencing a given object' (W3C Working Group, 2013, no pagination). Provenance definitions in the computer science domain often include accounts of data inputs or other resources employed (see e.g., Davidson and Freire, 2008), and very detailed descriptions of how the object has been modified and transformed (see e.g., Gehani et al., 2021 and W3C Working Group, 2013) intending to allow for the tracing connections between 'raw' data and products based on analysis of this data (Davidson and Freire, 2008; Pinheiro et al., 2013).

It can be noted that discussions of how to involve AI applications in archives management and the use of archives for scholarly or other purposes seem to indicate a possible intermingling of different archives- and computer science-based understandings of provenance and provenance data. At times, however, 'paradata' is used to describe the information that can be used to audit AI functions and interactions within the archival framework (see e.g., Davet et al., 2023; Franks, 2024; InterPARES Trust AI, forthcoming), possibly to distinguish this particular instance of process information from conventional archival provenance – a further indication of the (sometimes) closeness of the terms.

2.5 Discussion

The goal of this chapter was to examine the concept of paradata. The examination was done on the basis of a review of the etymology of the concept, and analyses of how paradata is defined and put to use in research practice in survey research and heritage visualisation research, two domains where paradata is a comparably established notion. Metadata and provenance data, two of paradata's closest conceptual siblings, were also reviewed alongside examples of relevant use cases so as to provide additional perspectives on the concept of paradata and how it can be understood.

It remains difficult, however, to arrive at an exhaustive description of the concept of paradata. This is not due to a lack of definitional options. Numerous studies have observed that there are many definitions of paradata discussed in multiple fields of study (Reilly et al., 2021), although none of them are in widespread use (e.g., Kreuter and Casas-Cordero, 2010; Nicolaas, 2011; Olson, 2013). Instead, the chapter indicates that there are several complexities at play that make it challenging to explain the concept. One major complexity is that while concepts always can be approached and analysed as such, they are also to some extent inextricably tied to practice (Moore, 2004). This means that any discussion of conceptual significance or definitions are tied to modes of doing and thinking in a particular professional arena or scholarly discipline, regulated by both specific practical circumstances and epistemic frameworks. As will be discussed further on, it is not certain if this heterogeneous array of paradata applications and meanings is a hindrance for grasping and putting the concept to use, or a resource that can be drawn on for the same purposes.

The second major complexity that makes it difficult to arrive at a precise rendering of the concept of paradata is that it co-exists with metadata and provenance in a complicated conceptual space, where the connections and boundaries between the concepts are blurred and shifting according to perspective. The complexities underpinning the difficulties of arriving at an encompassing and clear description of paradata also interconnect. This is visible in the many instances in the literature, where paradata is discussed as an instance of provenance data (Niccolucci et al., 2013) or metadata (Dahlström and Hansson, 2019), and many other intersections of the concepts are present (see e.g., Beacham, 2011; Huggett, 2012; Reilly et al., 2021).

2.5.1 Encompassing Paradata, Provenance Data and Metadata

The challenges of encompassing paradata notwithstanding, this chapter has shown that the concept has several core characteristics and also key correspondences to metadata and provenance data. General features of all three concepts are that they – like data and documentation, see Chapter 3 – exist through and in relation to conditions that are both social and material in nature, consisting of, to different extents, field-specific and field-overarching elements of scholarly practice, tools and systems, and epistemic frameworks. Paradata, provenance data and metadata are thus used and produced by both human and non-human actors by automatic or manual means, and they are, to a large extent, system-dependent in the sense that access, management and storage extensively relies on the purposeful functioning of supporting information systems (Force and Smith, 2021; Hansson and Dahlgren, 2021; Kim, 2021).

The literature also shows that all three data types can be represented 'in' data files and other forms of information, or exist in resources that are distinct from them – like metadata schemas or method descriptions in associated publications (De Oliveira et al., 2015; Pomerantz, 2015). Also, the discussed data types emerge in different forms and in different places: They can be highly structured (found in standards, data models) but also unstructured (present in datasets, work logs or notes) and comprise narrative or trace data. In terms of their temporal orientation, the concepts can be prescriptive and determine what paradata, provenance data or metadata should be documented when carrying out a certain task or process. They can also be retrospective and be used to discern and describe data interactions that are in the past or prospective and focused on speculating or stipulating future activities (Chapter 7; Cuevas-Vincenttin et al., 2016; Davidson and Freire, 2008; Ludäscher, 2016). Finally, paradata, provenance data and metadata are 'meta' concepts (cf. Schenk et al., 2009) in that they express the relationships and attributes of forms of information and other data or descriptive resources related to these items.

The relationship between paradata, provenance data and metadata on one hand and the forms of information that they describe on the other, is arguably – at least from a conceptual perspective – both their main designator and possibly their lowest common denominator. This chapter shows that the differences between the concepts are notable. The use cases of paradata, provenance data and metadata reviewed above support some observations about the relationship between the concepts as they manifest in research practice. A general dissimilarity between metadata and paradata and provenance data is that the former term describes the attributes of forms of information, while the latter two terms describe their histories of creation, curation, use and custody. In situations where the concepts are not considered to be distinct, metadata is most commonly attributed the highest order of abstraction. In these instances, provenance data (da Cruz et al., 2011; Curcin, 2017; Malik et al., 2010) and paradata (Dahlström and Hansson, 2019; Niccolucci et al., 2013; Pomerantz, 2015) are organised as metadata sub-types.

This is the only observable hierarchical relationship between the concepts. Paradata and provenance data are at times posited as alternatives to each other (Huggett, 2012), but several authors consider the concepts to be distinct, albeit closely related. The principal difference between paradata and provenance in these cases is that provenance has a stronger emphasis on the technical circumstances of data interactions. Paradata is instead seen to highlight the activities, processes and frameworks involved in interpreting and understanding data (D'Andrea and Fernie, 2013; Reilly et al., 2021).

The conceptual relationships most frequently discussed in the reviewed literature are those between metadata and paradata, and metadata and provenance data. Li and Sugimoto (2014) also suggest that metadata creation and description should be considered from the viewpoint of provenance, and that it would be valuable to record and keep. Reilly et al. (2021, p. 458) contrasts metadata, described as 'generally uncontentious static properties of data', to the more heterogeneous collection of data inputs and byproducts, scholarly activities and interpretative resources captured as paradata.

Studies in survey research show fairly uniform distinctions between paradata and metadata. Metadata is exemplified as providing information about survey-supporting elements, for example, questionnaires, sample designs, settings and configurations, and the web browsers and operating systems used (Barratt, 2016; Olson, 2013; Stieger and Reips, 2010). This is in contrast to paradata, which describes both how the surveys have been interacted with (scrolls, clicks, typing, call records) and the intellectual work involved in enacting the survey study (Barratt, 2016; Stieger and Reips, 2010). It is interesting to note that the relatively homogenous characterisation of paradata in survey research stands somewhat in contrast to approaches in other fields, where paradata is understood to encompass also the machinery, infrastructures, and tools involved in data creation, curation and use alongside information about their configurations (Huvila, 2022; Kreuter, 2013).

2.5.2 The Concept of Paradata

In conclusion, the concept of paradata as discussed in the literature is diverse. This chapter has shown that paradata encompasses a range of meanings and definitions. It is also conceptualised as being useful in relation to a various set of purposes and intents. Paradata's empirical referents – that is, the standards, data models and data or process descriptions that exemplify and instantiate it – are plentiful and assorted. Paradata is connected in close and complex ways to metadata and provenance data, and while some general observations can be made about how the concepts and their modes of use differ and are alike, it is difficult to draw any definitive boundaries between them. This does not mean, however, that there are not any purposeful approaches available that can be used to grasp the concept of paradata and to discern its possible implementations.

One approach is to consider paradata in a more abstract way. From this perspective, it is possible to determine that paradata is a concept that can be used to examine any information or data phenomenon in any work or leisure setting, although it has been most prominently used to examine scholarly settings and scholarly data in survey research, heritage visualisation research and information studies. Paradata is data about the full range of activities, resources and epistemic frameworks involved in creating, managing and using scholarly data. It can emerge in any form or format, and be created intentionally or as a secondary outcome of scholarly data interactions and processes. Paradata is useful for gaining insight into past data trajectories, processes and events. Purposeful paradata can facilitate a wide range of data management and reuse scenarios, and is an asset in examining data when assessing its relevance, reliability, accuracy, scope and content. From a more abstracted perspective, paradata differs from metadata in that it describes data processes, and metadata describes data. Paradata and provenance data are more alike in that both concepts are broadly concerned with the origins and processing histories of data, but provenance data is more strongly situated in the settings of archives, archaeology, art history and computer science which, as we have seen above, impacts what the data looks like, and how it is created and used.

Another approach is to consider paradata in a more tangible way, which also introduces significantly more changeability to the concept. In this sense, paradata emerges as a concept that is differently defined and applied across research settings and disciplines. In survey research, paradata showcases well-regimented expressions and modelings of past data trajectories and interactions that are akin to the computer science workflow-provenance research and standard-driven metadata descriptions. In other domains, paradata is a notably more fluid concept used as an exploratory and interpretative device (see e.g., Börjesson et al., 2022a; Reilly et al., 2021). Similarly to commonplace framings of metadata (see e.g., Mayernik, 2020; Tennis, 2008), paradata is in some settings data that is always created to function precisely as paradata. In other settings, it – like provenance data – is a 'by-product' of the activities of individuals, groups or institutions. Paradata also stands in other, more complex relationships to provenance data and metadata, and the intersections and similarities between the concepts are many. The significance of paradata and how it relates to metadata or provenance data has to be determined on a case-by-case basis, although there are some general patterns to how the concepts are employed together, as previously discussed in this chapter.

The way of thinking about paradata in a more tangible sense also points to paradata challenges that are important to discuss. In this view, both the definitional and the use case facets of paradata are understood to be bound to the practices and regimens of their setting of application. That being said, data like paradata always travel across several settings of application, where practices may contrast or clash (Brown and Duguid, 1996; Star and Griesemer, 1989). In relation to paradata, this might mean that there are gaps between the understandings and conceptualisations of paradata that risk causing paradata use becoming difficult. Such gaps can manifest also in varying levels of compatibility in information system design and data ontologies with particular paradata-related tasks, purposes and understandings. Examples include research communities with more or less matched comprehensions of paradata, and data models that render paradata in ways that do not match what is required for success in a particular use case (cf. Hansson and Dahlgren, 2021; Kim, 2021; Mayernik, 2011).

Related to this point are a range of often-present insufficiencies connected to the concept of paradata. One insufficiency is that paradata never is a 'reality-checking' implementation (Beacham, 2011, p. 51). No amount of paradata or combination of paradata can give complete access to data-interaction histories, and the work of, for example, reusing data is surely facilitated by paradata, but never fully driven and accomplished by paradata. Tasks involving the use of paradata to achieve some aim or result must always be supplemented also by other non-paradata resources and efforts.

Another insufficiency is that paradata itself is a data type that requires interpretation and sufficient interpretative conditions. This could be taken to mean that, theoretically, there would be reason to to supplement the paradata with additional paradata describing how and why it was created and documented (cf. Gant and Reilly, 2018; Huggett, 2020; Li and Sugimoto, 2014). This 'paradox ... of potentially infinite regression' (Huggett, 2020, p. 3) must, again, be considered in relation to practice where case-specific objectives and requirements of use, together with available resources to harness or create paradata, will be the actual factors limiting and shaping what interactions with paradata are relevant and possible.

The many definitions of and approaches to paradata are, in some respects, an obstacle for grasping and employing the concept. Equally, from a different viewpoint, it might not be considered desirable to lessen the complexities associated with paradata. As discussed later in this volume in Chapters 4–6, standards and other meta-framing attempts can be useful, but so also can the diversity of meanings and approaches to using paradata for various ends and means throughout paradata's many fields and scenarios of use. As observed by Furner (2020) in his discussion of the wealth of available metadata standards, it is important that connectivities exist between communities of concept use. Such connectivities can be built on the basis of clear and well-documented applications of the concept that make visible connections and disconnects across different scenarios of its application, as has been attempted in this chapter and which this volume pursues further in the following chapters.

References

Adkins L. and Adkins R. A. (1989). *Archaeological Illustration.* Cambridge: Cambridge University Press.

Andresen H. (2020). A discussion frame for explaining records that are based on algorithmic output. *Records Management Journal* 30(2), 129–141. https://doi .org/10.1108/RMJ-04-2019-0019.

Arshia A. H., Rasekh A. H., Moosavi M. R., Fakhrahmad S. M. and Sadreddini M. H. (2021). Traceability mining between unit test and source code based on textual analysis applied to software systems. Digital Scholarship *Humanities* 36(2), 268–285. https://doi.org/10.1093/llc/fqaa017.

Asuncion H. U. (2013). Automated data provenance capture in spreadsheets, with case studies. *Future Generation Computer Systems* 29(8), 2169–2181. https://doi.org/ 10.1016/j.future.2013.04.009.

Ballin M., Scanu M. and Vicard P. (2006). *Paradata and bayesian networks: A tool for monitoring and troubleshooting the data production process.* Rome: Università degli studi Roma Tre.

Barratt R. (2016). 3D reconstruction in archaeology: Using the future to understand the past in the present. Part 3: Sources and paradata. Available at https://archphotogrammetry .com/2016/06/25/part-3-sources-and-paradata (accessed 29 May 2024).

Beacham R. (2011). Concerning the paradox of paradata. Or, 'I don't want realism; I want magic!' *Virtual Archaeology Review* 2(4), 49–52.

Beacham R., Denard H. and Niccolucci F. (2006). An introduction to the London Charter. In *Papers from the Joint Event CIPA/VAST/EG/EuroMed Event.*

Bearman D. A. and Lytle R. H. (1985). The power of the principle of provenance. *Archivaria*, 21, 14–27.

Bentkowska-Kafel A., Denard H. and Baker D. (eds.) (2012). *Paradata and Transparency in Virtual Heritage.* Farnham: Ashgate.

Bernardi J., Usai P. C., Williams T. and Yumibe J. (eds.) (2021). *Provenance and Early Cinema.* Indianapolis: Indiana University Press.

Borgman C. L. (2012). The conundrum of sharing research data. *Journal of the American Society for Information Science and Technology* 63(6), 1059–1078. https://doi.org/10.1002/asi.22634.

Börjesson L., Huvila I. and Sköld O. (2022). Information needs on research data creation. *Information Research* 27. https://doi.org/10.47989/irisic2208.

Börjesson L., Sköld O., Friberg Z., Löwenborg D., Palsson G. and Huvila I. (2022a). Re-purposing excavation database content as paradata: An explorative analysis of paradata identification challenges and opportunities. *KULA: Knowledge Creation, Dissemination, and Preservation Studies* 62(3), 1–18. https://doi.org/10.18357/kula.221.

Börjesson L., Sköld O. and Huvila I. (2020). Paradata in documentation standards and recommendations for digital archaeological visualisations. *Digital Culture & Society* 6(2), 191–220. https://doi.org/10.14361/dcs-2020-0210.

Brown J. S. and Duguid P. (1996). The social life of documents. *First Monday* 1(1).

Buchanan S. A. (2016). *A Provenance Research Study of Archaeological Curation.* PhD dissertation. Austin: University of Texas at Austin.

Cameron S., Franks P. and Hamidzadeh B. (2023). Positioning paradata: A conceptual frame for AI processual documentation in archives and recordkeeping contexts. *Journal on Computing and Cultural Heritage* 16(4), 1–19. https://doi.org/10.1145/3594728.

Chao T. C. (2014). Enhancing metadatafor research methods in data curation. *Proceedings of the American Society for Information Science and Technology* 51(1), 1–4. https://doi.org/10.1002/meet.2014.14505101103.

Chrysanthi A., Berggren Å., Davies R., Earl G. P. and Knibbe, J. (2016). The camera 'at the trowel's edge': Personal video recording in archaeological research. *Journal of Archaeological Method and Theory* 23(1), 238–270. https://doi.org/10.1007/s10816-015-9239-x-015-9239-x.

Cook T. (1993). The concept of the archival fonds in the post-custodial era: Theory, problems and solutions. *Archivaria* 35, 24–37.

Couper M. P. (1998). Measuring survey quality in a CASIC environment. In *Proceedings of the Survey Research Methods Section,* 41–49.

Couper M. P. (2000). Usability evaluation of computer-assisted survey instruments. *Social Science Computer Review* 18(4), 384–396. https://doi.org/10.1177/08944393000180402.

Couper M. P. and Kreuter F. (2013). Using paradata to explore item level response times in surveys. *Journal of the Royal Statistical Society: Series A (Statistics in Society)* 176(1), 271–286. https://doi.org/10.1111/j.1467-985X.2012.01041.x.

Crosland M. P. (1962). *Historical Studies in the Language of Chemistry.* London: Heinemann.

da Cruz S. M. S., Paulino C. E., de Oliveira D., Campos M. L. M. and Mattoso M. (2011). Capturing distributed provenance metadata from cloud-based scientific workflows. *Journal of Information and Data Management* 2(1), 43–50.

Cuevas-Vincenttin V. et al. (2016). *ProvONE: A PROV Extension Data Model for Scientific Workflow Provenance.* Available at http://jenkins-1.dataone.org/jenkins/view/Documentation%20Projects/job/ProvONE-Documentation-trunk/ws/provenance/ProvONE/v1/provone.html (accessed 29 May 2024).

Curcin V. (2017). Embedding data provenance into the Learning Health System to facilitate reproducible research. *Learning Health Systems* 1(2). https://doi.org/10.1002/lrh2.10019.

Dahlström M. and Hansson J. (2019). Documentary provenance and digitized collections: Concepts and problems. *Proceedings from the Document Academy* 6(1), 1–11. https://doi.org/10.35492/docam/6/1/8.

D'Andrea A. and Fernie K. (2013). CARARE 2.0: A metadata schema for 3D cultural objects. In *2013 Digital Heritage International Congress (DigitalHeritage)*. New York: IEEE, 137–143. https://doi.org/10.1109/DigitalHeritage.2013.6744745.

Davet J., Hamidzadeh B. and Franks P. (2023). Archivist in the machine: Paradata for AI-based automation in the archives. *Archival Science* 23, 275–295. https://doi.org/10.1007/s10502-023-09408-8.

Davidson S. B. and Freire J. (2008). Provenance and scientific workflows: Challenges and opportunities. In *Proceedings of the 2008 ACM SIGMOD International Conference on Management of Data*. New York: ACM. https://doi.org/10.1145/1376616.1376772.

Day M. (2002). *Cedars Guide to Preservation Metadata*. Bath: University of Bath.

De Oliveira D., Silva V. and Mattoso M. (2015). How much domain data should be in provenance databases? In *Proceedings of the 7th USENIX Conference on Theory and Practice of Provenance*. Berkeley, CA: USENIX Association.

Dell'Unto N., Leander A. M., Dellepiane M., Callieri M., Ferdani D. and Lindgren S. (2013). Digital reconstruction and visualization in archaeology: Case-study drawn from the work of the Swedish Pompeii Project. In *2013 Digital Heritage International Congress (DigitalHeritage)*. New York: IEEE, 621–628. https://doi.org/10.1109/DigitalHeritage.2013.6743804.

Denard H. (2016). A new introduction to the London Charter. In Bentkowska-Kafel A, Denard H. and Baker D. (eds.), *Paradata and Transparency in Virtual Heritage*. Farnham: Ashgate.

Doerr M., Stead S. and Theodoridou M. (2016). *Definition of the CRMdig: An Extension of CIDOC-CRM to support provenance metadata*. Available at https://cidoc-crm.org/lrmoo/sites/default/files/CRMdig_v3.2.1.pdf (accessed 29 May 2024).

Doerr M. and Theodoridou M. (2011). CRMdig: A generic digital provenance model for scientific observation. In *TAPP11: 3rd USENIX workshop on the Theory and Practice of Provenance*.

Drachsler H. etal. (2012). *D8. 1 Review of Social Data Requirements*. Report written in the Open Discovery Space project.

Durrant G. B., D'Arrigo J. and Steele F. (2011). Using paradata to predict best times of contact: Conditioning on household and interviewer influences. *Journal of the Royal Statistical Society: Series A (Statistics in Society)* 174(4), 1029–1049. https://doi.org/10.1111/j.1467-985X.2011.00715.x.

Edwards R., Goodwin J., O'Connor H. and Phoenix A. (2017). *Working with Paradata, Marginalia and Fieldnotes: The Centrality of By-Products of Social Research*. Cheltenham: Edward Elgar Publishing.

Efthymiou A., Fragaki G. and Markos A. (2015). Exploring the meaning and productivity of a polysemous prefix: The case of the Modern Greek prepositional prefix para-. *Acta Linguistica Hungarica Acta Linguistica Hungarica* 62(4), 447–476. http://dx.doi.org/10.1556/064.2015.62.4.4.

Faniel I. and Yakel E. (2017). Practices do not make perfect: Disciplinary data sharing and reuse practices and their implications for repository data curation. In Johnston L. R. (ed.), *Curating Research Data: Practical Strategies for Your Data Repository*. Chicago, IL: ACRL, 103–126.

Fear K. and Donaldson D. R. (2012). Provenance and credibility in scientific data repositories. *Archival Science* 12(3), 319–339. https://doi.org/10.1007/s10502-012-9172-7.

Franks, P. (2024). The crucial role of paradata in AI governance. In Duranti L and Rogers C (eds.), *Artificial Intelligence and Documentary Heritage*. Vancouver: InterPARES Trust AI.

Force D. C. and Smith R. (2021). Context lost: Digital surrogates, their physical counterparts, and the metadata that is keeping them apart. *The American Archivist*, 84(1), 91–118. https://doi.org/10.17723/0360-9081-84.1.91.

Furner J. (2020). Definitions of 'metadata': A brief survey of international standards. *Journal of the Association for Information Science and Technology* 71(6), E33–E42. https://doi.org/10.1002/asi.24295.

Gant S. and Reilly P. (2018). Different expressions of the same mode: A recent dialogue between archaeological and contemporary drawing practices. *Journal of Visual Art Practice* 17(1), 100–120. https://doi.org/10.1080/14702029.2017.1384974.

Gehani A., Ahmad R., Irshad H., Zhu J. and Patel J. (2021). Digging into big provenance (with SPADE). *Communications of the ACM* 64(12), 48–56.

Geiger R. S. and Ribes D. (2011). Trace ethnography: Following coordination through documentary practices. In *Proceedings from the 44th Hawaii International Conference on System Sciences*. New York. IEEE, 1–10. https://doi.org/10.1109/HICSS.2011.455.

Genette G. and Maclean M. (1991). Introduction to the paratext. *New Literary History* 22(2), 261–272. https://doi.org/10.2307/469037.

Gilliland A. J. (2008). Setting the stage. In Baca M. (ed.), *Introduction to Metadata*. Los Angeles, CA: Getty Research Institute, 1–19.

Gitelman L. (ed.) (2013). *'Raw Data' is an Oxymoron*. Cambridge, MA: MIT Press.

Greenberg J. (2003). Metadata and the world wide web. In Drake M. A. (ed.), *Encyclopedia of Library and Information Science*, 2nd ed. New York: Dekker, 1876–1888.

Hansson K. and Dahlgren A. (2021). Open research data repositories: Practices, norms, and metadata for sharing images. *Journal of the Association for Information Science and Technology* 73(2), 303–316. https://doi.org/10.1002/asi.24571.

Hjørland B. (2018). Data (with big data and database semantics). *Knowledge Organization* 45(8), 685–708. https://doi.org/10.5771/0943-7444-2018-8-685

Huggett J. (2012). Promise and paradox: Accessing open data in archaeology. In Mills C., Pidd M. and Ward W. (eds.), *Proceedings of the Digital Humanities Congress 2012*. Sheffield: Humanities Research Institute. http://dx.doi.org/10.17613/qc5d-9x46.

Huggett J. (2020). Capturing the silences in digital archaeological knowledge. *Information* 11(5), 278. https://doi.org/10.3390/info11050278.

Huvila I. (2012). The unbearable complexity of documenting intellectual processes: Paradata and virtual cultural heritage visualisation. *Human IT* 12(1), 97–110.

Huvila I. (2014). Archaeologists and their information sources. In Huvila I. (ed.), *Perspectives to Archaeological Information in the Digital Society*. Uppsala: Uppsala universitet, Institutionen för ABM, 25–54.

Huvila I. (2022). Improving the usefulness of research data with better paradata. *Open Information Science* 6(1), 28–48.

Huvila I., Andersson L. and Sköld O. (2022). Citing methods literature: Citations to field manuals as paradata on archaeological fieldwork. *Information Research* 27(3). https://doi.org/10.47989/irpaper941.

Huvila I., Andersson L. and Sköld O. (eds.). (2024). *Perspectives on Paradata: Research and Practice of Documenting Data Processes*. Cham: Springer.

Huvila I., Greenberg J., Sköld O., Thomer A., Trace C. and Zhao X. (2021a). Documenting information processes and practices: Paradata, provenance metadata, life-cycles and pipelines. *Proceedings of the Association for Information Science and Technology* 58(1), 604–609. https://doi.org/10.1002/pra2.509.

Huvila I. and Sköld O. (2021). Choreographies of making archaeological data. *Open Archaeology* 7(1), 1602–1617. https://doi.org/10.1515/opar-2020-0212.

Huvila I., Sköld O. and Andersson L. (2023). Knowing-in-practice, its traces and ingredients. In Cozza M. and Gherardi S. (eds.), *The Posthumanist Epistemology of Practice Theory: Re-imagining Method in Organization Studies and Beyond*. Cham: Palgrave Macmillan, 37–69. https://doi.org/10.1007/978-3-031-42276-8_2.

Huvila I., Sköld O. and Börjesson L. (2021b). Documenting information making in archaeological field reports. *Journal of Documentation* 77(5), 1107–1127. https://doi.org/10.1108/JD-11-2020-0188.

International Council on Archives (2000). *ISAD(G): General International Standard Archival Description*. Paris: International Council on Archives.

International Council on Archives (2004). *Multilingual Archival Terminology: Provenance*. Paris: International Council on Archives.

InterPARES Trust AI (forthcoming). *Terminology Database: Paradata*. Vancouver: InterPARES Trust AI.

Kalová T. (2020). Creating needs-based metadata and research data management services: Exploring the requirements of scientists. *Young Information Scientist* 5, 31–46. https://doi.org/10.25365/yis-2020-5-3.

Kansa S. W., Atici L., Kansa E. C. and Meadow R. H. (2020). Archaeological analysis in the information age: Guidelines for maximizing the reach, comprehensiveness, and longevity of data. *Advances in Archaeological Practice* 8(1), 40–52. doi:10.1017/aap.2019.36.

Khazraee E. (2019). Assembling narratives: Tensions in collaborative construction of knowledge. *Journal of the Association for Information Science and Technology* 70(4), 325–337. https://doi.org/10.1002/asi.24133.

Kim Y. (2021). A study of the roles of metadata standard and data repository in science, technology, engineering and mathematics researchers' data reuse. *Online Information Review* 45(7), 1306–1321. https://doi.org/10.1108/OIR-09-2020-0431.

Kreuter F. (ed.) (2013). *Improving Surveys with Paradata: Analytic Uses of Process Information*. Chichester: John Wiley & Sons.

Kreuter F. and Casas-Cordero C. (2010). *Paradata. Rat für Sozial- und Wirtschaftsdaten (RatSWD) working paper*. Berlin: RatSWD.

Lemieux V. L. (2016). Provenance: Past, present and future in interdisciplinary and multidisciplinary perspective. In Lemieux V. (ed.), *Building Trust in Information*. Cham: Springer, 3–45. https://doi.org/10.1007/978-3-319-40226-0_1.

Li C. and Sugimoto S. (2014). Provenance description of metadata using PROV with PREMIS for long-term use of metadata. In *International Conference on Dublin Core and Metadata Applications*, 147–156. https://doi.org/10.23106/dcmi .952136486.

Lopez-Menchero V. M. and Grande A. (2011). The principles of the Seville Charter. In *CIPA Symposium Proceedings*, 2–6.

Ludäscher B. (2016). A brief tour through provenance in scientific workflows and databases. In Lemieux V (ed.), *Building Trust in Information*. Cham: Springer, 103–126. https://doi.org/10.1007/978-3-319-40226-0_7.

Lyberg L. (2009). *The paradata concept in survey research*. Presentation. Available at https://csdiworkshop.org/wp-content/uploads/2020/03/Lybert2011CSDI.pdf (accessed 29 May 2024).

MacNeil H. (2008). Archivalterity: Rethinking original order. *Archivaria* 66(0 SE - Articles):1–24.

Malik T., Nistor L. and Gehani A. (2010). Tracking and sketching distributed data provenance. *In 2010 IEEE Sixth International Conference on e-Science*. New York: IEEE, 190–197. https://doi.org/10.1109/eScience.2010.51.

Matei S. A. and Hunter L. (2021). Data storytelling is not storytelling with data: A framework for storytelling in science communication and data journalism. *The Information Society* 37(5), 312–322. https://doi.org/10.1080/01972243.2021.1951415.

Mayernik M. S. (2011). Metadata tensions: A case study of library principles vs. everyday scientific data practices. *Proceedings of the Association for Information Science and Technology* 47(1), 1–2. https://doi.org/10.1002/meet.14504701337.

Mayernik M. S. (2020). Metadata. *Knowledge Organization* 47(8), 696–713. https://doi.org/10.5771/0943-7444-2020-8-696.

Michetti G. (2016). Provenance: An archival perspective. In Lemieux V. (ed.), *Building Trust in Information*. Cham: Springer, 59–68. https://doi.org/10.1007/978-3-319-40226-0_3.

Missier P. (2017). Provenance standards. In Liu L. and Özsu M. T. (eds.), *Encyclopedia of Database Systems*. New York: Springer, 1–8.

Moore H. L. (2004). Global anxieties: Concept-metaphors and pre-theoretical commitments in anthropology. *Anthropological Theory* 4(1), 71–88. https://doi.org/10.1177/1463499604040848.

Morgan C. and Winters J. (2015). Introduction: Critical blogging in archaeology. Internet *Archaeology* 39. https://doi.org/10.11141/ia.39.11.

Mudge M. (2016). Transparency for empirical data. In Bentkowska-Kafel A, Denard H. and Baker D. (eds.), *Paradata and Transparency in Virtual Heritage*. Farnham: Ashgate, 252–263.

Niccolucci F., Beacham D., Hermon S. and Denard, H. (2010). Five years after: The London Charter revisited. In Artusi A., Joly M., Lucet G., Pitzalis D. and Ribes A. (eds.), *The 11th International Symposium on Virtual Reality, Archaeology and Cultural Heritage*. Graz: The Eurographics Association, 101–104.

Niccolucci F., Felicetti A., Amico N. and D'Andrea, A. (2013). Quality control in the production of 3D documentation of monuments. In *Built Heritage 2013 Monitoring Conservation Management*. Milano: Centro per la Conservazion, 864–873.

Nicolaas G. (2011). *Survey paradata: A review*. Review paper. Southampton: NCRM.

Olson K. (2013). Paradata for nonresponse adjustment. *The Annals of the American Academy of Political and Social Science* 645(1), 142–170. https://doi.org/10.1177/0002716212459475.

Online Etymology Dictionary. (2023). -para (prefix). Available at www.etymonline.com/word/para-#etymonline_v_7162 (accessed 29 May 2024).

Online Etymology Dictionary. (2024). data (noun). Available at www.etymonline.com/word/data#etymonline_v_782 (accessed 29 May 2024).

Oxford English Dictionary. (2023). para- (prefix). https://doi.org/10.1093/OED/3136200135 (accessed 29 May 2024).

Oxford English Dictionary (2024). data (noun). https://doi.org/10.1093/OED/7999740343 (accessed 29 May 2024).

Phillips D. and Smit M. (2021). Toward best practices for unstructured descriptions of research data. *Proceedings of the Association for Information Science and Technology* 58(1), 303–314.

Pinheiro R., Holanda M., Araujo A. P. F., Walter, M. E. and Lifschitz, S. (2013). Automatic capture of provenance data in genome project workflows. In *2013 IEEE International Conference on Bioinformatics and Biomedicine*, 15–20. https://doi.org/10.1109/BIBM.2013.6732621.

Pomerantz J. (2015). *Metadata*. Cambridge, MA: MIT Press.

Post C. and Chassanoff A. (2021). Beyond the workflow: Archivists' aspirations for digital curation practices. *Archival Science* 21(4), 413–432. https://doi.org/10.1007/s10502-021-09365-0.

Reilly P., Callery S., Dawson I. and Gant S. (2021). Provenance illusions and elusive paradata: When archaeology and art/archaeological practice meets the phygital. *Open Archaeology* 7(1), 454–481. https://doi.org/10.1515/opar-2020-0143.

Richards-Rissetto H. and Landau K. (2019). Digitally-mediated practices of geospatial archaeological data: Transformation, integration, & interpretation. *Journal of Computer Applications in Archaeology* 2(1), 120–135. http://doi.org/10.5334/jcaa.30.

Ronzino P., Hermon S., and Niccolucci F. (2012). A metadata schema for cultural heritage documentation. *Electronic Imaging & the Visual Arts*. Florence: Firenze University Press, 36–41. http://doi.org/10.1400/187333.

Rösch F. (2021). From drawing into digital: On the transformation of knowledge production in postexcavation processing. *Open Archaeology* 7(1), 1506–1528. https://doi.org/10.1515/opar-2020-0211.

Schenk S., Dividino R. and Staab S. (2009). Reasoning with provenance, trust and all that other meta knowledge in OWL. In Freire J., Missier P. and Sahoo S. S. (eds.), *Proceedings of the First International Workshop on the role of Semantic Web in Provenance Management (SWPM 2009), collocated with the 8th International Semantic Web Conference (ISWC- 2009)*.

Sendelbah A., Vehovar V., Slavec A. and Petrovčič A. (2016). Investigating respondent multitasking in web surveys using paradata. *Computers in Human Behavior* 55, 777–787. https://doi.org/10.1016/j.chb.2015.10.028.

Sharma S. (2019). *Paradata, Interviewing Quality, and Interviewer Effects*. PhD dissertation. Ann Arbor: University of Michigan.

Siqueira J. and Martins D. L. (2022). Workflow models for aggregating cultural heritage data on the web: A systematic literature review. *Journal of the Association for Information Science and Technology* 73(2), 204–224. https://doi.org/10.1002/asi.24498.

Sköld O., Börjesson L. and Huvila, I. (2022). Interrogating paradata. *Information Research* 27. https://doi.org/10.47989/colis2206.

Smiraglia R. P. (2005). Introducing metadata. *Cataloging & Classification Quarterly*, 40(3–4), 1–15. https://doi.org/10.1300/J104v40n03_01.

Star S. L. and Griesemer J. R. (1989). Institutional ecology, 'translations' and boundary objects: Amateurs and professionals in Berkeley's Museum of Vertebrate Zoology, 1907-39. *Social Studies of Science* 19(3), 387–420. https://doi.org/10.1177/030631289019003001.

Stieger S. and Reips U.-D. (2010). What are participants doing while filling in an online questionnaire: A paradata collection tool and an empirical study. *Computers in Human Behavior* 26(6), 1488–1495. https://doi.org/10.1016/j.chb.2010.05.013.

Sundberg H. (2013). Process based archival descriptions: Organizational and process challenges. *Business Process Management Journal* 19(5), 783–798. https://doi.org/10.1108/BPMJ-Jan-2012-0002.

Sweeney S. (2008). The ambiguous origins of the archival principle of 'provenance'. *Libraries & the Cultural Record* 43(2), 193–213. www.jstor.org/stable/25549475.

Tennis J.T. (2008). *Metadata in the Chain of Preservation Model: Draft Metadata Specification Model*. InterPARES 2 working paper.

The London Charter Organization (2009a). *The London Charter for the computer-based visualisation of cultural heritage*. Available at https://londoncharter.org (accessed 29 May 2024).

The London Charter Organization (2009b). *The London Charter for the computer-based visualisation of cultural heritage: Principle 4 - Documentation*. Available at https://londoncharter.org/principles/documentation.html (accessed 29 May 2024).

Tompkins V. T., Honick B. J., Polley K. L. and Qin J. (2021). MetaFAIR: A metadata application profile for managing research data. *Proceedings of the Association for Information Science and Technology* 58(1), 337–345. https://doi.org/10.1002/pra2.461.

Ullah I. I. T. (2015). Integrating older survey data into modern research paradigms: Identifying and correcting spatial error in 'Legacy' datasets. *Advances in Archaeological Practice*, 3(4), 331–350. https://doi.org/10.7183/2326-3768.3.4.331.

W3C Working Group (2013). *PROV Model Primer*. Available at www.w3.org/TR/prov-primer (accessed 29 May 2024).

Wall G. and Hale A. (2021). Art & archaeology: Uncomfortable archival landscapes. *The International Journal of Art & Design Education* 39(4), 770–787. https://doi.org/10.1111/jade.12316.

West B. T. (2011). Paradata in survey research. *Survey Practice* 4(4). https://doi.org/10.29115/SP-2011-0018.

White L. (2017). Provenance of museum objects. In McDonald J. D. and Michael L.-C. (eds.), *Encyclopedia of Library and Information Sciences*, 4th ed. Boca Raton: CRC Press, 3756–3765.

Zeng M. L. and Qin J. (2016). *Metadata*. Chicago, IL: American Library Association.

3

Paradata 'In the Wild'

How and Where Paradata Emerges in Research Documentation

Olle Sköld and Lisa Andersson

3.1 Introduction

All manners of data-driven activities and processes, including analytical, curatorial and scholarly work, require access to data that can be used for the task at hand. Access to relevant and usable data is, however, not a primordial state of affairs in the sense that it is without preconditions. Instead, it ultimately rests on the user's ability to determine what data looks like, how it can be accessed, and whether it is task-relevant or not. The literature describing data and work with data in different settings offers an abundance of examples. Knorr-Cetina (1999) and Berg (1996) show how physicians have to sift through large amounts of signs, tactile and visual information, and outputs from medical machinery, physical examinations, as well as the patient's responses to clinical background questions to identify the data relevant to diagnose the medical condition at hand. In other settings, where different goals and methods are at play, similar situations emerge: Latour (1999) depicts how a group of Earth scientists arrives at a field site located at the crossroads of a savanna and the Amazonian rainforest and – by engaging in observation, indexing, cataloguing and sample-taking – transforms the vast complex of potential data offered at the site, manifested in tree varieties, different types of bushes, plants and soil types into a scholarly dataset pertinent to the question the expedition set out to answer: Is the rainforest advancing or retreating? Previous chapters in this volume have established paradata as a heterogeneous phenomenon with a broad range of examples and conceptual constructions and use cases, including facilitating secondary use of research data by offering insights into the practices and processes of data creation, curation and use (Huvila, 2022; Sköld et al., 2022). For paradata to become useful in supporting data reuse applications, however, it (like data) must first be identified and accessed, and just as in working out what vegetation and soil compositions are relevant for understanding the dynamics of Amazonian ecosystems, the identification of paradata is a context-sensitive task that is not particularly straightforward in the sense that what paradata is relevant and important will notably vary from use case to use case.

It has been suggested that in research-based data making one of the most valuable resources for identifying paradata is research documentation, that is, the many documents, datasets, notes, communications, drafts and documentary fragments that are produced during the course of scholarly work and stored in data repositories, email inboxes, hard-drive folders, and office shelves and cupboards (Borgman, 2012; Frank et al., 2015; Gant and Reilly, 2018; Huggett, 2012; Weber et al., 2012). Two approaches to identifying paradata in research documentation can be identified in the literature that this chapter will draw on. The first approach (paradata 'as thing'; cf. Buckland, 1991) is based on the idea that paradata can be documented, stored, managed, retrieved and used, and entails looking for descriptors and identifiers in research documentation indicating the existence of paradata (Faniel and Yakel, 2017; Huvila et al., 2022a; Huvila and Sköld, 2023). These descriptors and identifiers can be of different kinds. Nominally universal and domain-agnostic paradata identifiers exist in standards, schemes, guidelines, conceptual models and other instructions of how to describe and systematise data and, of course, in the corresponding datasets normalised by implementing these instructions (Börjesson et al., 2020; Mayernik, 2016; Zimmerman, 2008). For example, The London Charter (The London Charter Organization, 2009) and CIDOC CRM (Doerr et al., 2007) are a guideline and a standard regulating the description of archaeological visualisations and cultural heritage resources, respectively. They suggest that decisions and implicit and explicit reasoning underpinning them should be documented along with actions and events important to understanding the provenance of the item described. Paradata identifiers and descriptors are not solely found in highly structured data and data descriptions schemas, however, but are also present in more loosely organised datasets that are not systematic, but systematised to the extent required to enable sufficient analysis in their settings of origin (Baker and Yarmey, 2009; Börjesson et al., 2022b; Gitelman, 2013).

The second approach to identifying paradata suggested by earlier studies (paradata 'as practice') is to track paradata use cases and to learn from the gaze of paradata users where paradata emerges and how it is mobilised into action (Latour and Woolgar, 1979; Pasquetto et al., 2019; Shankar, 2009). This way of locating paradata emphasises domain knowledge and contextual insights on a micro-meso-macro gradient (research projects, research data collaborations, disciplinary epistemic horizons) as essential resources in identifying paradata. The approach draws on a longer line of research on scholarly data that stresses that while (para)data certainly is tangible and exists within a framework of material dependencies, it is also a malleable phenomenon that manifests itself differently across use settings and disciplinary contexts depending on what the specificities of the task requiring (para)data are (Borgman, 2015; Pinch and Bijker, 1984; Wallis et al., 2013).

Drawing on insights in tracing paradata in research documentation, the aim of this chapter is to show how and where paradata emerges in data documentation and what this paradata might look like. The chapter's approach to identifying paradata draws on and intertwines the two approaches outlined above. The analysis of how paradata is identified is informed by a comprehensive interview study done within the auspices of the CAPTURE project of how archaeologists and archaeological research data professionals locate, access and use paradata for reuse purposes (i.e., building on the paradata as practice perspective). One of the main objectives of the chapter is to facilitate more tangible understandings of what paradata (as a thing) is and how it can be located. Further, this chapter assumes that paradata can be present in documentation such as notes and log files, but also in oral briefings and other interactions between colleagues. Chapter 1 outlined the scope and rationales underpinning how the present book engages with paradata and Chapter 2 provided a deep-dive into the concept of paradata. This chapter offers an overview of practical examples of paradata that anticipates both the walk-through of formalised methods for identifying, capturing and documenting paradata offered in Chapters 4 and 5, and the approaches to managing paradata discussed in Chapter 6.

The chapter is organised as follows. First, literature on three topics is reviewed to create a framework for discussing how and where paradata emerges in research documentation. The topics reviewed are foundational perspectives on data, contextual perspectives on data, and how science and scholarly work can be understood from the viewpoints of documents and documentation. After that, a practice-led study of paradata in research documentation is presented on the basis of the CAPTURE interview study (Börjesson and Sköld, 2021; the study has been previously and differently reported in e.g., Börjesson, 2021 and Börjesson et al., 2022a) conducted in 2020–2021 and comprising thirty-one interviews.[1] Table 3.2 presents the key

---

[1] The semi-structured interviews were held in Swedish and English, and all translations have been done by the chapter authors.

findings of the chapter and describes what research documentation can be consulted to identify and extract paradata. The table also describes key characteristics of the paradata sources and the access affordances that impact how they can be located and used.

3.2 Understanding (Para)data

Scholarship on data can provide important resources for starting to think about what paradata might be and how it emerges in research documentation. Several of the frameworks and perspectives used to probe data as a notion and as something that is a part of human doings and ongoings in research and other areas of work and activity can also be useful for approaching paradata. Like paradata, data is a slippery concept. It is also, and to a much greater extent than paradata, a powerful operationaliser in the scholarly arena as, the 'substance' that is managed and curated (e.g., Koesten et al., 2020), described (e.g., Hjørland, 2023), collected, searched for (e.g., Gregory et al., 2019), analysed and interpreted (e.g., Leonelli and Tempini, 2020). Although data is a term often used to denote a general property of scholarly work and a key occurrence in academic research and its ecosystem of related activities, data is also something that can be thought about and approached as a thing (Buckland, 1991). This way of thinking emphasises the physical media, including the material strata that make up digital data (Kirschenbaum, 2008), where the data is recorded or otherwise present. Data as a thing appears in different shapes and across scholarly disciplines and the wider domains of labour and leisure. Beyond the examples of soil samples and data generated in medical examinations offered above, scholarly data can be the recorded interactions of high-energy particles (Knorr-Cetina, 1999), artefacts and observations made and documented during archaeological field excavations (Huvila, 2014), and the reports and publications coming out of already completed studies to be used for data aggregation purposes (Faniel and Yakel, 2017).

The breadth and complexity of the challenges related to discussing what data 'is' can be illustrated further. Heritage data is a term used to refer to the holdings of archives, libraries, museums, and other heritage institutions and organisations (Bruseker et al., 2017). Different modes of data work have been observed to be important parts of, for instance, the co-productive activities of videogame players (Sköld, 2017; Steinkuehler and Duncan, 2008; Warmelink, 2013) and people invested in self-tracking their daily, non-labour activities (Abtahi et al., 2020; Trace and Zhang, 2020). Scholarship concerned with defining data has stressed that while it is a complex notion (see e.g., Carlson and Anderson, 2007), it fundamentally signifies representations ('evidence' as per Birnholtz and Bietz, 2003, no pagination; 'facts' or 'observations' as per Rowley, 2007, p. 170; 'measurements' as per Zimmerman, 2008, p. 633) that describe the characteristics of things, events, and processes (e.g., Beretta, 2024; Rowley, 2007). Although it has been argued that data should always be understood as a social and cultural phenomenon in the sense that no set of data is without a context of production (Birnholtz and Bietz, 2003; Borgman, 2012; Gitelman, 2013; Hjørland, 2018), several attempts have been made to explain what data is by highlighting that data can potentially exist without a conceivable context of use. From this perspective, data can be independent of whether or not conditions are in place for understanding its contents or structure and putting it to use in a relevant way (Rowley, 2007). This is in contrast to a notion like information, which is generally (but not always, see e.g., Wallis et al. 2013) understood to have a higher degree of innate interpretability even though its usefulness and modes of interaction with the setting of use is anything but monolithic and vary widely from context to context (see e.g., Hjørland, 2023).

3.3 Understanding (Para)data in Context

There are numerous studies that further add to the complexity of what data is by stressing the inextricably contextual nature of data. Although this way of thinking about data encompasses an extensive range of perspectives and emphases, data here comes across as something that is always enmeshed with human affairs and that has to be understood by delving not only into the data itself but also taking into account what is done with data, through data, and by data in different settings of activity and work (Borgman, 2012; Hilgartner and Brandt-Rauf, 1994; Latour, 1987). In this view, data becomes data when it is mobilised into the practices that engage with it to achieve some result or to reach some goal (Berg, 1996; Birnholtz and Bietz, 2003; Oliver et al., 2024). These data practices can be those of making and interpreting data (Berg and Bowker, 1997; Huvila et al., 2021a; Huvila et al., 2021c), but also of, for example, adding marginalia (Edwards et al., 2017) and curating, aggregating, or visualising data (Börjesson et al., 2022b; Sköld et al., 2022). Data is not simply a resource in data practices, but an impactful agent that affects the outcomes and procedure of the practice of which it is a part, that is, creating and maintaining boundaries between groups of users and different forms of data use (Brown and Duguid, 1996; Huvila, 2011; Harvey and Chrisman, 1998) including the shaping of ethics and politics (Börjesson et al., 2020;

Olson, 2002) and impacting the ways in which data is organised (Nadim, 2021), circulated (Kansa and Kansa, 2021) and reused (Pasquetto et al., 2019). Some studies underline the sociomaterial nature of data. From this perspective, data's social – relating to the full range of data work and data-related activities – and material – that is, the infrastructural and technological – dimensions have to be considered in tandem when attempting to grasp what data is and what data does in its different settings of use (e.g., Berg, 1996; Pinch and Bijker, 1984). Data and data practices blend, cojoin, and collate into assemblages of social and material data doings that are continuously negotiated and to different extents local in flux (Law, 1993; Pickering, 1995).

Relating specifically to what underpins data identification, the context in which data is produced has been shown to greatly impact what is required for data to be captured and successfully reused by parties other than those involved in its making (Borgman, 2012; Durrant et al., 2011). Data is always entangled with the setting where it came from – a setting which is constituted in turn by certain methodological choices and implementations, theoretical interests, research purposes, institutional factors and technical know-how (Berg and Goorman, 1999; Faniel and Zimmerman, 2011; Van House, 2002b). If data is thought about and put to work in an environment framed by other epistemic horizons and approaches, challenges may arise that impact the usability of the data unless mitigated. Examples of challenges include difficulties in understanding what the data signifies, how it can be interpreted, and to what extent it is purposeful and trustworthy (Baker and Yarmey, 2009; Faniel and Jacobsen, 2010; Rolland and Lee, 2013; Yakel et al., 2013). Using various kinds of data descriptions in order to elucidate what is considered to be, for identification and usability, the central elements of the data is considered to be one of the main ways to bring the horizons of data makers and data reusers closer together. Thus, data useful in one setting can also be useful (albeit possibly in different ways) in another (Baker and Yarmey, 2009; Carlson and Anderson, 2007; Zimmerman, 2008). Data descriptions that decrease the 'distance-from-origin' (Baker and Yarmey, 2009, p. 13) between data makers and data reusers can be free-form or structured to varying degrees using, for example, standards and recommendations. However, all have to navigate variations on the same dilemma: From one data reuse scenario to the next, it is difficult to know what information is required to bridge the gap between the locales where data is first made and used and the secondary-use contexts (Carlson and Anderson, 2007; Faniel and Zimmerman, 2011; Zimmerman, 2008). Additionally, metadata schemas and standards that are deemed to be purposeful in one domain may not work equally well in another (Birnholtz and Bietz, 2003; Fear and Donaldson, 2012; Yakel et al., 2013).

3.4 Tracing the Interplay between Research and Research Documentation

For paradata created and generated during the course of research work, research documentation is one of the main sources from which it can be harvested. Identifying documentation as a source of paradata reflects a fundamental tenet of sociomaterial insight into the practices and processes of scholarly knowledge-making: namely that documentation is something present and notably, but differently (Becher, 1989; Knorr-Cetina, 1999), involved in all major steps of the research lifecycle (see e.g., Latour and Woolgar, 1979; Trace, 2011). The overall centrality of documentation and systems of documentation in human epistemic endeavours is also highlighted by research that examines how knowledge is made and negotiated in broader contexts of labour and leisure beyond the scope of science (Harper, 1998; Law and Lynch, 1988; Levy, 2001).

It has been similarly noted that research documentation is valuable for purposes of paradata collection and use (Geiger and Ribes, 2011; Hodges, 2021; Sköld, 2018). Documents and documentation can manifest in many different forms and contain information about any number of things, as is shown by a range of information studies research (see e.g., Briet, 2006; Lund, 2009). The ubiquity and importance of documentation in knowledge-making stems not principally from document 'aboutness' (Brown and Duguid, 1996; Hjørland, 2000), although aboutness has been underlined as being of importance (e.g., Buckland, 2018), but rather from how documentation functions epistemically and socially (Lund, 2010).

In academic research settings, documentation can vary in how it functions and appears across disciplines. It is understood to be a material, historically situated, and genre-bound resource in scholarly work that simultaneously and in various ways supports, coordinates and perpetuates many of the defining practices of research (research design, data collection and analysis, ethical constraints, the reporting of findings and results; see e.g., Cragin and Shankar, 2006). Documentation is also the principal scholarly deliverable of science in the form of books, papers in scholarly journals, and datasets (Frohmann, 2004a; Knorr-Cetina, 1999; Trace, 2011). In addition to emerging as scholarly end products, the major part of research documentation is composed of documents created for supporting purposes during the course of scientific activity. Examples include field diaries, notes and sketches, and other scholarly by-products and marginalia (Edwards et al., 2017; Huvila et al., 2021a; Shankar, 2009; Spedding and Tankard, 2021).

Research examining the production of scholarly documentation during scientific work has identified overarching issues affecting the extent to which documentation offers useful and usable paradata. One such issue is that a large part of the documentation arising from research activities is created to serve project- or research-specific purposes, which often do not consider the need to support secondary data use by any party not already involved in the original data production (Börjesson et al., 2022b; Sköld et al., 2022). For paradata present in research documentation, this means that access and identification of supporting resources to be able to interpret the paradata in sufficient context are likely to be pervasive challenges.

Another issue concerns the ability of expert insiders to explain data work and appearance. A major obstacle for identifying and using paradata in research documentation is the bridging of 'insider' and 'outsider' horizons of data insights and understandings. Sometimes, even expert insiders have trouble explaining what precisely their work with data looks like and why they do the things they do (Ciborra and Lanzara, 1994; Shepherd and Rudd, 2014). This is especially the case if the audience belongs to disciplinary domains or subdomains with different epistemic and methodological hallmarks (Faniel and Yakel, 2017; Niu, 2009; Pardo et al., 2006) or levels of in-field proficiency (Faniel et al., 2012; Yakel et al., 2013). The degrees of similarity and difference between the contexts of paradata making and paradata use are important broad-scope parameters in explaining the potential and challenges of paradata local-isation and use (Borgman, 2012; Faniel and Zimmerman, 2011). However, studies of facilitating factors and barriers of data reuse among, for example, archaeologists (Faniel et al., 2013), ecologists (Zimmerman, 2008), earthquake engineers (Faniel and Jacobsen, 2010), medical researchers and space physi-cists (Birnholtz and Bietz, 2003) have shown which paradata characteristics researchers find useful for facilitating understanding of what a dataset manifests and how it can be engaged with secondary-use purposes. Paradata containing information about how a dataset has been collected, processed (Borgman, 2012; Börjesson et al., 2022a; Rolland and Lee, 2013), and organised (Börjesson et al., 2022a; Yoon, 2014a) – including explanations of variables (Rolland and Lee, 2013) and concepts (Faniel et al., 2012) with a high degree of explanatory potential – emerges as valuable in several settings of use, although there are variations in the findings across themes and emphases.

Similarly useful is paradata underpinning facets such as the background and goals of the research producing the data (Borgman, 2012; Niu, 2009). Alongside paradata quality, coverage, findability and completeness impacting the success of data reuse attempts (Faniel et al., 2016; Faniel and Yakel, 2017) are the personal elements of the individual data reusers. Examples of personal elements include the degree of required data-related skills (Niu, 2009) and literacies (Börjesson, 2021; Kim and Yoon, 2017), and perceptions of data usefulness, sufficiency of resources supporting the data reuse venture, degrees of trust in the data (Faniel and Jacobsen, 2010; Yoon, 2014a), and the credibility of the data and its makers (Faniel et al., 2016; Franks, 2024; Huvila, 2020).

Several studies have adopted different approaches to determining how paradata can be identified in research documentation of both the end product and supporting resources. These studies show that paradata can be identified in the full range of digital and physical research documentation, from papers to reports and monographs, from notes in databases and datasets to diaries and codebooks (e.g., Börjesson et al., 2022b; Niu, 2009; Sköld et al., 2022), as well as the visual representations (including photographs but also other types of visual representations like maps and drawings) underlined as important representations of scholarly practices and processes by Huggett (2023) and Huvila et al. (2023a). The breadth of documented paradata corresponds to how researchers document research practices and processes, something which is done in many ways, for many purposes, using many different means (Huvila et al., 2021c; Huvila et al., 2022a; Knorr-Cetina, 1999).

The paradata itself can also emerge differently. Börjesson et al. (2022b) note that paradata can be either explicit and manifested in descriptions of how certain operations impacting the resulting research data were planned and executed, or indirect evidence by which data actions, deliberations and processes can be traced (see also Huvila et al., 2023a). Due to the potential richness of paradata stemming from the many traces of data practices and processes in datasets, it has been suggested that 'messy' and non-harmonised datasets might not be a hindrance to data reuse (e.g., Richards et al., 2021) but actually an asset in facilitating insight into what measures were taken in its creation and preparation (Börjesson et al., 2022b). Paradata can, for instance, be identified in missing information and incompleteness that, while often being detrimental to paradata quality (West and Sinibaldi, 2013), via information gaps and otherwise non-available and non-interpretable information, can be used to some extent as useful paradata due to it to reflecting the priorities, methods, and abilities supporting the original data-making endeavour (Huvila et al., 2023b; Ullah, 2015). Normalised and harmonised datasets are easier to make interoperable, which would open up opportunities for identifying and aggregating paradata in large corpuses of research documentation (Gunnarsson, 2020; Kintigh, 2006). There is a risk of over-standardising datasets (Plantin and Thomer, 2023), however, when in different ways adapting them to standards for enhanced interoperability (Maron and Feinberg, 2018). In this way, dataset normalisation, harmonisation and standardisation can mean that potentially useful paradata is cleaned away in the data curation process (Börjesson et al., 2022).

3.5 Following Practice: How Archaeologists and Archaeological Research Data Professionals Identify Paradata

The interview study of how archaeologists and archaeological research data professionals use and create paradata exemplifies how information qualifying as paradata provides information about a varied set of scholarly practices and processes, and is heterogeneous in the sense that it emerges in research documentation with different characteristics and access affordances. The following section will examine the three types of documentation that were most commonly consulted by the interviewees as sources of paradata, and illustrate the descriptive qualities and what practices and processes that the paradata that was obtained from these types provide information about. The document types are: method descriptions, references and structured information. They occur in several interconnected forms and shapes across many types of research documentation, as shown in Table 3.1.

3.5.1 Method Descriptions

The interviewed researchers and data professionals commonly consult various types of 'method descriptions' in the documentation when working to identify paradata in research documentation. Method descriptions occur in several kinds of research documentation and are differently manifested in terms of how extensive the descriptions are and where they can be located and accessed.

Table 3.1 *A selection of the documentation types that the researchers and archaeological research data professionals in the CAPTURE interview study identified as paradata sources*

Documentation type	Documentation type description	Prevalent instances of research documentation
Method descriptions	Accounts of the actions and deliberations involved in creating research data	Journal articles, monographs, reports, notes, working logs, email messages
References	Codes or other identifiers that serve as connectors between items of research documentation	References to scholarly publications, datasets, authors, data authors
Structured information	Information organised according to a standard or other organisational principles	Standards, local standards, data dictionaries, domain ontologies, scripts and code

Method Descriptions in Reporting Documentation

And I just thought, "Oh no, [the georeference coordinates are] wrong".
[- - -] But then I went and found the original paper and I checked
the coordinates and the coordinates in the database are actually the
coordinates that are in the paper, they were just wrong. But the paper
was from 1992. So, people were not using GPS then. (Interview no. 7)

Researchers and data professionals ubiquitously use method descriptions in
published (journal articles, monographs) and unpublished (reports, manuals
and guides, theses and dissertations) scholarly outputs as sources of paradata.
Method descriptions in these types of scholarly reporting documentation are
often easy to identify and examine, with the exceptions of older and undigi-
tised items. They are fairly homogenous in the sense that descriptions account
for the main elements of research processes by reflecting the guiding research
questions and framing of the inquiry or task, methods and materials, interpretative resources, and results in method and materials sections and similar
passages. The paradata identified in the method descriptions of scholarly
reporting documentation is broad in scope and reflects the practices and
processes of how the data has been created, used and curated in a way that is
narratively and semantically comprehensible. To some extent, it is also formalised and genre-bound, although the scope, detail and format of the paradata
can vary. Some reporting documentation is highly standardised, while other
method descriptions are free-form and provisional, reporting observations and
reflections that stem from different forms of investigative and analytical
activities, including fieldwork. Notes and field notes of this nature are not
the final reporting documentation of the research processes they come from,
but are an important building block for it. They contain descriptions of how
research methods have been employed in empirical research and what results
emerged out of the process.

Paradata about the procedures and means involved in creating primary (previously non-existing) data in an empirical setting like a field site or laboratory,
including instruments and instrument settings, are often identified in the method
descriptions of reporting documentation. Data-use paradata is also present there
and offers insights into how the data has been analysed to support the results
presented in, for instance, the article or report. The main elements of management paradata available in the method descriptions of reporting documentation
provide information about the procedures involved in the aggregation and
integration of available data resources. Examples of such sources include bodies
of source documents and collections of already created research data that are
aggregated into composite datasets and databases.

Method Descriptions in Auxiliary Documentation

And those sorts of things, decisions and exceptions and strange stuff, that is what we document while talking about it, and by having that discussion be part of the [project] records. (interview no. 19)

Paradata can also be identified in the methods descriptions of auxiliary documentation. While paradata in the method descriptions of reporting documentation emerges from the relationship between the documentation and the modes of scholarly work reported there, the researchers and data professionals also identify paradata in method descriptions of other types of documents. Rather than being one of the final outputs of a research process, these types of documents have intermediate or supporting characteristics. They are created and used to document, guide and otherwise support the research being done. Auxiliary documentation of this kind encompasses a broad range of research documentation, from highly structured and detailed files to sparse hand-written notes and documentary fragments.

The method descriptions where paradata can be identified in auxiliary research documentation similarly vary in comprehensiveness, format and accessibility. Comprehensive method descriptions in auxiliary documentation are often similar to those present in reporting documentation in that the descriptions have narrative structures and are written for audiences other than the author. In contrast to reporting documentation, however, method descriptions in auxiliary documentation are usually primarily intended for internal or project-specific applications. As a result, they are less formalised and have, for instance, a substantial presence of abbreviated forms of notes and comments, and they generally require more domain knowledge to understand and use.

A recurrent type of auxiliary documentation with comprehensive method descriptions is task and procedure documentation. This documentation can be shared working logs of project team members, in which paradata is present in the form of research activities formulated and tracked objectives, documentation of data management procedures and underpinning decisions stored in joint online resources such as internal wikis or repositories.

Method descriptions present in the entire body of notes and drafts produced during the course of scholarly work can also be used to identify paradata. These method descriptions come in the form of sketches that outline implemented methodologies or workflows, records of how a dataset has been analysed, enriched with metadata or otherwise managed. Email messages are another source of comprehensive method information consulted to identify paradata and, likely due to the prevalence of email communication in scholarly work, paradata about a broad range of research activities can be identified there – from paradata about how research data has been categorised and described to the steps of data analysis and creation.

Less comprehensive method descriptions in auxiliary documentation are characterised by often being produced only to support the person writing them. They are very informal and use large amounts of shorthand and abbreviations. The method paradata in less comprehensive auxiliary documentation is not narrative but trace-like, representing isolated actions or disassociated pieces of method paradata, and it requires a high degree of domain familiarity to be informative. Examples from the interview study include communicating the lack of precision in the geolocation of finds by putting three zeroes at the end of the related GIS coordinates, and using certain signifiers like dashes and question marks to indicate interpretative uncertainty in dataset items.

3.5.2 References

References in Scholarly Publications

And if it's something quite specific and well-defined, then those citations tend to be really solid and [. . .] like, okay, you know, here is the canonical article that establishes why this particular term is something that we record [in the dataset]. And then some things that are like, okay, well, that's just kind of general domain knowledge, those tend to get citations in kind of introductory handbooks to, you know, the handbook to archaeological specimens or whatever it is. (interview no. 12)

Another commonly consulted source of paradata are diverse formal and informal references. References in research documentation function in interlocking ways: either by the reference itself offering insight into research practices and processes, or by referring the researcher to the publication or referenced item where the paradata can be identified.

Paradata emerging from references in the first instance is only accessible with significant domain familiarity. A reference to landmark publications with large impact on subsequent works produced in its line of research can signal that the research output where the reference is present conforms to certain methodological traditions or modes of thought. Additionally, a reference to well-known datasets in a specific area of research – one example from the interview study is *Kong Valdemars Jordebog*, a Danish fourteenth-century census book containing, among other things, land ownership information not available in other sources – might also provide trace information about how the data has been created, curated and used for study and what contextual elements have impacted the dataset.

In the second instance, researchers identify paradata in references by engaging with the items that the references point at. These items can be published or unpublished texts, datasets or parts of a datasets and not seldom they provide paradata of a narrative nature, such as method descriptions. Access affordances and the paradata provided vary between different kinds of references, and references present in datasets and in scholarly literature, respectively, are the most prevalent kinds.

References in Datasets

> Well, there are find coordinates [in the aggregated dataset] and included are also three additional types of references to other data sources: the ID of find post in the [Swedish National Heritage Board's database for archaeological sites and monuments] if it's available [- - -], a reference to publications appended to the data [. . .], and a museum collection inventory number – that's the most important thing, so that the [physical finds] can be located. (Interview no. 27)

The references present in datasets that researchers and data managers use to identify paradata refer to both literature and other datasets. References to other datasets often occur in datasets that themselves are the result of aggregation or integration data work, where multiple data sources have been merged or otherwise connected into a structure that can be consulted as a whole. These references are used by researchers to identify paradata about the individual datasets to better understand the research work that created them, or to understand how the aggregated dataset has been assembled. There are also internal references that link the segments of a dataset, and which can offer insights into how the dataset and its parts are related to each other. Datasets in database environments have tables that are linked together by identifiers, and beyond offering search functionalities these links can be used as paradata because they provide information about how the data in the tables is connected. Examples include how the results presented in one table connect to underpinning method descriptions or other research process elements in another table.

References in datasets to literature are employed to identify similar paradata, namely information about how the dataset has been created including definitions of variables and descriptions of stances and decisions taken. In addition to this, references in literature are also used to learn how related datasets have been created, used and curated. Most commonly, this literature reports the results of research based on the data in question, as is explained in the previous section. References embedded in the method descriptions can offer more detailed insight into the scholarly processes that shaped the supporting dataset. References in scholarly literature that refer to datasets can be used in order to gain access to the paradata in the dataset itself, including gaining a better understanding of how the data has been described and engaged in the analytic process.

References to Authors and Data Authors

> Yeah, I mean I would say probably the most important information that I would add to this project [dataset] description is the credits [of the data author]. (interview no. 18)

A common position among the researchers and data professionals interviewed in the study is that references to the actors involved in data authorship – names as well as laboratory affiliation of the individuals – are highly useful to elicit paradata. Although the name alone of a data author can provide information about the contents of a dataset and modes of work involved in producing it, the main way to gain paradata through data authorship references is to communicate with data authors. Data authors can give access to several important paradata sources, such as information about the techniques, methods, software and instruments employed, as well as other rich context and process information. Advantages to sourcing paradata via authorship references are that the data authors can explain facets of the research process that are rarely documented and otherwise difficult to obtain. Such facets include the exploratory parts of the research process that are seldom reflected in the final research outputs, and underlying disciplinary norms and domain knowledge that are difficult to discern and articulate but with impact on the data created.

3.5.3 Structured Information

'Structured information' is the third documentation type of great importance for the modes of paradata use found in the interview study. The 'reference' documentation type is fairly homogenous by being mainly of a trace rather than a narrative character, and being principally formalised. The structured information used to identify paradata, on the other hand, is akin to the 'method descriptions' documentation type in being considerably varied. Structured information that can be used to access paradata range from technical and descriptive standards to different degrees formalised local conventions for describing and presenting data including scripts and code, and semantic typologies like data dictionaries and domain ontologies.

Standards and 'Local Standards'

I know that for [the] CIDOC CRM [standard], there are many options with that ontology to document procedural information such as who did what, when, with what data. (interview no. 11)

Researchers and data professionals identify paradata in research documentation by looking for standards employed and referenced. Standards are used as interpretative tools that, due to their nominal status as institutionally backed and highly organised descriptors of how scholarly actions should be performed – CIDOC CRM and geolocation standards are the most commonly occurring examples in the study – can be used to gain insight into settings of scholarly data work across sites, disciplines and time. Standards can yield paradata about how datasets have been described by providing the supporting metadata principles. They can also show how the components of an aggregated dataset have been linked together through standards that establish and describe research tasks, processes or other categories present in the integrated datasets. Standards are also consulted in order to identify paradata about how data has been analysed and created, including how instruments and computational tools have been calibrated and what their operating conditions were like during the time of data creation.

Apart from standards, there are many other established ways of creating, using and managing data that are described in research documentation, and are sought by researchers to identify paradata. These 'local standards' vary more in the extent to which they are formalised and documented than do institutionalised standards. They also have more local application: in complex and large-scale research tasks as well as more limited ones, local standards are sometimes used in the data collection and description work of individual researchers. Occasionally, they coordinate the scholarly efforts of researcher groups or networks. The paradata provided by local standards is similar in type to the paradata than can be identified in standards, but showcases a broader scope in that, in addition to data on data creation, description and management, research contexts and modes of data use, it provides a greater extent of narrative and trace paradata about group attitudes, idiosyncratic approaches to different scholarly tasks. Local standards have similarly diverse access affordances that can be described sparingly or comprehensively, and can be found in the often internally kept auxiliary documentation produced within research projects and accessible in online repositories and other online resources.

Semantic Typologies

Yes. I am quite specific on that, because I think it's very important to be specific on what kind of terms and stuff you use, also so other people know exactly what you mean when you call something "orange". Or when you call something "angular", what you mean with it. (interview no. 8)

Semantic typologies of different varieties are another prevalent form of structured information in research documentation used to identify paradata. These typologies offer paradata that is, on a general level, similar to that identified in standards and local standards – it tells the reader about the main phenomena that exist within the area that the typologies encompass and details what the relationships between the phenomena are in a way that is often largely formalised. In contrast to standards and local standards, the semantic typologies are principally oriented towards mapping areas and domains of conceptual knowledge and are less concerned with the practices and processes of how research data is created, curated or used. Semantic typologies are useful sources of paradata, providing insights into the scope, pivotal concepts and relationships between concepts that have informed data work in research projects and research data collaborations. This paradata presents the opportunities to better grasp the epistemic horizons of a certain research venture, and enables purposeful comparisons and data integration, by providing definitions of notions and parameters that signify one significance of a range of possible significances.

Semantic typologies in research documentation that have been collected or managed over an extended period of time can also offer paradata about research procedures, where changing ways of describing data or defining terms and parameters traces reconsiderations and other changing modes of work. Instances of semantic typologies found in research documentation are data dictionaries, which provide definitions of impactful terms, variables and parameters present in a dataset; domain ontologies, which frequently map high-level entities comprising a certain data domain; and scope notes, which offer paradata about the area of empirical reality that the dataset describes along with the main conceptual vocabulary and methodologies used to interpret and study it.

Codes and Scripts

So, I expect the reader to start in the R Markdown file and then kind of navigate through the rest of the compendium according to the code that I've written in there. And perhaps, like reverse the past, reverse engineer my analysis from the R Markdown, which is kind of the recipe that brings all the bits and pieces together. (interview no. 30)

Codes and scripts are an additional instance of structured information used to identify paradata in research documentation. These are written, for example, to analyse, visualise, aggregate or otherwise process and use research data using, for example, Excel formulas, and code in the R or Python programming languages. The paradata in codes and scripts shares characteristics with paradata in standards, local standards and semantic typologies. Even though the code or scripts themselves may differ in terms of how well documented they are and to what degree commands and functions have been stringently implemented, the programming and scripting languages are in a fundamental sense documented and described in a way that is meant to transcend different areas of operation and implementation.

Code and scripts – especially codes and scripts that have been written to be transparent – are also consulted to trace what operations were performed on the datasets involved, and to understand why the resulting outputs look the way they do. These operations can provide information about established modes of work in a manner similar to standards and local standards. They may also make it possible to determine what parameters or variables were defined in the preprocessing stages of scholarly data work and to see how they support in the resulting analysis or visualisation.

3.6 How Can Paradata in Research Documentation Be Identified, and What Does It Look Like?

The basic premise of this chapter is that knowing how to identify data useful for solving the task at hand, and being able to know what this data might look like, are important conditions of successful (para)data procurement. The observations from the CAPTURE interview study add to the significance of this starting point by reinforcing the characterisation suggested by previous research that the work of science to large extents resembles work of and with documentation (Frohmann, 2004a; Shankar, 2009). The interview observations also show that paradata of many kinds can be identified in a broad range of the scholarly documents and snippets of documentation like out-of-context notes and potentially informative traces of acts and events available in such documentation (see also, e.g., Huvila et al., 2021a; Huvila et al., 2023a; Niu, 2009).

From this outset we can examine how paradata in research documentation might be identified, and to describe paradata's potential appearance from the two perspectives of paradata as thing and paradata as practice. The former perspective directs attention towards how paradata is physically manifested in research documentation; the latter emphasises how paradata is involved in and emerges from the modes of work and activities enacted by the interviewed researchers and data professionals. Together these perspectives highlight related but distinct facets of paradata available 'in the wild' of research documentation, how it might be identified, and what it might look like.

3.6.1 Paradata as Thing

When approaching the instances of paradata described in the interview study from the data as thing perspective, paradata emerges as method descriptions (in e.g., journal articles, monographs, unpublished reports and dissertations, and in notes, work logs and emails), references (in and between e.g., datasets and publications), and structured information (in e.g., standards, local standards, code and scripts) examined for their information about past research practices and processes.

Table 3.2 summarises where paradata is identified in research documentation and provides examples of key sources to consult in the capture of paradata. The table also describes the overarching characteristics of the paradata that can be extracted from these sources alongside the sources' access affordances. In the table, 'paradata access affordance A' signifies that the paradata sources are accessible in online public access catalogues, publication or preprint repositories, or open data repositories. 'Paradata access affordance B', on the other hand, shows that the paradata sources are accessible by consulting data authors or data authoring organisations. If the paradata sources require significant domain knowledge to access they are marked as having 'paradata access affordance C'. Access affordances referenced within parenthesis signifies that it is present to a lesser extent.

Corresponding and complementary to the results of earlier inquiries into paradata in research documentation (Börjesson et al., 2022b; Huvila et al., 2021c; Huvila et al., 2022b), the document types emerging from the analysis in the preceding section contains several kinds of paradata. The kinds of paradata range from paradata about how research data was created, including both machine use and research steps and methods employed, data aggregation and curation and analysis procedures, to how the data has been organised and structured. Although method descriptions, references and structured information alongside the prevalent instances of paradata manifestations they collate are examples of paradata identifiers signalling that the presence of paradata can be reasonably expected, the paradata may vary considerably in terms of aboutness. That is to say, there might be data creation paradata, data curation paradata, data organisation paradata and so on but the paradata may also

Table 3.2 *An overview of how to identify and access paradata in research documentation based on the results of the CAPTURE interview study*

Where paradata is identified	Key sources to consult	Paradata characteristics	Paradata access affordances
In method descriptions	Published reporting documentation like journal articles and scholarly monographs	The paradata describes the principal activities and resources involved in data creation, curation and use	A
	Unpublished reporting documentation like reports, manuals, guides, theses and dissertations	The paradata is akin to the paradata in method descriptions of published reporting documentation, but more varied in comprehensiveness and content	A, B
	Auxiliary research documentation like notes, work logs, drafts, email messages, internal documentation of research procedures	The paradata describes often discrete activities or resources involved in data creation, curation, and use with significant variances in comprehensiveness, structure and format	B, C
In references	References in published and unpublished reporting documentation; the referenced literature	The paradata describes a wide range of paradata principally informing about what literature is discussed with and drawn upon, and in what respects	A
	References in datasets including databases; the referenced datasets and databases	The paradata describes how datasets are linked to each other and to literature, and how dataset components are linked	A, B, C
In consultations with data authors	Data authors and data authoring organisations	Data authors or data authoring organisations can provide broad-range paradata that partly may not be otherwise accessible	A, B
In structured information	Standards in published and unpublished reporting documentation; the referenced standard	The paradata describes how data has been described, structured, created, curated and used	A, B

Table 3.2 (*cont.*)

Where paradata is identified	Key sources to consult	Paradata characteristics	Paradata access affordances
	'Local' standards in published and unpublished reporting documentation	The paradata describes how data has been described, structured, created, curated and used, but will significant variances in comprehensiveness	A, (B), C
	Semantic typologies like ontologies, data dictionaries, scope notes, concept mappings	The paradata describes the significance and scope of concepts and conceptual structures	A, (B)
	Codes and scripts like R code, Python code, Excel formulas	The paradata describes detailed data creation and processing steps	A, (B)

exhibit a range of other characteristics along intersecting gradients of formalisation, comprehensiveness and scope. The paradata can be highly formalised as shown, for instance, in data created or described using geolocation or other standards, or be free-form in structure and content as in notes and sketches intended for use within a research project or group. Both standardised and free-form paradata is rule-bound, however, albeit by different sets of constraints and with different degrees of formalisation; 'informal' documentation like email messages, notes and notations in databases may also be tied to paradata genres and adhere to localised and more idiosyncratic standards or ways of organising, relating and documenting terms, variables or research procedures (Börjesson et al., 2022b; Huvila et al., 2022a).

As observed by Maron and Feinberg (2018) and Birnholtz and Bietz (2003), data impacted by standards and guidelines may also operationalise these in different ways and to different extents, resulting in paradata that may be less formalised than expected. Similarly, paradata in certain document types and in certain regards appear more comprehensive than others, such as method descriptions in reporting documentation vis-à-vis trace-like notations of actions in a work log. It may be that while the method descriptions better adhere to the established way of reporting how a study was planned and enacted, the work log may yield less processed and, within a more limited scope, fuller and better serialised expressions of what was done during the course of a study.

3.6.2 Paradata as Practice

Paradata in research documentation can also be considered from the perspective of practices. In the interviews there are two practices that particularly come into play: how archaeologists and archaeological data professionals create paradata in research documentation, and how they identify it.

When it comes to the practice of creating paradata, several things can be observed. Firstly, paradata can be created with the objectives of several audiences in mind (Faniel and Zimmerman, 2011; Huvila and Sköld, 2023). While it may be difficult to clearly map categories of underpinning intentionality to what paradata emerges from different document types, there are some patterns that are striking. Paradata in the method descriptions and references of published reporting documentation (monographs, journal articles) are more likely to be created with an audience in mind that is external to the local setting of the reported research task. The narratives of what activities, decisions and deliberations took place, and how as well as when, provided by this paradata can be expected to be, to some extent, shaped by the regimes of scholarly discourse and expectation that vary across research traditions and disciplines (Huvila et al., 2021c; Shankar, 2007).

There is also paradata that is similarly embedded in the context where it was created, but where the hallmarks of its embeddedness are distinct – and akin. This paradata has strong processual characteristics in that it was created to support a particular process, for example, data analysis, aggregation or organisation. It can be identified in material such as notes and shorthand annotations in datasets, and in data structures that correspond to modes of work that are exercised within very local circumstances where the intended paradata stakeholders are few, comprising only the paradata creator and possibly members of a research group.

It can also be observed that paradata creators document paradata using a range of strategies. These strategies involve different document locations, approaches, and means (Huvila et al., 2022a; Sköld et al., 2022). Some strategies produce results, such as references and method descriptions in published outputs, data work informed by standards, or more regimented unpublished items like reports, that vary less in terms of what the paradata looks like and how it can be identified. Others display a larger degree of idiosyncrasy and variety.

In the interview study, paradata that describes sequences of events, even if described rudimentarily or with little narrative structure, is more often self-contained and available in documentation separate from datasets or publications. Paradata documented in formats more closely resembling traces and marginalia tends to be present in a broader range of locations in and across datasets and collections of documents (Edwards et al., 2017; cf. Sköld, 2017). In many cases, there is some degree of structure to paradata traces and marginalia, which can be used to identify and interpret them. This structure is often anchored in local modes of documenting research practices and processes that are themselves to a lesser degree documented or institutionalised beyond their immediate context of creation.

The interview study also highlights some patterns in the practices of identifying paradata: the interviewees identify paradata among data authors and contributors, in the gaps and relationships between research documentation, and in research documentation. Consulting data authors and contributors is a crucial strategy in the practice of identifying paradata. It is not always possible to carry out, for example, because data authors or contributors cannot be contacted or because it is difficult to determine, especially in large datasets, who was responsible for what data task or operation. While consulting the people involved in data creation, curation and use is an approach that has the potential to yield detailed and comprehensive paradata, it is not always successful even if contact between paradata maker and paradata user can be established. The interviews reveal that the questions meant to facilitate locating and using paradata risk being framed within the horizon of paradata use to the extent that they are difficult to answer from a data creator's perspective. The reason for this is that questions can be closely tied to, for example, the research objectives, methodologies and modes of reasoning pertinent to the inquiry that the paradata is supposed to support, and these can be very different from the research setting from which the paradata originated (Rolland and Lee, 2013; Van House, 2002b; Voss, 2012).

Paradata is also identified in the gaps and relationships of research documentation, in the sense that the relationship between different parts of the same resource, for example, multiple entries in a database, or between several kinds of documentation can outline past data events. This practice is very useful in that it can be used to grasp undocumented or not insufficiently documented elements of data work in a broad range of documentation types. This can be done regardless of their degree of formalisation, comprehensiveness and scope, by serialising and tracing change and constants in all of the documentation types discussed above and presented in Table 3.2.

Another way of identifying paradata 'in between' research documentation resembles the 'reputational cues' that Huvila argues inform credibility assessments of research documentation (2020, no pagination; see also Berg and Goorman, 1999; Faniel et al., 2016; Fear and Donaldson, 2012). This method involves considering if there are some elements (the data author, the research project the documentation comes from, the documentation itself) that are institutionalised or otherwise well enough established within their domains to allow for making inferences regarding what the data is about, and how it has been accumulated, created or managed. To determine if such inferences can be made, it is necessary to have sufficient domain insight and understanding of the social and practical circumstances of the research work in order to be able to determine if there are reputational cues and what paradata they might offer.

In the same way that it is a common strategy to consult paradata in different documentation types that address relevant but not identical things (Börjesson et al., 2022a; Niu, 2009; Yoon, 2014b), it is rare to use discrete approaches to identifying paradata. Instead, paradata is often identified by consulting data documentation and data authors and contributors in some combination, and attempting to discover patterns in the research documentation that can offer useful insights into the scholarly data processes of interest (Fear and Donaldson, 2012; Huvila et al., 2021c). The interview study similarly shows that paradata from one source is rarely sufficient to answer all process queries. The usefulness of paradata rests to a significant extent on the degree to which it can be connected to other paradata or to what is known about how it is created and commonly used in the field of interest.

3.6.3 Paradata as Thing, Paradata as Practice

The two perspectives on paradata explored above are simultaneously distinct and connected. As a thing, paradata emerges in different forms and with varying scope, comprehensiveness and degrees of formalisation across many of the document types produced during the life cycles of research enterprises – from preparation to reporting, data management and sharing. It is useful to approach paradata as 'a thing' for the purposes of identification and localisation, but it is also useful for the same purposes to consider paradata as being a connected data entity that – in line with numerous studies in data and document scholarship (Borgman, 2012; Frohmann, 2004a; Latour, 1987; Shankar, 2009) – is integrally a part of practices of paradata creation and use.

While Chapter 7 continues the theorisation of paradata as a thing-and-as-practice by tying in to the thoroughgoing notion of working knowledge, encompassing both practices and paradata phenomena, it can here be concluded that having insight into the regimes of scholarly discourse and work that impacts how paradata is created and manifested in scholarly documentation is likely to be helpful in knowing how paradata can be identified and what it looks like in a certain discipline or area of research. Together with familiarity of how and where researchers in the domain of interest locate paradata, knowledge of paradata practices emerges as an important resource in the interpretative work of understanding and using the identified paradata as documentation of past research events and processes.

The discussion of paradata as 'thing' or 'practice' also ties in to the distinction made in Chapter 6, exploring the issue of how paradata can be managed in data repositories, between 'core' and 'potential' paradata. Core paradata refers to paradata that is generally understood as such, see, for example, the 'method descriptions' data type outline above or the more well-defined use of the paradata concept emerging in survey research as shown in Chapter 2. Potential paradata, by contrast, is information about research practices and processes that is not purposely created as paradata, but that might be used as paradata in particular circumstances. Examples drawn from the present chapter include auxiliary documentation, which potentially can be consulted for paradata but that is made for the purposes of supporting research processes. The thing-practice framework used to discuss paradata in this chapter is principally a theoretical tool that enables paradata to be discussed as a data entity that is identifiable from a nominally domain-agnostic vantage point, while retaining the non-essentialist stance that paradata is something that is ultimately sought, identified and put to use within the auspices of particular practices. The distinction between core and potential paradata signifies the extent to which certain paradata categories are conventionalised. The two frameworks, however, inform each other. When paradata is discussed in a thing-y way, it is likely also 'core' paradata in the sense that it is mobilised as such in a broad range of research and data management practices. The paradata potential of 'potential' paradata, on the other hand, is also ultimately based on the extent to which it is – or has the ability to become – a part of the activities and processes taking place within either data management or research-aligned practice.

The framing of paradata as 'thing' *and* as 'practice' also directs attention towards technical and epistemic usefulness thresholds that are relevant for identifying and using paradata in research documentation (cf. the access affordances presented in Table 3.2). The thresholds are connected to each other but emphasise different fundamental conditions of successfully consulting research documentation to identify and access paradata to learn about past data work. This learning is done by navigating the network of 'participants, practices, artefacts and social arrangements' that make up the social and technical underpinnings of scholarly knowing (Van House, 2002a, p. 111; see also Kim and Yoon, 2017 and Huvila et al., 2023a).

Passing the technical and epistemic usefulness thresholds would mean that the paradata identified and harvested can be used to serve the purposes for which is was sought out, which will vary from one data reuse scenario to the next (cf. Pasquetto et al., 2019). The technical usefulness threshold represents baseline possibilities of accessing and interacting with paradata in research documentation (see e.g., Börjesson et al., 2022b; Niu, 2009; Wallis et al., 2013). It involves having the appropriate software tools for opening and browsing the research documentation, including the means to circumvent issues relating to proprietary or legacy data formats, and the overarching issue of gaining access to the documentation in cases where it is not openly or otherwise available. Given the wide distribution of research documentation across media and locations shown in the CAPTURE interview study and in previous research (Börjesson et al., 2022b; Faniel and Yakel, 2017; Sköld et al., 2022), the access affordances can vary between documentation types.

The epistemic usefulness threshold, on the other hand, underlines the degree of affinity between the epistemic horizons of paradata creation and paradata use. In organisational terms, the former is often related to the original project or venture where the data and paradata were created, and the latter relates to data reuse attempts at a later point in time, during which researchers are seeking to understand how the data came into being, and how it was curated and used. While matters of documentation access and interaction expressed in relation to the technical usefulness threshold are complex and span a range of issues and conditions depending on, for instance, who tries to identify what research-documentation paradata for what purposes, the epistemic usefulness threshold ties into the mechanisms of knowing as they relate to understanding, which arguably has a different kind of complexity attached to it. Familiarity with the context in which the paradata was created (discipline, mode of research, theoretical auspices; Baker and Yarmey, 2009; Berg and Goorman, 1999; Faniel and Zimmerman, 2011; Sköld et al., 2022), methodologies and techniques employed (Faniel et al., 2013; Fear and Donaldson, 2012; Huvila and Sköld, 2023), basic dataset descriptors (scope and provenance Borgman, 2012; Börjesson et al., 2022a; Rolland and Lee, 2013) how the data has been organised (Birnholtz and Bietz, 2003; Börjesson et al., 2020; Maron and Feinberg, 2018), and with the data-creating organisation, researcher or research team (Faniel and Jacobsen, 2010; Huvila, 2020; Yakel et al., 2013; Yoon, 2014a) are all resources that can be utilised in the work of locating paradata in research documentation and in increasing its usefulness by creating the conditions for interpreting the paradata in dialogue with its intended functionalities and modes of production (Huvila et al., 2021c).

How useful paradata 'in the wild' can be identified, and what such paradata might look like, ultimately depends on the nature of the research for whose purposes the paradata is sought, and the characteristics of the obtainable research documentation. Research documentation varies enormously across disciplines but also between different research endeavours within the same discipline and area of research. However, knowing how to mobilise the resources necessary to attain the technical and epistemic usefulness thresholds is key in identifying and using paradata in purposeful ways in many data reuse scenarios.

Being able to 'read' research documentation for paradata is a competence that is sociotechnically organised and, as underscored by Law and Lynch (1988), Niu (2009), and Kansa and Kansa (2021), a practice that can be trained. Variance in intellectual and epistemic traditions or in how methods are applied and data created or managed will always be present, but as this chapter explains there are also structures that are technically and epistemically pervasive and can be used as markers when consulting research documentation for paradata – for example, commonplace documentation types and 'genres' or recurring patterns in how paradata is recorded in these documentation types. The discussion of the ability to see, read and interact with paradata in the pursuit of multiple purposes as a competency and as a state of mind is continued in Chapters 6 and 8, where paradata literacies and paradata mindsets are discussed, respectively.

Returning to the initial discussion about differences between data and information, it can be observed that paradata crucially functions as data, in the sense that it carries the potentiality of use, but that this potentiality is realised (that is, being made informative) when it is mobilised into the practices of identifying and using paradata for reuse purposes. From this perspective, paradata emerges as an interpretable property of the connections that can be made between, within and throughout the available research documentation and the technical and epistemic resources of the party or parties collating and reading the paradata.

It does remain important to ask *how paradata can be identified* and what documentation types might be useful to collect. A complementing inquiry of equal importance might be *how paradata can be made useful* by tracing the linkages between available types of research documentation, what is known about the context from which the paradata emerged, and how the links apply to the data reuse venture at hand.

References

Abtahi P., Ding V., Yang A. C., Bruzzese T., Romanos A. B., Murnane E. L., Follmer, S. and Landay J. A. (2020). Understanding physical practices and the role of technology in manual self-tracking. *Proceedings of the ACM on Interactive, Mobile, Wearable and Ubiquitous Technologies* 4(4). https://doi.org/10.1145/3432236

Baker K. S. and Yarmey L. (2009). Data stewardship: Environmental data curation and a web-of-repositories. *International Journal of Digital Curation* 4(2), 12–27. https://doi.org/10.2218/ijdc.v4i2.90

Becher T. (1989). *Academic Tribes and Territories: Intellectual Enquiry and the Cultures of Disciplines*. Milton Keynes: Society for Research into Higher Education.

Beretta F. (2024). Semantic data for humanities and social sciences (SDHSS): An ecosystem of CIDOC CRM extensions for research data production and reuse. arXiv preprint arXiv:2402.07531. https://doi.org/10.48550/arXiv.2402.07531

Berg M. (1996). Practices of reading and writing: The constitutive role of the patient record in medical work. *Sociology of Health & Illness* 18(4), 499–524. https://doi.org/10.1111/1467-9566.ep10939100

Berg M. and Bowker G. (1997). The multiple bodies of the medical record: Toward a sociology of an artifact. *The Sociological Quarterly* 38(3), 513–537. https://doi.org/10.1111/j.1533-8525.1997.tb00490.x

Berg M. and Goorman E. (1999). The contextual nature of medical information. *International Journal of Medical Informatics* 56(1), 51–60. https://doi.org/10.1016/S1386-5056(99)00041-6

Birnholtz J. P. and Bietz M. J. (2003). Data at work: Supporting sharing in science and engineering. In *Proceedings of the 2003 ACM International Conference on Supporting Group Work*, 339–348. https://doi.org/10.1145/958160.958215

Borgman C. L. (2012). The conundrum of sharing research data. *Journal of the American Society for Information Science and Technology* 63(6), 1059–1078. https://doi.org/10.1002/asi.22634

Borgman C. L. (2015). *Big Data, Little Data, No Data: Scholarship in the Networked World*. Cambridge, MA: MIT Press.

Börjesson L. (2021). Legacy in the making: A knowledge infrastructural perspective on systems for archeological information sharing. *Open Archaeology* 7(1), 1636–1647. https://doi.org/10.1515/opar-2020-0213

Börjesson L., Huvila I. and Sköld O. (2022). Information needs on research data creation. *Information Research* 27. https://doi.org/10.47989/irisic2208

Börjesson L. and Sköld O. (2021). Interview dataset metadata for 'The making and use of paradata: An interview study'. Uppsala University DiVA. Available at https://urn.kb.se/resolve?urn = urn:nbn:se:uu:diva-455730

Börjesson L., Sköld O., Friberg Z., Löwenborg D., Palsson G. and Huvila I. (2022b). Re-purposing excavation database content as paradata: An explorative analysis of paradata identification challenges and opportunities. *KULA: Knowledge Creation, Dissemination, and Preservation Studies* 62(3), 1–18. https://doi.org/10.18357/kula.221

Börjesson L., Sköld O. and Huvila, I. (2020). Paradata in documentation standards and recommendations for digital archaeological visualisations. *Digital Culture & Society* 6(2), 191–220. https://doi.org/10.14361/dcs-2020-0210

Briet S. (2006). What is documentation? In Day R. E., Martinet L. and Anghelescu H. G. B. (eds.), *What is Documentation? English Translation of the Classic French Text*. Lanham, MD: Scarecrow Press.

Brown J. S. and Duguid P. (1996). The social life of documents. *First Monday* 1(1). https://firstmonday.org/ojs/index.php/fm/article/download/466/387

Bruseker G., Carboni N. and Guillem A. (2017). Cultural heritage data management: The role of formal ontology and CIDOC CRM. In Vincent M., López-Menchero Bendicho V., Ioannides M. and Levy T. (eds.), *Heritage and Archaeology in the Digital Age*. Cham: Springer. https://doi.org/10.1007/978-3-319-65370-9_6

Buckland M. (1991). Information as thing. *Journal of the American Society for Information Science* 42(5), 351–360. https://doi.org/10.1002/(SICI)1097-4571 (199106)42:5<351::AID-ASI5>3.0.CO;2-

Buckland M. (2018). Document theory. *Knowledge Organization* 45(5), 425–436. https://doi.org/10.5771/0943-7444-2018-5-425

Carlson S. and Anderson B. (2007). What are data? The many kinds of data and their implications for data re-use. *Journal of Computer-Mediated Communication* 12(2), 635–651. https://doi.org/10.1111/j.1083-6101.2007.00342.x

Ciborra C. U. and Lanzara G. F. (1994). Formative contexts and information technology: Understanding the dynamics of innovation in organizations. *Accounting, Management and Information Technologies* 4(2):61–86. https://doi.org/10.1016/0959-8022(94)90005-1

Cragin M. H. and Shankar K. (2006). Scientific data collections and distributed collective practice. *Computer Supported Cooperative Work* 15(2), 185–204. https://doi.org/10.1007/s10606-006-9018-z

Doerr M., Ore C.-E. and Stead S. (2007). The CIDOC conceptual reference model: A new standard for knowledge sharing. In *Proceedings from the 26th International Conference on Conceptual Modeling*, 83, 51–56.

Durrant G .B., D'Arrigo J. and Steele F. (2011). Using paradata to predict best times of contact, conditioning on household and interviewer influences. *Journal of the Royal Statistical Society Series A: Statistics in Society* 174(4), 1029–1049. https://doi.org/10.1111/j.1467-985X.2011.00715.x

Edwards R., Goodwin J., O'Connor H., and Phoenix A. (2017). *Working with Paradata, Marginalia and Fieldnotes: The Centrality of By-Products of Social Research*. Northampton, MA: Edward Elgar Publishing.

Faniel I., Kansa E., Whitcher Kansa S., Barrera-Gomez J. and Yakel E. (2013). The challenges of digging data: A study of context in archaeological data reuse. In *Proceedings of the 13th ACM/IEEE-CS Joint Conference on Digital Libraries*, 295–304. New York: ACM. https://doi.org/10.1145/2467696.2467712

Faniel I. and Yakel E. (2017). Practices do not make perfect: Disciplinary data sharing and reuse practices and their implications for repository data curation. In Johnston LR (ed.), *Curating Research Data, Volume One: Practical Strategies for Your Data Repository*, 103–126. Chicago, IL: ACRL.

Faniel I. and Zimmerman A. S. (2011). Beyond the data deluge: A research agenda for large-scale data sharing and reuse. *The International Journal of Digital Curation* 1(6), 58–68. https://doi.org/10.2218/ijdc.v6i1.172

Faniel I. M. and Jacobsen T. E. (2010). Reusing scientific data: How earthquake engineering researchers assess the reusability of colleagues' data. *Computer Supported Cooperative Work* 19(3), 355–375. https://doi.org/10.1007/s10606-010-9117-8

Faniel I. M., Kriesberg A. and Yakel E. (2012). Data reuse and sensemaking among novice social scientists. *Proceedings of the American Society for Information Science and Technology* 49(1), 1–10. https://doi.org/10.1002/meet.14504901068

Faniel I. M., Kriesberg A. and Yakel E. (2016). Social scientists' satisfaction with data reuse. *Journal of the Association for Information Science and Technology* 67(6), 1404–1416. https://doi.org/10.1002/asi.23480

Fear K. and Donaldson D. R. (2012). Provenance and credibility in scientific data repositories. *Archival Science* 12(3), 319–339. https://doi.org/10.1007/s10502-012-9172-7

Frank R. D., Yakel E. and Faniel I. M. (2015). Destruction/reconstruction: preservation of archaeological and zoological research data. *Archival Science* 15(2), 141–167. https://doi.org/10.1007/s10502-014-9238-9

Franks, P. (2024). The crucial role of paradata in AI governance. In Duranti L. and Rogers C. (eds.), *Artificial Intelligence and Documentary Heritage*. Vancouver: InterPARES Trust AI.

Frohmann B. (2004). *Deflating Information: From Science Studies to Documentation*. Toronto: University of Toronto Press.

Gant S. and Reilly P. (2018). Different expressions of the same mode: A recent dialogue between archaeological and contemporary drawing practices. *Journal of Visual Art Practice* 17(1), 100–120. https://doi.org/10.1080/14702029.2017.1384974

Geiger R. S. and Ribes D. (2011). Trace ethnography: Following coordination through documentary practices. In *Proceedings from the 44th Hawaii International Conference on System Sciences*. New York: IEEE. https://doi.org/10.1109/HICSS.2011.455

Gitelman L. (2013). *'Raw Data' is an Oxymoron*. Cambridge, MA: MIT Press.

Gregory K. M., Cousijn H., Groth P., Scharnhorst A. and Wyatt S. (2019). Understanding data search as a socio-technical practice. *Journal of Information Science* 46(4), 459–475. https://doi.org/10.1177/0165551519833718

Gunnarsson F. (2020). Digitalisation and its impact on archaeological knowledge production. In Hansson J. and Svensson J. (eds.), *Doing Digital Humanities: Concepts, Approaches, Cases*. Växjö: Linnaeus University Press, 27–44.

Harper R. H. R. (1998). *Inside the IMF: An Ethnography of Documents, Technology, and Organisational Action*. San Diego, CA: Academic Press.

Harvey F. and Chrisman N. (1998). Boundary objects and the social construction of GIS technology. *Environment and Planning A: Economy and Space* 30(9), 1683–1694. https://doi.org/10.1068/a30168

Hilgartner S. and Brandt-Rauf S. I. (1994). Data access, ownership, and control: Toward empirical studies of access practices. *Knowledge* 15(4), 355–372. https://doi.org/10.1177/107554709401500401

Hjørland B. (2000). Documents, memory institutions and information science. *Journal of Documentation* 56(1), 27–41. https://doi.org/10.1108/EUM0000000007107

Hjørland B. (2018). Data (with big data and database semantics). *Knowledge Organization* 45(8), 685–708. https://doi.org/10.5771/0943-7444-2018-8-685

Hjørland B. (2023). Description: Its meaning, epistemology, and use with emphasis on information science. *Journal of the Association for Information Science and Technology* 74(13), 1532–1549. https://doi.org/10.1002/asi.24834

Hodges J. A. (2021). Forensically reconstructing biomedical maintenance labor: PDF metadata under the epistemic conditions of COVID-19. *Journal of the Association for Information Science and Technology* 72(11), 1400–1414. https://doi.org/10.1002/asi.24484

Huggett J. (2012). Promise and paradox: Accessing open data in archaeology. In Mills C., Pidd M. and Ward E. (eds.), *Proceedings of the Digital Humanities Congress 2012: Studies in the Digital Humanities*. Sheffield: HRI Online Publications. http://dx.doi.org/10.17613/qc5d-9x46

Huggett J. (2023). Extending discourse analysis in archaeology: A multimodal approach. In Gonzalez-Perez C., Martin-Rodilla P. and Pereira-Fariña M. (eds.), *Discourse and Argumentation in Archaeology: Conceptual and Computational Approaches*. Cham: Springer. https://doi.org/10.1007/978-3-031-37156-1_8

Huvila, I. (2011). The politics of boundary objects: Hegemonic interventions and the making of a document. *Journal of the American Society for Information Science and Technology* 62(12), 2528–2539. https://doi.org/10.1002/asi.21639

Huvila I. (2014). Archaeologists and their information sources. In Huvila I. (ed.), *Perspectives to Archaeological Information in the Digital Society*. Uppsala: Uppsala University, Department of ALM, 25–54.

Huvila I. (2020). Information-making-related information needs and the credibility of information. *Information Research*, 25(4). https://doi.org/10.47989/irisic2002

Huvila I. (2022). Improving the usefulness of research data with better paradata. *Open Information Science* 6(1), 28–48. https://doi.org/10.1515/opis-2022-0129

Huvila I., Andersson L., Fulton C., Haider J. and Harviainen J. T. (2023a). Managing information gaps and non-information. *Proceedings of the Association for Information Science and Technology* 60(1), 793–798. https://doi.org/10.1002/pra2.863

Huvila I., Andersson L., and Sköld O. (2022a). Citing methods literature: Citations to field manuals as paradata on archaeological fieldwork. *Information Research* 27(3). https://doi.org/10.47989/irpaper941

Huvila I., Börjesson L., and Sköld O. (2022b). Archaeological information-making activities according to field reports. *Library & Information Science Research* 44(3). https://doi.org/10.1016/j.lisr.2022.101171

Huvila I., Greenberg J., Sköld O., Thomer A., Trace C. and Zhao X. (2021a). Documenting information processes and practices: Paradata, provenance metadata, life-cycles and pipelines. *Proceedings of the Association for Information Science and Technology* 58(1), 604–609. https://doi.org/10.1002/pra2.509

Huvila I. and Sköld O. (2023). A fieldwork manual as a regulatory device: Instructing, prescribing and describing documentation work. *Journal of Information Science*. https://doi.org/10.1177/01655515231203

Huvila I., Sköld O., and Andersson L. (2023b). Knowing-in-practice, its traces and ingredients. In Cozza M. and Gherardi S. (eds.), *The Posthumanist Epistemology of Practice Theory*. Cham: Palgrave Macmillan. https://doi.org/10.1007/978-3-031-42276-8_2

Huvila I., Sköld O. and Börjesson L. (2021). Documenting information making in archaeological field reports. *Journal of Documentation* 77(5), 1107–1127. https://doi.org/10.1108/JD-11-2020-0188

Kansa E. and Kansa S. W. (2021). Digital data and data literacy in archaeology now and in the new decade. *Advances in Archaeological Practice* 9(1), 81–85. https://doi.org/10.1017/aap.2020.55

Kim Y. and Yoon A. (2017). Scientists' data reuse behaviors: A multilevel analysis. *Journal of the Association for Information Science and Technology* 68(12), 2709–2719. http://doi.org/10.3886/E100404V1

Kintigh K. (2006). The promise and challenge of archaeological data integration. *American Antiquity* 71(3), 567–578. http://doi.org/10.2307/40035365

Kirschenbaum M. G. (2008). *Mechanisms: New Media and the Forensic Imagination.* Cambridge, MA: MIT Press.

Knorr-Cetina K. (1999). *Epistemic Cultures: How the Sciences Make Knowledge.* Cambridge, MA: Harvard University Press.

Koesten L., Simperl E., Blount T., Kacprzak E. and Tennison J. (2020). Everything you always wanted to know about a dataset: Studies in data summarisation. *International Journal of Human-Computer Studies* 135. https://doi.org/10.1016/j.ijhcs.2019.10.004

Latour B. (1987). *Science in Action: How to Follow Scientists and Engineers through Society.* Cambridge, MA: Harvard University Press.

Latour B. (1999). Circulating reference: Sampling the soil in the Amazon Forest. In *Pandora's Hope: Essays on the Reality of Science Studies.* Cambridge, MA: Harvard University Press, 25–79

Latour B. and Woolgar S. (1979). *Laboratory Life: The Social Construction of Scientific Facts.* Beverly Hills, CA: Sage.

Law J. (1993). *Organising Modernity: Social Ordering and Social Theory.* Hoboken, NJ: Wiley.

Law J. and Lynch M. (1988). Lists, field guides, and the descriptive organization of seeing: Birdwatching as an exemplary observational activity. *Human Studies* 11(2/3), 271–303.

Leonelli S. and Tempini N. (eds.) (2020). *Data Journeys in the Sciences.* Cham: Springer.

Levy D. M. (2001). *Scrolling Forward: Making Sense of Documents in the Digital Age.* New York: Arcade Pub.

Lund N. W. (2009). Document theory. *Annual Review of Information Science and Technology* 43, 399–432. https://doi.org/10.1002/aris.2009.1440430116

Lund N. W. (2010). Document, text and medium: Concepts, theories and disciplines. *Journal of Documentation* 66(5), 734–749. https://doi.org/10.1108/00220411011066817

Maron D. and Feinberg M. (2018). What does it mean to adopt a metadata standard? A case study of Omeka and the Dublin Core. *Journal of Documentation,* 74(4), 674–691. https://doi.org/10.1108/JD-06-2017-0095

Mayernik M. S. (2016). Research data and metadata curation as institutional issues. *Journal of the Association for Information Science and Technology* 67(4), 973–993. https://doi.org/10.1002/asi.23425

Nadim T. (2021). The datafication of nature: Data formations and new scales in natural history. *Journal of the Royal Anthropological Institute* 27(1), 62–75. https://doi.org/10.1111/1467-9655.13480

Niu J. (2009). Overcoming inadequate documentation. *Proceedings of the American Society for Information Science and Technology* 46(1), 1–14. https://doi.org/10.1002/meet.2009.145046024

Oliver G., Cranefield J., Lilley S. and Lewellen M. J. (2024). Understanding data culture/s: Influences, activities, and initiatives: An Annual Review of Information Science and Technology (ARIST) paper. *Journal of the Association for Information Science and Technology* 75(3), 201–214. https://doi.org/10.1002/asi.24737

Olson H. A. (2002). *Power to Name: Locating the Subject Representation in Libraries.* Boston: Kluwer.

Pardo T. A., Cresswell A. M., Thompson F. and Zhang J. (2006). Knowledge sharing in cross-boundary information system development in the public sector. *Information Technology and Management* 7(4), 293–313. https://doi.org/10.1007/s10799-006-0278-6

Pasquetto I. V., Borgman C. L. and Wofford M. F. (2019). Uses and reuses of scientific data: The data creators' advantage. *Harvard Data Science Review* 1(2). https://doi.org/10.1162/99608f92.fc14bf2d

Pickering A. (1995). *The Mangle of Practice: Time, Agency, and Science.* Chicago: University of Chicago Press.

Pinch T. J. and Bijker W. E. (1984). The social construction of facts and artefacts: Or how the sociology of science and the sociology of technology might benefit each other. *Social Studies of Science* 14(3), 399–441. https://doi.org/10.1177/0306312840140030

Plantin J.-C. and Thomer A. (2023). Platforms, programmability, and precarity: The platformization of research repositories in academic libraries. *New Media & Society.* https://doi.org/10.1177/14614448231171767

Richards J. D., Jakobsson U., Novák D., Štular B. and Wright, H. (2021). Digital archiving in archaeology: The state of the art. *Internet Archaeology* 58. https://doi.org/10.11141/ia.58.23

Rolland B. and Lee C. P. (2013). Beyond trust and reliability: Reusing data in collaborative cancer epidemiology research. In *Proceedings of the 2013 Conference on Computer Supported Cooperative Work.* New York: ACM, 435–444. https://doi.org/10.1145/2441776.2441826

Rowley J. (2007). The wisdom hierarchy: Representations of the DIKW hierarchy. *Journal of Information Science* 33(2), 163–180. https://doi.org/10.1177/0165551506070706

Shankar K. (2007). Order from chaos: The poetics and pragmatics of scientific record-keeping. *Journal of the American Society for Information Science and Technology* 58, 1457–1466. https://doi.org/10.1002/asi.20625

Shankar K. (2009). Ambiguity and legitimate peripheral participation in the creation of scientific documents. *Journal of Documentation,* 65(1), 151–165. https://doi.org/10.1108/00220410910926167

Shepherd N. G. and Rudd J. M. (2014). The influence of context on the strategic decisionâmaking process: A review of the literature. *International Journal of Management Reviews* 16(3), 340–364. https://doi.org/10.1111/ijmr.12023

Sköld O. (2017). Getting-to-know: Inquiries, sources, methods, and the production of knowledge on a videogame wiki. *Journal of Documentation* 73(6), 1299–1321. https://doi.org/10.1108/JD-11-2016-0145

Sköld O. (2018). *Documenting Videogame Communities: A Study of Community Production of Information in Social-media Environments and its Implications for Videogame Preservation.* PhD dissertation. Uppsala: Department of ALM, Uppsala University.

Sköld O., Börjesson L. and Huvila I. (2022). Interrogating Paradata. *Information Research,* 27. https://doi.org/10.47989/colis2206

Spedding P. and Tankard P. (eds.) (2021). *Marginal Notes: Social Reading and the Literal Margins*. Basingstoke: Palgrave Macmillan.

Steinkuehler C. and Duncan S. (2008). Scientific habits of mind in virtual worlds. *Journal of Science Education and Technology* 17(6), 530–543. https://doi.org/10.1007/s10956-008-9120-8

The London Charter Organization (2009) *The London Charter for the Computer-Based Visualisation of Cultural Heritage.* Available at https://londoncharter.org (accessed 12 April 2024).

Trace C. B. (2011). Documenting work and working documents: Perspectives from workplace studies, CSCW, and genre studies. In Sprague, R. H. Jr. (ed.), *Proceedings from the 44th Hawaii International Conference on System Sciences.* New York: IEEE. https://doi.org/10.1109/HICSS.2011.170

Trace C. B. and Zhang Y. (2020). The quantified-self archive: Documenting lives through self-tracking data. *Journal of Documentation* 76(1), 290–316. https://doi.org/10.1108/JD-04-2019-0064

Ullah I. I. T. (2015). Integrating older survey data into modern research paradigms: Identifying and correcting spatial error in 'legacy' datasets. *Advances in Archaeological Practice* 3(4), 331–350. https://doi.org/10.7183/2326-3768.3.4.331

Van House N. A. (2002a) Digital libraries and practices of trust: Networked biodiversity information. *Social Epistemology* 16(1), 99–114. https://doi.org/10.1080/026917220210132833

Van House N. A. (2002b). Trust and epistemic communities in biodiversity data sharing. In *Proceedings of the 2nd ACM/IEEE-CS Joint Conference on Digital Libraries,* 231–239. https://doi.org/10.1145/544220.544270

Voss, B. L. (2012). Curation as research: A case study in orphaned and under- reported archaeological collections. *Archaeological Dialogues* 19(2), 145–169. https://doi.org/10.1017/S1380203812000219

Wallis J. C., Rolando E. and Borgman C. L. (2013). If we share data, will anyone use them? Data sharing and reuse in the long tail of science and technology. *PLoS ONE* 8(7). https://doi.org/10.1371/journal.pone.0067332

Warmelink H. (2013). *Online Gaming and Playful Organization.* New York: Routledge.

Weber N. M., Baker K. S., Thomer A. K., Chao T. C. and Palmer C. L. (2012). Value and context in data use: Domain analysis revisited. *Proceedings of the American Society for Information Science and Technology* 49(1):1–10. https://doi.org/10.1007/s10502

West B. T. and Sinibaldi J. (2013). The quality of paradata: A literature review. In Kreuter F (ed.), *Improving Surveys with Paradata: Analytic Uses of Process Information.* Hoboken, NJ: Wiley. https://doi.org/10.1002/9781118596869.ch14

Yakel E., Faniel I., Kriesberg A. and Yoon A. (2013). Trust in digital repositories. *The International Journal of Digital Curation* 8(1), 1–14. https://doi.org/10.2218/ijdc.v8i1.251

Yoon A. (2014a). End users' trust in data repositories: Definition and influences on trust development. *Archival Science* 14(1), 17–34.

Yoon A. (2014b). 'Making a square fit into a circle': Researchers' experiences reusing qualitative data. *Proceedings of the American Society for Information Science and Technology* 51(1), 1–4. https://doi.org/10.1002/meet.2014.14505101140

Zimmerman A. S. (2008). New knowledge from old data: The role of standards in the sharing and reuse of ecological data. *Science, Technology, & Human Values* 33(5), 631–652. https://doi.org/10.1177/0162243907306704

4

Methods for Generating and Documenting Paradata

Ying-Hsang Liu and Isto Huvila

4.1 Introduction

Using appropriate methods to capture adequate paradata on data generation practices and processes is an essential step in facilitating reuse of data and understanding the practices and processes of data creation. In the previous chapters of this volume, we have delved into discussing the notion of paradata (Chapter 2) and where it can be found across data documentation (Chapter 3).

An analysis conducted by Juneström and Huvila as part of the CAPTURE project revealed two major categories of methods relevant for data creators to generate paradata: prospective and in-situ ones. Prospective paradata generation takes place before a practice or process is enacted whereas in-situ refers to paradata generation at the time when an activity takes place. Many prospective methods are prescriptive. Specifically, prescriptive methods aim to create structured approaches for directing forthcoming data generation activities. These methods include enforcing the use of formal metadata standards and knowledge representation frameworks (ontology building), registered reports and prescriptive workflows.

In-situ methods involve generating paradata simultaneously with the creation of data. Such approaches include narrative descriptions through note-taking and data storytelling, recordings such as photographs and audio-visual recordings, and the automatic logging of activities.

In this chapter, we will explore how data creators can generate task-appropriate paradata on various practices and processes related to data creation, management and use. The aim of this chapter is to provide insights into methods that can be adopted and adjusted by researchers and data managers to capture paradata across various disciplinary contexts and study scenarios.

Besides offering practicable advice on how to generate and document para-data, these methods serve as examples of diverse approaches that can be employed to enhance methodological transparency in data creation processes, ensuring the understandability, and for instance, accuracy, replicability and credibility of research. The suitability of these approaches depends on the type of transparency sought and the intended purpose of creating and using the paradata. Key references and further reading are provided after each method description.

4.2 Methods Descriptions

The set of methods described in this chapter were chosen based on a scoping review of paradata generation practices in research activities from a wide range of disciplines. Many other methods exist than those covered in this chapter. Some are specific to particular domains, such as survey research (cf. Chapter 2) and meta-analysis, with established approaches on how to document for them relevant aspects of research-related practices and processes (Kreuter, 2013; Schmid et al., 2021). A preliminary framework of paradata generation developed at the beginning of the CAPTURE project formed a baseline for identifying methods of paradata documentation and generation (Huvila, 2022). This was supplemented by reviewing a large number of articles sourced from project team members over the first four years of the project. The goal was to understand how paradata is generated in different settings and how different approaches eventually could be applied to create different types of paradata.

The chapter starts with formal metadata, a section that is also longest, to discuss the approach that is systematically promoted as the principal method for comprehensive documentation of data and a key premise for its findability, accessibility, interoperability and reusability (Wilkinson et al., 2016). Techniques that are specific to certain disciplines and study contexts are mentioned briefly when relevant, to illustrate their potential for wider application (e.g., protocol registration for clinical trials and experimental protocols in life sciences). However, many such methods that are particularly domain specific have generally been excluded from this chapter to maintain its focus on general principles and approaches with potential relevance across a broader range of domains. However, it is important to note that disciplinary specificity does not necessarily imply a lack of broader relevance. Some approaches originating from specific fields, like registered reports in social psychology, clearly have the potential to inform practices far beyond their initial context.

The following sections introduce and discuss five categories of methods for generating and documenting paradata: 1) formal metadata; 2) narrative descriptions; 3) recordings; 4) logging; and 5) planning and workflows.

4.2.1 Formal Metadata

Formal metadata refers to data descriptions produced according to standards that establish consistent criteria, methods, processes and practices for describing resources for particular purposes, including data structures, data contents, data values and means of data exchange (Zeng and Qin, 2022). It is one of the principal approaches used for describing and organising information and data. Formal metadata systems provide context and consistency for data descriptions. They are often called 'authority files'. A formal metadata system may be specific for one organisation, national or international consortia, or associations and cover a subject specialty or a broader discipline. Formal metadata systems are often organised in tree structures in which the metadata terms (concepts) are arranged hierarchically from the broad to the narrow, or by relationships indicating states of connectedness. Relationships can be associative, relational or equivalent (for synonymous terms). Formal metadata systems provide both descriptions of terms and rules for their use. Formal metadata makes data and paradata easier to manage and contributes to its discoverability and retrievability. It also aids in identifying and differentiating between similar and dissimilar resources. Key instruments of formal metadata include data dictionaries, label sets, controlled vocabularies and metadata standards.

Data Dictionaries and Label Sets

A data dictionary is a tool that provides detailed information about the structure, meaning and relationships of variables within a dataset for describing data contents. For survey research it might include, for example, the types of data (e.g., numerical, categorical and free text), wording of survey questions, question types (e.g., multiple choice, Likert scale and rating scale) and the meaning of the data values. Relevant information for other types of research varies but may include comparable documentation of data types, terms, methods and descriptions of data.

A data dictionary helps to capture details of a data collection process more comprehensively, improves consistency and provides means to turn implicit practices explicit. From a paradata perspective, data dictionaries are especially helpful for addressing data users' needs (cf. the need of knowledge organisation and representation paradata in Börjesson et al., 2022). They help users understand how a dataset is organised, the conventions and considerations applied when it was structured, the process of transforming data into knowledge and how this knowledge is represented.

The primary limitations of data dictionaries are their lack of long-term stability. They are created at one point of time but as people start using new terms, old terms change meaning and are abandoned; the dictionaries become obsolete. Also, while they enable data creators to articulate their assumptions, contextualise datasets and delineate the scope of the data, they often fall short in documenting the social, political and historical contexts of their creation (Poirier, 2022). When creating a data dictionary, it is difficult to know what contextual facets need to be described and to what extent. Further, they often incorporate assumptions their creators might not recognize or deem necessary to document. Consequently, in practice, data dictionaries are less reliable than commonly assumed (Poirier, 2022).

Label sets, either included in data dictionaries or held separately, classify data or information by predefined categories or groups. Labels are specific words, expressions or notations that are assigned to data points to categorise them. For example, whenever survey participants' highest level of education is discussed, a standardised terminology can be used to organise education programmes and related qualifications by levels in a way similar to how biology uses standardised names based on binomial nomenclature to classify species by genus and species names.

For documenting survey paradata, comparable standardised expressions can refer to the names of specific methods of data collection, management and analysis, such as collecting individual data points online, by telephone or by mail. Examples of applicable labels include 'structured face-to-face interview', 'online questionnaire survey', or a 'semi-structured telephone interview'. To clarify their meaning, they need to be accompanied with a detailed procedural description in a label set. Similarly, labels can be used to standardise the names of the procedures of recording variables on a new scale (e.g., Min-Max scaling, standardisation or robust scaling for common procedures), normalised, or when new variables are computed from earlier ones, for instance, by multiplying values of an earlier variable or by calculating the current age of survey participants based on their date of birth.

As a part of the description of categorical variables, label sets can be documented within a data dictionary. Sufficient documentation of data using data dictionaries and label sets is crucial for data harmonisation. This contributes so that the variables described are self-explanatory enough for other researchers to reuse the data, and that the results are replicable across studies. A typical example of a label set in survey research is the description of labels for various education levels that can be based, for example, on the list of qualifications in the International Standard Classification of Education (ISCED 2011). This set may also specify whether participants were asked to select the highest level of education attained or completed, or for example, to indicate all types of education they have completed. Diagnostic research uses classifications and label sets for similar purposes, such as to provide labels for different stages of cancer that can be used to describe diagnoses.

A clear challenge is determining what constitutes sufficient detail and how to be reasonably certain that the label descriptions are understandable for their intended users. Producing workable label sets is usually possible within a single domain with shared vocabulary and concepts whereas it tends to be difficult in interdisciplinary research where such an understanding is lacking.

Controlled Vocabularies

Controlled vocabularies are useful for consistently describing data contents by unifying the various terms used to describe the same concept (Liu and Wacholder, 2017; Svenonious, 1986; Zeng and Qin, 2022). Controlled vocabularies have been developed for many domains, such as MeSH[1] (Medical Subject Headings) for biomedical domain, INSPEC Thesaurus[2] for the engineering and information technology fields, and European Language Social Science Thesaurus (ELSST)[3] for the social sciences. A major benefit of using controlled vocabularies for documenting paradata is that they enable consistent indexing and retrieval of resources, and to distinguish between documentation of practices and processes (paradata) and the documentation of documents describing them.

For example, in the biomedical domain, the MeSH term 'Clinical Trial Protocol' is a preferred term (i.e. controlled) for other term variants, including 'Clinical Trial Protocols', 'Trial Protocol' and 'Trial Protocols' to document a specific 'Publication Type' that reports a clinical trial protocol. A different term – 'Clinical Trial Protocols as Topic' – is used to describe a clinical study, including the study's objectives, design and methods. In the context of data repositories, the adoption of controlled vocabularies by open repository software can enhance the interoperability across repositories. For example, both 'clinical study' (referring to research reports) and 'clinical trial data' (referring to data from a clinical trial study) are controlled terms of Resource Types in COAR[4] (Confederation of Open Access Repositories) Controlled

---

[1] https://meshb.nlm.nih.gov/.   [2] www.theiet.org/publishing/inspec/guides-and-support.
[3] https://elsst.cessda.eu/.   [4] https://vocabularies.coar-repositories.org/.

Vocabularies, making distinctions among different types of resources in data repositories.

Many controlled vocabularies contain elements relevant for expressing paradata, but so far few paradata-specific vocabularies exist. One exception is the Data Practices and Curation Vocabulary (DPCVocab), which can be useful for characterising research data practices like data collection and generation, processing and analysis. This vocabulary helps achieve more consistent data descriptions among curators, data producers, system developers and other stakeholders involved in the data curation process (Chao et al. 2015). Another example of a scheme with direct relevance to the documentation of paradata is a recently developed annotation scheme for characterising research data practices in the disciplines of sociology, economics physics and biology (Lee et al. 2023). This scheme includes research data practices of collecting, processing, analysing, representing and publishing or citing data, along with the dimensions of action, object and instrument. The finding that each type of research data practice varies across disciplines regarding action (e.g., interview, gather or observe), object (e.g., participant, tissue or circuit) and instrument (e.g., questionnaire, centrifuge or tensor) can be further developed for paradata-specific vocabularies applicable to specific domains.

The primary advantage of using a controlled vocabulary is that it can help to enhance the consistency of paradata documentation, facilitate the development and sharing of a common understanding of concepts used to describe practices and processes, and make paradata more transparent and easier to compare and integrate with data from multiple sources. To embed the use of controlled vocabularies within the work routine, the design of controlled vocabularies can be enhanced and guided by investigating people's interactions with information within their information-seeking activities and constraints (Mai 2008). However, the usefulness of a controlled vocabulary is limited by the search interface design and extensive training required for using it effectively for information searching in various domains (Golub et al. 2023; Liu and Wacholder 2017). Further, accommodating new concepts quickly is challenging and the maintenance and update of controlled vocabularies are resource-intensive, requiring inputs from domain experts.

Metadata Standards

Metadata standards for research data documentation exist across disciplines, although not universally, with many domains lacking dedicated specifications. These standards incorporate elements relevant for describing practices and processes, that is, paradata, to varying degrees. Domain- or discipline-specific standards are typically more effective at describing data generation practices and processes at a higher level of granularity than cross-disciplinary standards, as shown in the specificity of the paradata-related metadata elements in Table 4.1.

For example, Darwin Core and NetCDF Climate and Forecast (CF) Metadata Conventions enable more consistent descriptions of biodiversity data by providing a vocabulary standard for describing practices and processes in great detail. In contrast, many general metadata standards are far less detailed. For example, the WHO Trial Registration Data Set is a standard for describing clinical trials. It stipulates on the inclusion of some contextual information on the data collection process in a trial study, including descriptions of clinical interventions, study type and recruitment of participants. For observational studies in the social, economic and behavioural sciences, the broader methodology and processing details can be documented using the Data Documentation Initiative (DDI) Codebook standard, which describes the variables, files, source material and study level information.

While lists of metadata terms and descriptions of terms are comprehensible for humans, they are difficult to process using computer programmes. In other words, they are not machine-readable. Machine-readability facilitates automatic processing of formal metadata, and effective searching and linking of metadata terms. It is particularly useful for processing large amounts of data and data descriptions.

Metadata schemas are specifications developed to make metadata terms and vocabularies machine-readable, that is, readable and processable by computer programmes. They provide an implementation blueprint for a metadata standard by encoding a metadata element set into a machine-readable format, much like putting together the pieces of a puzzle (Zeng and Qin, 2022). Encoding metadata schemas involves converting metadata elements into a structured, machine-readable format, such as XML (Extensible Markup Language) which is currently the lingua franca for storing and exchanging information across systems. One possible application of using metadata standards to generate and document paradata is that they can be encoded and be made machine-readable, which will facilitate data exchange among the resources.

Examples of machine-readable metadata schemas with potential relevance to documentation of paradata include the Encoded Archival Description (EAD)[5] developed for encoding information on archival records in the XML format, including paradata-relevant information of their provenance, and many others. Schema.org,[6] another widely used metadata schema for structured data

---

[5] www.loc.gov/ead/.   [6] https://schema.org/.

Table 4.1 *A selective list of metadata standards for research data documentation*

Metadata standards	Discipline/ domain	Type of research	Metadata elements useful for describing paradata
Darwin Core (DwC)[1]	Biological diversity	Observational studies	• Occurrence • Organism • MaterialEntity • MaterialSample • Event • Location • GeologicalContext • Identification • Taxon • MeasurementOrFact • HumanObservation • MachineObservation • …

NetCDF Climate and Forecast (CF) Metadata Conventions[2]	Climate science	Observational studies	• Description of the Data
			  ○ Units
			  ○ Ancillary Data
			• Coordinate Types
			• Coordinate Systems and Domain
			• Data Representative of Cells
			• Reduction of Dataset Size
			• …

WHO Trial Registration Data Set[3]	Biomedical research	Observational and interventional studies	• Countries of Recruitment • Health Condition(s) or Problem(s) Studied • Intervention(s) • Key Inclusion and Exclusion Criteria • Study Type (including study design) • Sample Size • Recruitment Status • …
Data Documentation Initiative (DDI), DDI-Codebook	Social, behavioural, economic and health sciences	Observational study	• anlysUnit (unit of analysis) • codeBook • cohort • collMode (mode of data collection) • dataProcessing • instrumentDevelopment • …

[1] www.tdwg.org/standards/dwc/.
[2] http://cfconventions.org/cf-conventions/cf-conventions.html.
[3] www.who.int/clinical-trials-registry-platform/network/who-data-set.

in the web pages about datasets, can be used to enhance data integration by search engines. Schema.org is not explicitly a paradata schema but includes types and properties useful for representing diverse aspects of practices and processes, including the type Action for describing 'actions' performed directly or indirectly by agents on 'objects', making it practical especially for many less complex documentation needs.

As envisioned by Tim Berners-Lee, the inventor of the World Wide Web, scientific papers published on the Semantic Web would contain machine-readable content (Berners-Lee and Hendler, 2001). The Resource Description Framework (RDF)[7] has emerged as an alternative general framework for representing and linking data based on a simple data model that uses subject-predicate-object expressions to make statements about resources and their qualities. For example, one might state that Amy (person, subject) created (predicate) a dataset A (object). Linked Open Data (LOD) employs these standards, including RDF, to link resources and resource descriptions together and make them openly available to the world (Nurmikko-Fuller, 2023). The RDF-star extension to RDF is a framework to make assertions about RDF statements, providing a mechanism to describe, for example, their origins and intellectual underpinnings (Rupp et al. 2024). Standardised encoding and open linking provide opportunities for both dissemination and utilisation of paradata. They also enable the use of formal metadata elements across individual standards and vocabularies to enrich documentation of practices and processes.

The goal of using controlled vocabularies, metadata standards, and schemas is to enhance data publishing interoperability. For example, Google's Dataset Search[8] can understand Schema.org and the equivalent structures represented in W3C's Data Catalog Vocabulary (DCAT)[9] format, an RDF-based specification for describing and publishing data catalogues on the web. However, there are gaps in the controlled vocabularies that limit their applicability for describing paradata with pre-defined terms in metadata schemas, such as lack of support for incorporating external controlled vocabularies (Wu et al., 2023) and the difficulty of making legacy vocabularies machine-readable to support the findability, accessibility, interoperability and reusability of data (Cox et al., 2021). As the practice of publishing research datasets as part of research outputs becomes increasingly common, adopting appropriate metadata schemas can facilitate the sharing and publishing of crucial information on practices and processes underpinning the creation, management and use of datasets.

---

[7] www.w3.org/RDF/.   [8] https://datasetsearch.research.google.com/.
[9] www.w3.org/TR/vocab-dcat-3/.

Ontologies and Knowledge Graphs

Unlike metadata schemas, which aim to describe resources and their attributes, ontologies provide a structured framework for representing knowledge within and across domains, capturing the semantics of data. They enable the definition, naming and representation of entities (including concepts and data), and the relationships between them. As a standard language for representing ontologies in the Semantic Web, The Web Ontology Language (OWL)[10] is a knowledge representation language with tools to create Semantic Web ontologies that can be utilised in the development knowledge graphs,[11] that is, a network of interlinked knowledge entities.

One of the major knowledge graphs, Google's Knowledge Graph[12] is a critical component of its search engine. It functions as a database of interlinked pieces of information and is used to source facts about people, places, things, events and their relationships shown on the search engine results pages. For example, typing 'Eiffel Tower' into Google search box will display a panel showing a selection of facts about the Eiffel Tower, such as its location, address, height, date of construction started, opening date and architects. The usefulness of ontologies and knowledge graphs for documentation of paradata lies in their ability to provide a formal representation of all types of metainformation in a single framework. This ensures that paradata is not isolated from other documentation but that they are instead complementary to each other and can be queried together.

Many domain-specific ontologies include mechanisms for documenting and developing specific documentation schemes to represent information about complex practices and processes. There are also dedicated process- and practice-oriented ontologies. For example, PROV is a group of specifications developed for the exchange of provenance information across systems (PROV-Overview 2013). Process Specification Language is another process ontology developed and used for documenting industrial manufacturing processes (ISO 18629–1:2004).

The use of ontologies and knowledge graphs can be illustrated with an example from the cultural heritage domain. The CIDOC Conceptual Reference Model (CRM)[13] is a widely used formal ontology for documenting cultural heritage data. It can be used to produce a knowledge graph that makes connections among researchers, data and practices in a network of relations

---

[10] www.w3.org/OWL/.

[11] There is no firm consensus of a definition knowledge graph and consequently, how they are distinct from, for example, ontologies (cf. Huck 2022).

[12] https://support.google.com/knowledgepanel/answer/9787176?hl=en.

[13] www.cidoc-crm.org/.

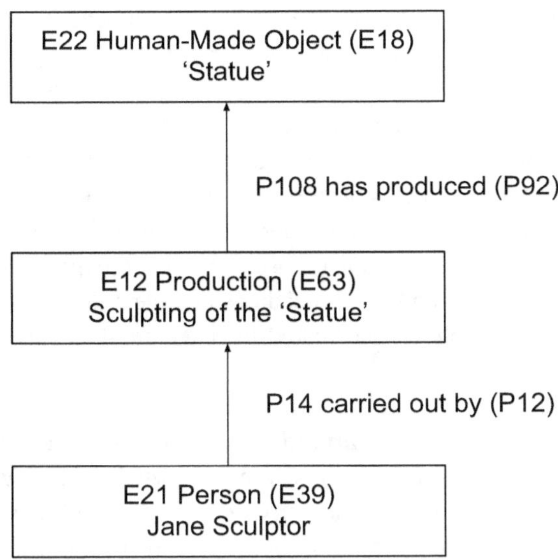

Figure 4.1 Knowledge graph of an artwork titled 'Statue' incorporating simple paradata.

(Oldman and Tanase, 2018). A knowledge graph based on CIDOC CRM can include paradata to incorporate information on the processes involved in creating, collecting and curating cultural heritage data, such as how, when and under what conditions the data was gathered or digitised.

Figure 4.1 shows the knowledge graph of an artwork, entitled 'Statue' representing simple paradata about its production. Further paradata about the sculpture, copies, drawings and photographs of it but also further details such as how the 'Statue' has been referred to in the literature can also be stored in the graph. The uniqueness of multiple originals in the archival ecosystem provides a digital space for studying the history of art (Caraffa et al. 2020). CIDOC CRM is an extensible ontology meaning that it can easily incorporate additional types. A number of CIDOC CRM extensions have been developed including, for instance, CRMdig for documenting provenance information (Doerr et al. 2016; Theodoridou et al. 2010), CRMpe for cross-research-infrastructure information (Bruseker et al., 2017b), CRMsci for information about scientific observation, measurements and processed data in descriptive and empirical sciences (Doerr et al., 2014), and CRMInf on argumentation and inference making in descriptive and empirical sciences (Stead and Doerr, 2015).

A similar example to CIDOC CRM, in the biomedical domain, is the SMART Protocols Ontology that can be used for representing information about the practices and processes related to experimental protocols (Giraldo et al., 2018). An experimental protocol is essentially a recipe for an experiment, detailing its method and design. The SMART ontology includes data elements relevant to documenting paradata, providing means for describing the execution of protocols and procedures, as well as relevant material artefacts such as laboratory equipment, consumables and software. Figure 4.2 offers an overview of the elements and relations within the SMART Protocols Ontology, illustrating how it can be used to encode experimental protocols consisting of procedures and sub-procedures and their elements. It also shows how individual protocols can be linked to other protocols and the literature through a set of relationships.

Advantages and Limitations of Formal Metadata

Formal metadata is useful for representing knowledge both within specific disciplinary and study contexts and across domains. Its primary advantage in documenting paradata lies in how it contributes to standardising vocabulary, concepts and labels and documentation of practices and processes, which improves the discoverability and interoperability of documentation. Formal metadata-based documentation of paradata allows for making paradata machine-readable and technically compliant to the FAIR (Findability, Accessibility, Interoperability, Reuse) principles for data management (Wilkinson et al., 2016) which are increasingly embraced by funding agencies and research administrative authorities around the world. When a specific term from a documentation standard is consistently used to refer to the same practice or process, all descriptions of that method can be found simultaneously. Similarly, when a standard stipulates what needs to be documented, it is more likely that the particular information will be available for its users, provided data creators follow the standard. When described using formal metadata, research data can be found in digital data repositories, accessible for digital data analysis in open formats, technically and semantically interoperable through metadata standards, and easier to reuse when accompanied by appropriate data licensing information.

One of the major drawbacks of formal metadata is that not all practice and process knowledge is easy to formalise in an ontology. There is a risk of data loss when nuances are not captured by formal terms and relationships. Uncertainties are similarly difficult to formalise. In this sense, formal metadata works best for the representation of a subset of facets of practices and processes that all key stakeholders can agree upon.

Formal data documentation is also hampered by the broader limitations that are inherent to objectivisation of knowledge. All formalisations enact a

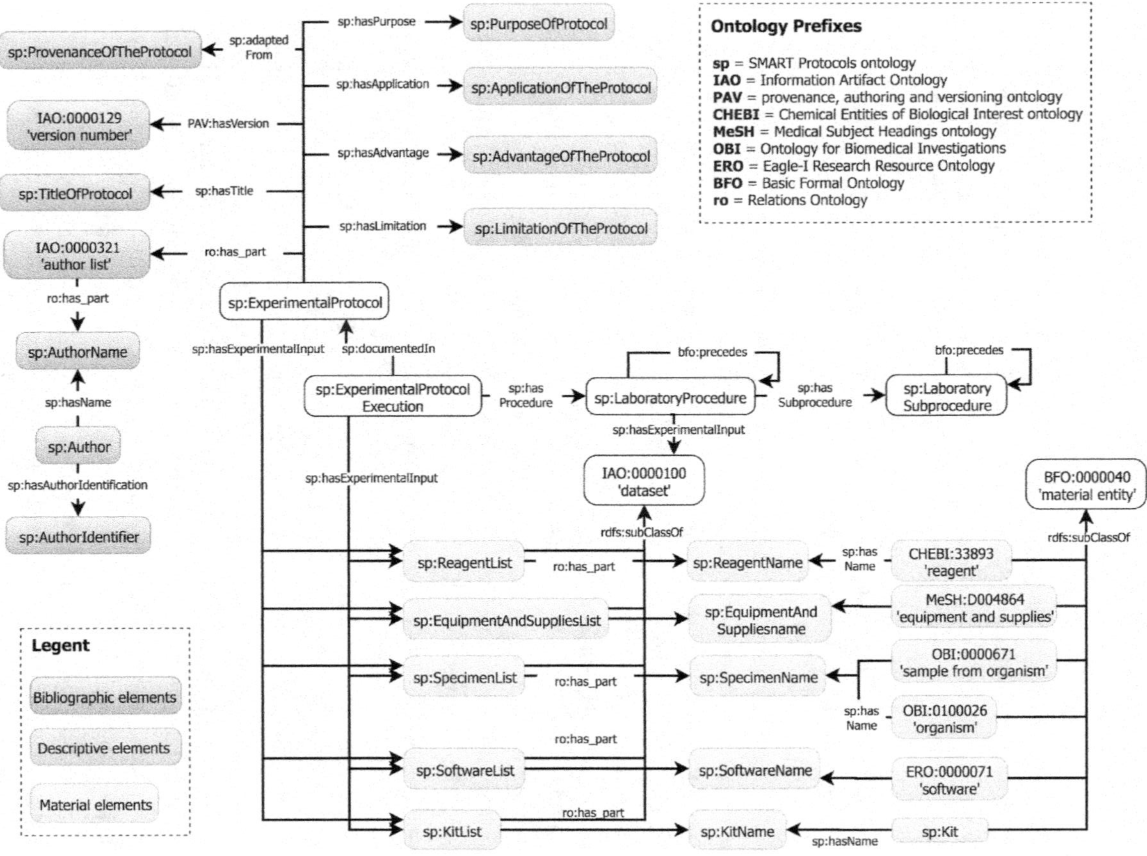

Figure 4.2 Hierarchical organisation of data elements in the SMART Protocols Ontology, sourced from Giraldo et al. 2018 (Image: CC BY 4.0 DEED Attribution 4.0 International).

multitude of cultural and discursive assumptions that are inherent and specific to particular domains and communities. Differences can be found between countries, research disciplines and professional communities but also between diverse sub-specialties within the same discipline. Different communities use different words to describe similar aspects of practices without necessarily being cognisant of their disparities.

For example, archaeologists interviewed in the CAPTURE project highlighted many examples of such differences. A prime example is the naming and temporal bounds of historical periods in different European countries. The term 'Middle Ages' might refer to a period of time that begins several centuries earlier in southern Europe compared to the Nordic countries. There are also parallel categorisation systems that are used independently by particular communities, sometimes without awareness of the existence of multiple classification methods. Many of the assumptions and discursive conventions are also invisible, unconscious and difficult to articulate for community members, leading to gaps in documentation and communication within data standards. A seemingly tidy surface can easily give a false impression of comprehensiveness. The danger of false security is, as Baird remarks, 'in the things the system does not know where to put or how to classify, or in the metadata it does not think to write' (Baird 2023, p. 19).

Another practical complication is that formal data documentation is resource-intensive and it is debatable to what extent all data and associated paradata need to be documented in a minute level of formal detail. Ontology development projects tend to require significant resources and multiyear research funding arrangements, involving a team of researchers with various areas of expertise, such as project managers, domain experts, software engineers and project scientists (e.g., Chao et al., 2015; Hyvönen, 2023; Oldman and Tanase, 2018).

At the same time, however, the development of templates for individual standards and reusable tool sets can make it easier for even a relatively non-technical researcher to utilise ontologies for paradata documentation. The Finnish Sampo-model (Hyvönen, 2023) and the long series of accordingly titled cultural heritage linked open data portals exemplify how an ontology toolkit can be deployed to facilitate work with a broad variety of documentation across multiple contexts. Because of the complications of applying formal metadata to document paradata, especially in cases when established standards are yet to be developed, it is advisable to consult research data and data documentation experts. However, when used mindfully and with care, controlled vocabularies and metadata standards can significantly enhance the transparency of research practices and processes for data publishing.

Key References and Further Reading

- Chao T. C., Cragin M. H. and Palmer C. L. (2015). Data Practices and Curation Vocabulary (DPCVocab): An empirically derived framework of scientific data practices and curatorial processes. *Journal of the Association for Information Science and Technology* 66(3), 616–633. https://doi.org/10.1002/asi.23184. The vocabulary can serve as lingua franca to facilitate communication among the stakeholders in data practices and curatorial processes.
- Nurmikko-Fuller T. (2023). *Linked Data for Digital Humanities,* London: Routledge. https://doi.org/10.4324/9781003197898. A monograph that introduces linked open data in the context of digital humanities, written in non-technical language.
- Zeng M. and Qin J. (2022). *Metadata, 3rd ed.* Chicago: ALA Neal-Schuman. An authoritative and clear introduction to metadata, ranging from fundamental concepts to metadata standards.

4.2.2 Narrative Descriptions

Narrative descriptions encompass written descriptions of connected events for data creation processes, including in the laboratory and field environments, diary keeping, marginalia and fieldnotes. Note taking may go beyond narratives and often involves recording individual data points and pieces of information. We return briefly to this aspect of field notes in the following section when discussing recording as a method of paradata generation.

In field sciences, notebooks and diaries have traditionally been the primary means of documenting both field observations and contextual information, including information on the fieldwork process that can be termed paradata (Canfield, 2011; Rytter et al., 2020). Since the turn of the millennium, digital-, audio- and video-based note taking using mobile phones and in some cases dedicated devices has become increasingly common. In the CAPTURE project, Kaiser has experimented with a prototype of an audio-to-text note-taking application for documenting archaeological fieldwork paradata. Note-taking and narrative descriptions are also prevalent in survey research (Edwards et al., 2017) and laboratory notebooks in natural and life science experiments (Rheinberger, 2023).

Narratives of practices and processes can be documented in various forms and formats, such as in annotations to data, research materials, diaries, research reports and publications, and notebooks. They can also be found in secondary documents and artefacts relating to a practice or process (e.g., Lin, 2021). In many disciplines, the published narratives of research processes tend to be sparse. Methods sections published in research articles are often brief, focusing on essential content as dictated by author guidelines and disciplinary conventions. However, in disciplines like anthropology, it is conventional to produce extensive methodological reflections as a part of what Geertz (1973) famously termed 'thick description'. While usually only short passages of such descriptions find their way to research publications, book-length studies sometimes also allow researchers to write chapter-length descriptions of methods and the research process (e.g., chapter 4 in Smith, 2020).

Narrative descriptions are often combined with illustrations, diagrams, photographs and other types of content as part of a single document. For example, written notes and sketches recorded in notebooks and experiment sheets can be useful for documenting initial and work-in-progress findings and conceptualisations of data. Tracking how descriptions of findings and concepts evolve over time can help both note-takers and others follow the research process. Paradata recorded in lab notebooks and experiment logs facilitate the transition of data from the lab bench to journal articles, research reports etc., using tools such as lists, tables, curves and graphs for combining and summarising data points, observations and experimental results (Rheinberger, 2023).

In field sciences, note-taking is useful for accurately recording observations since the richness of contextual information captures the various conditions and contexts that shape field research experiences and findings (Emerson et al., 2011). It is recommended to promptly document detailed field notes after fieldwork, preferably within twenty-four hours (Williamson 2018). The intended audience matters as well. Working notes need only to be understandable for their author, while notes for external audiences should be written with their intended readers in mind. The language must be appropriate and understandable for an audience that includes both those who plan to reuse data and those who are merely searching for it. Further, it is important to write stand-alone descriptions with enough context and a clear structure (Phillips and Smit, 2021) to ensure that their readers do not need to find and access a lot of additional documentation to understand the descriptions.

In addition to the notes documenting field observations (field notes), other note-taking approaches, such as method notes (reflections on techniques used and their descriptions) and theory notes (ideas about the observed phenomena and their connections with the theoretical framework) are useful for capturing the data creation process (Chatman, 1992). Notably, the use of method notes reflects a growing trend towards reflexivity in social research by examining the researcher's influence on both the research process and its results (Goodwin et al., 2017).

Besides documenting the practical steps taken during a research process, paradata captured in fieldnotes offers researchers a means to introspectively reflect on their own biases and preconceptions throughout the research process, making them transparent to others. Ortlipp (2008) describes her use of reflective journals in documenting qualitative research providing both theoretical insights and practical advice. In archaeology, the reflexive diaries recorded during the Çatalhöyük project (in Anatolia) from the 1990s until 2010s in text and video (Sandoval, 2020), exemplify narrativising data creation process for increased reflexivity.

The relevance of narrative descriptions for documenting paradata lies in the deep embeddedness of narratives in how people understand and communicate their experiences. Dourish and Cruz (2018) emphasise that data is never self-explanatory; it needs to be narrated to give it shape and meaning. Various techniques of data storytelling have been developed to narrate data during processes of interpretation and meaning-making (Dykes, 2020; Knaflic, 2019; Matei, 2021). In this sense, narrative descriptions go beyond mere note-taking and function as thinking aids for their creators. They can also give paradata shape and meaning, mobilise it and help to put it to work. This applies both within the domain crafting the narrative and as a meta-story (Holtorf, 2020) of how the domain portrays itself to external audiences.

Key References and Further Reading

- Dourish P. and Cruz E. G. (2018). Datafication and data fiction: Narrating data and narrating with data. *Big Data & Society* 5(2), 1–10. https://doi.org/10.1177/2053951718784083. An article that discusses the use of narratives in data-driven analysis from the perspective of ethnographic practices.
- Emerson R. M., Fretz R. I. and Shaw L. L. (2011). *Writing Ethnographic Fieldnotes, 2nd ed.* Chicago: University of Chicago press. A manual that provides clear and detailed instructions on writing and processing fieldnotes in ethnographic research.
- Rheinberger H.-J. (2023). *A Phenomenology of Experimentation.* Chicago: University of Chicago Press. An insightful research monograph of experimentation and elements of experimental research including traces, models, grafting and note-taking.

4.2.3 Recordings

Besides developing narrative descriptions, practices and processes can also be captured concurrently through various means, such as photographs, audio, video and 3D data capture. The forms of paradata generation share the common feature of active and purposeful generation of a real-time 'record' of a practice or process. In this sense they can be termed *recordings*. These types of recordings can also be captured using text, either in narrative form or as a series of notes or data points recorded either hand-written on paper or pro forma sheets or digitally in a database.

For instance, during fieldwork documentation, anthropologists take photographs and make films to document their interactions with study participants, cultural artefacts, and the local environment. These photographs and films provide insights into the research process and help interpret the data collected for both data makers and reusers.

When rich enough, they can provide a 'thick depiction', akin to a thick description (Hann, 2021), incorporating multiple levels of interpretations and documentation of the subject of study *and* the study process in one. Such recordings can help to disclose at the best minute details of both data generation practices and processes and their underpinning theories and ideologies. Investigating the colonial legacy in anthropological audiovisual materials, for example, has revealed inherent Western biases and colonial power dynamics by analysing their inception and aesthetics (Giglitto et al. 2023).

As such, recordings provide contextual information and paradata about the research setting and including the environment, interactions between researchers and participants, and non-verbal cues that may not be captured in written notes alone. Whenever audio or video recording does not lead to ethical dilemmas regarding the protection of the privacy and security of involved individuals or groups, they are effective options for generating rich descriptions of practices and processes.

Recordings can document the procedures followed during data collection, including interview techniques, experimental protocols and observational methods. For example, in qualitative studies using interview techniques, audio and video recordings are typically used (Mason, 2018). Researchers can cross-reference interview transcripts and analyses with the recordings to confirm their accuracy. In quantitative studies based on surveys and experiments, recordings are used to ensure that the experiment protocols are followed closely and in interview research, that the interviewer does not deviate from the interview guidelines (Kunz et al., 2024). In observational studies, recordings can capture real-time behaviour, interactions and events in naturalistic settings. The advantage of recording is the ability to collect data that might be impossible or difficult to capture otherwise due to time constraints and the need to engage in concurrent activities. Recordings serving as paradata for documentation of procedures thus contribute both to transparency and replicability in research and in general, of practices and processes.

There is, however, another layer to add. As digital recording devices become increasingly accessible, there is growing recognition of the importance of paradata about recordings. For example, live broadcasting of theatrical events leads to complex documentation processes, in which para-documents (i.e., documents related to a play beyond its core content, such as audience reactions to the primary text), have enriched the impact of a single performance (Abbott and Read, 2017).

One limitation of this approach is the complexity of recordings, which may require the creation and maintenance of paradata specifically for the recording process. This can result in a proliferation of documentation (including documentation of documentation), posing challenges for the management of data and paradata (see Dawson and Reilly, 2019 for reference).

In cultural heritage contexts, 3D scanning methodologies and technologies are increasingly recognised as valuable tools for artefact documentation (Homburg et al. 2021). For example, since 3D scanning accurately captures the exact dimensions and intricate surface details of artefacts, enhanced 3D representations of coins can be achieved by integrating fine photometric details from photographic images with precise geometric data from a 3D laser scanner (MacDonald et al., 2017). The accuracy of such data is high, exceeding the current possibilities of generating comparable information from photographs using photogrammetry, a technique for obtaining information on the physical properties of objects depicted in photographs and video. From paradata perspective, the advantage of both 3D scanning and photogrammetry is not the accurate representation of artefacts per se, but rather the possibility to document a process, for example, the progress of an archaeological excavation or change in natural landscapes, using a series of scans undertaken at different points in time.

In addition to the potential overall quality and accuracy of 3D scanning outputs, capturing paradata in 3D recording practices is important as they provide context and support the reasoning process behind the creation and interpretation of final 3D visualisations (Demetrescu et al., 2023; Opgenhaffen 2022). Further, 3D models have also been proposed as a potentially fruitful approach to knowledge integration, comparable to knowledge graphs, by providing an interface to different forms of knowledge pertaining to both physical and abstract entities.

As interpretative representations, 3D recordings offer a form of knowledge production distinct from those based on text and linear one- or two-dimensional narratives (Derudas, 2021; Sullivan, 2020). Multiple examples of prototypes exist that aim to help archaeologists envision and theorise how different physical elements and multisensory considerations recorded in 3D models may have influenced the sensory experience of a particular archaeological site. Viewers can interact with the data via metadata accessible through the online 3D browser, as well as through documentary metadata and paradata provided in the model's comprehensive publication (Sullivan, 2020, 2023).

Overall, paradata documentation through recording can enhance the transparency and replicability of practices and processes and support data interpretation. A major disadvantage is the large amounts of data generated, which can be difficult to manage and interpret, as evidenced by the video diaries recorded at the Çatalhöyük excavation (Sandoval, 2020). The information density of recordings is not necessarily high and it can take a lot of time to find relevant evidence. Some of these problems can be alleviated by careful planning of what, how and when to record, and by documenting recordings for searchability and findability. The retrieval and summarisation of information from recordings can also be facilitated by artificial intelligence techniques, though there are likely to be limits in the level of detail and precision that automation can achieve in interpretative tasks.

Ethical considerations must also be taken into account before recording everything, since recording can interfere with both legal and ethical bounds of individual privacy. This includes both those who intentionally recorded and those incidentally present when practices and processes are recorded. Recordings can also be easily misused for surveillance and evaluation of individuals' work even if not originally intended for such purposes.

Despite these challenges, recording – particularly when guided by a careful documentation strategy – offers a powerful method for enhancing the comprehensiveness of paradata. Even if a recording is never completely raw, as it is underpinned by multiple choices of what, how and when to record, it provides opportunities to capture aspects of practices or processes in real-time rather than planning them in advance or narrating them afterwards.

Key References and Further Reading

- Sant, T. (ed.) (2017). *Documenting Performance: The Context and Processes of Digital Curation and Archiving*. London; New York: Bloomsbury Methuen Drama. A broad collection of papers addressing the issues of documenting processes in drama and performance studies highlighting many pertinent issues of the documentation of practices and processes independent of domain and context.
- Opgenhaffen L. (2022). Archives in action: The impact of digital technology on archaeological recording strategies and ensuing open research archives. *Digital Applications in Archaeology and Cultural Heritage* 27, e00231. https://doi.org/10.1016/j.daach.2022.e00231. A journal article featuring a

detailed account of recording research processes that emphasises the need for transparency in the digital recording process, advocating for a thorough documentation of the decisions and techniques used in creating 3D models.

4.2.4 Logging

Logging is closely affiliated to recording as a method for generating paradata. Log files (also known as system logs) are documents created in real time during an on-going practice or process. Unlike recordings, which result from deliberate acts of recording, logging is automatic and generated by registering events and actions within a computer system or software application. As researchers extensively utilise digital devices and applications for data collection, processing and analysis, log files provide a straightforward method for automatically collecting evidence of these processes.

Since the advent of paradata during the data collection process, computer-assisted social survey research has received more attention from survey methodologists (Durrant and Kreuter, 2013). For example, survey researchers using computer-assisted personal interview (CAPI) software programs for data collection can automatically log numerous parameters related to interviews, such as time spent on each question, keystrokes, types of events and the person's role in the study. CAPI has been particularly useful for helping researchers manage fieldwork activities by collecting the paradata of timestamps, GPS (Global Positioning System) coordinates and interviewer characteristics. For example, the collection and analysis of paradata of interviewers' movements in the field using automatically logged GPS (Global Positioning System) coordinates can ensure that sampling protocols are followed correctly (Choumert-Nkolo et al., 2019).

Additionally, the collection and analysis of such paradata as response times in web-based surveys can reveal respondents' difficulties of understanding individual questions asked or the effort they invest in taking the survey (Kunz et al. 2024). Paradata of mouse movements have also been used to predict question difficulty in online surveys by taking into account individual differences in mouse-tracking measures, though there is some room for improvement in accuracy with this technique (Fernández-Fontelo et al., 2023). Incorporating such paradata into survey research not only enhances the integrity of data collection processes but also provides insights into respondent behaviour and fieldwork management.

Besides survey research, logs can generate practice and process data also in various other contexts and domains. Logging is currently being tested for capturing interactions with large language models (e.g., Trippas et al., 2024) and in the field called Robotic Process Automation, to log work processes in minute detail (Fani Sani et al., 2023). In scientific and scholarly field research, many digital measuring devices from digital cameras to GPS units, log significant amounts of information besides primary photographic or spatial data. For example, photographs shared on social media platforms like Instagram can be used to study the everyday experiences and sensory perceptions of participants in the field by asking them to take pictures and posing them short questions about their feelings and experiences relating to the topics of the photographs (Shortt and Warren, 2020). In education research, the log files from large-scale cognitive assessments of adult compentencies have been analysed to extract process indicators of test-taking, such as total time on task, time to first action, and the number of interactions, to infer the underlying cognitive processes (Goldhammer et al., 2020). Logging extends to data analysis in virtual research environments that help to collect detailed data on minute steps of data management and use (Bentkowska-Kafel et al., 2012; Sant, 2017).

One of the major challenges with logging is to ensure the coherence of logged information. Blockchain technology provides a robust and secure framework for ensuring the integrity of the logged activities by algorithmically guaranteeing the immutability of logged information and the transparency of activities visible to all relevant parties on a decentralised network (Swan 2015). Envisioned as an alternative to having a trusted third-party to guarantee the practical irreversibility of financial transactions – that a payment once made cannot be undone – blockchain allows what Lemieux describes as trustless trust. While blockchain really makes erasing once recorded information of transactions impractical rather than completely impossible, it provides a method to produce a trustworthy record of consequent activities that stands on its own without an institution or individual to guarantee its integrity (Lemieux, 2022). Since every transaction is registered in a block that connects to prior transactions, a sequential, immutable chain is created. A major benefit of blockchain is how it can be utilised for maintaining the integrity of log files, or paradata in general. All steps of a data creation, management or use are registered and cannot be altered afterward.

Moreover, the blockchain itself incorporates paradata through supplementary or metadata associated with blockchain transactions and operations, including contextual information about the transactions registered on the blockchain, such as timestamps, transaction metadata and participant identities. So far, blockchain technology has been used for diverse purposes ranging from safeguarding patient privacy and data security by storing and sharing 3D augmented reality surgical navigation data through peer-to-peer decentralised technology (Batchu et al., 2023) to ensuring the integrity of archival records (Lemieux 2019). However, the effectiveness and trustworthiness of blockchain systems heavily rely on comprehensive and accurate documentation, as it is often challenging to ascertain the presence, type and location of records within these systems (Lemieux, 2022).

Logging shares many benefits and concerns with recording regarding its usefulness for generating paradata. The primary benefit is its automation, which requires no effort from data creators. This leaves room for directing the conscious human effort to documentation tasks that are difficult or impossible to automatise.

However, similarly to recording, there are ethical issues related to logging practices and processes and keeping logs, especially due to the invisibility of paradata generation. Another challenge with retrieving paradata from log files is that the log files themselves are seldom self-explanatory. Depending on the log, extensive contextual information on both the device or system and its use may be necessary for the logs to make sense to their eventual users. We will return to this final question later in Chapter 5 of this volume when discussing how to use quantitative methods to backtrack past practices and processes.

Key References and Further Reading

- Kunz T., Daikeler J. and Ackermann-Piek D. (2024) Interviewer-observed paradata in mixed-mode and innovative data collection. *International Journal of Market Research* 66(1), 14–26. https://doi.org/10.1177/14707853231184742. A journal article introduces the interviewer-observed paradata in mixed-mode data collection methods.
- Lemieux V. L. (2022) *Searching for Trust: Blockchain Technology in an Age of Disinformation*. Cambridge: Cambridge University Press. A book that discusses the relation of record-keeping, blockchain technologies and trust and emphasises the need for thorough record-keeping and associated documentation and transparency in blockchain systems as a premise to establish and maintain the authenticity of archival records.

4.2.5 Research Plans

In the preceding sections, we have delved into methods for generating paradata either during or directly following practice or process. An alternative approach is to produce documentation in advance. Juneström and Huvila's analysis suggests that this approach can be used either to delineate potential future activities or to prescribe them in advance.

One of the most common approaches to prescribing and prospectively describing practices and processes is by planning and producing corresponding documents, that is, different types of plans. To illustrate plans and their potential function as sources of paradata, this section takes a closer look at data management plans, registered reports, experimental protocols and clinical trial registries.

Data management plans (DMPs), as a type of research plan, are useful for prospectively generating paradata on data-related practices and processes. They provide a structured framework and promote standardised documentation practices to support data sharing and reuse. DMPs serve as structured descriptions of activities that are expected to be followed to reach a particular outcome in research data management, guiding researchers in planning their work.

The increasing use of DMPs has been influenced by funding agencies seeking to enhance transparency of research and promote the sharing and reuse of research data (Smale et al. 2020). It has been posited that to make research data findable, accessible, interoperable and re-usable (FAIR), a well-constructed DMP should describe research data management procedures planned for an entire research project, with particular attention to the collection, processing and generation of data, applied methodologies and standards, data sharing and open access, and data curation and preservation, with a guideline and template to follow.[14]

The effectiveness of DMPs for researchers can be hampered by stakeholder tensions and the generic nature of templates. If aligned with researchers' paradata needs and discipline-specific norms and data practices, they have the potential to be useful for both their creators and the reusers of documented datasets (Kvale and Pharo, 2020; Smale et al., 2020). In contrast, if reduced to mere administrative paperwork, their value is likely to remain questionable. Overall, if implemented properly and aligned to support the planning of relevant aspects of data creation, management and use, DMPs can function as useful devices for eliciting prospective paradata, which in turn can improve transparency of data creation, management and use practices to promote the sharing and reuse of data.

As an alternative form of research plan, registered reports provide detailed plans for a research study, subjected to peer review and publicly registered before execution. These reports outline research questions, hypotheses, methodology, data collection methods and data analysis techniques (Nosek and Lakens, 2014). Registering a research protocol in advance can assist researchers adhere to a predetermined procedure, thus resulting in more accurate documentation of the process compared to a retrospective description (Huvila and Sinnamon, 2022). To improve the computational reproducibility

---

[14] Guidelines on FAIR Data Management in Horizon 2020 http://dx.doi.org/10.25607/OBP-774

of registered reports in statistical data analysis, recommended practice is to include a codebook in data files, annotating and structuring the code for clarity, ensuring reproducibility of codes post-revisions, and listing required software packages and versions (Obels et al., 2020). Pre-registered reports are a useful starting point for replicating experimental studies and comparing research findings across studies. Including a codebook in data files and associated paradata in procedures of data analysis can improve computational reproducibility of shared data, thus enhancing methodological transparency and data sharing and reuse.

Experimental protocols are a related approach to pre-registered reports used in experimental research, with the goal of functioning as a recipe for running an experiment. Their specifics and level of detail can vary by laboratories and publications even if they are expected to follow discipline-specific norms (Giraldo et al., 2018). They are expected to provide a description that is sufficiently thorough to give enough information for an external colleague to replicate an experiment. Similarly to registered reports, their prominent aim is to improve transparency and reproducibility of research by prompting data creators to describe their procedures prior to data generation and mobilsing research findings from the laboratory bench to the research publication (Rheinberger, 2023). Their major advantage is in their potential to reduce the number of unplanned ad hoc changes to plans that do not end up being documented. Their principal drawback is that they reduce the flexibility of research work thus making them less suitable for qualitative and exploratory research based on the rationale of adapting data generation methods to the evolving research situation.

As a final example of a plan, clinical trial registries are publicly accessible online databases that provide access to information regarding clinical trials prior to their initiation. As an alternative form of research plans, their focus is on documenting details of clinical trials, including study descriptions, participation criteria and study plans (experimental design and outcome measures).

The purpose of trial registries is to disseminate information concerning clinical trial research, thereby contributing to enhancing the transparency and quality of trials. Registries are typically specific to countries or regions, such as ClinicalTrials.gov, provided by the National Library of Medicine (NLM) in the USA, the Australian New Zealand Clinical Trials Registry (ANZCTR) (www.anzctr.org.au/), and the European Union Clinical Trials Register (currently transitioning to the Clinical Trials Information System, CTIS) (https://euclinicaltrials.eu/search-for-clinical-trials/?lang=en) for trials conducted in the European Union (EU) and European Economic Area (EEA). Additionally, the

World Health Organization (WHO) manages the International Clinical Trials Registry Platform (ICTRP) (https://trialsearch.who.int/), which serves as an aggregator of registries worldwide. Like registered reports, a registration process is in place. However, there is generally no peer-reviewing process and the policies of whether the information is entered by investigators and research sponsors or national authorities with authorisations and ethics reviews included depend on the registry.

The clinical trial registries are useful resources for other researchers conducting meta-analysis studies, developing healthcare guidelines or seeking collaborative research opportunities (Liu et al., 2023). Clinical trial registries offer valuable access to pre-initiation information about trials, including paradata about the various aspects of the trial process, which in turn helps to enhance the methodological transparency on trial studies. As a highly specific and resource-intensive approach to documenting planned research, the approach lacks transferability to domains where a comparable level of regulation and formalisation of data generation is not feasible. At the same time, they show how planning can be a highly effective method of generating detailed paradata to stipulate forthcoming data creation.

Key References and Further Reading

- DeVito N. J., Morley J., Smith J. A., Drysdale H., Goldacre B. and Heneghan C. (2024) Availability of results of clinical trials registered on EU Clinical Trials Register: Cross sectional audit study. *BMJ Medicine* 3(1). https://doi.org/10.1136/bmjmed-2023-000738. A study that describes how the European Union Clinical Trials Register (EUCTR) functions as a repository for accessing unique trial results and can support literature searching for systematic review studies.
- Gajbe S. B., Tiwari A., Gopalji and Singh R. K. (2021) Evaluation and analysis of Data Management Plan tools: A parametric approach. *Information Processing & Management* 58(3), 102480. https://doi.org/10.1016/j.ipm.2020.102480. This article provides a comprehensive review of data management tools and guides the selection of tools that best suit the researchers' needs.
- Nosek B. A. and Lakens D. (2014) Registered reports: A method to increase the credibility of published results. *Social Psychology* 45(3), 137–141. https://doi.org/10.1027/1864-9335/a000192. This article provides an overview of the concept of registered reports and discusses their rationales and use for enhancing the transparency and credibility of experiments in social psychology.

4.2.6 Prospective Workflows

In addition to (research) plans that vary in their degree of formality, prospective workflows represent a future-oriented technique for describing and, often in parallel, prescribing planned practices and processes. Similar to plans, this approach is useful for generating prospective or potential paradata (cf. Chapter 6) – documentation of forthcoming activities that ultimately becomes paradata when the practice or process is enacted.

In the literature on procedural workflows, a workflow refers to the series of tasks or steps involved in completing a particular process or achieving a specific goal. Workflows provide a structured approach to organising and executing work efficiently to accomplish desired outcomes. They are particularly popular in contexts incorporating repetitive tasks that need to be executed repeatedly in the same order, such as consecutive steps in scientific experiments, industry and computational tasks.

Workflow-based approaches systematically outline the steps to accomplish specific tasks and detail how individuals and automated processes and practices should be executed to achieve a specific goal. In IT, computational workflows are usually executable, containing all necessary information to carry out and complete a task as a whole. In contrast, human workflows often document only key steps of a workflow, omitting details deemed unnecessary for a human executing the task.

Figure 4.3 shows a visual representation of a workflow diagram (Activity Diagram) that can be converted to machine-readable code, for example, in Unified Modelling Language (UML). Workflow diagrams are formal diagrammatic models that aim to provide comprehensive documentation of a process. The diagram can be visualised to facilitate the recording, sharing and explanation of protocols used in generating results, selected outcomes and summarising courses of action (Blaise and Dudek, 2023).

Likewise, to make the research results easier to verify, the workflow of managing research data can be semi-automated in a workflow management system to meet specified external and internal requirements of the documentation of data (Miksa et al., 2021). However, to direct the actual workflow – that is, how tasks are executed – the adoption of a workflow management system must be embedded in the daily work practice of its users, requiring both engagement and resources.

Workflows are frequently depicted using machine-readable diagrams to enhance their discoverability by automated systems (Weigel et al., 2020). The surge in digital data processing and analysis has led to an increasing demand for adequate documentation of computational workflows. Supporting

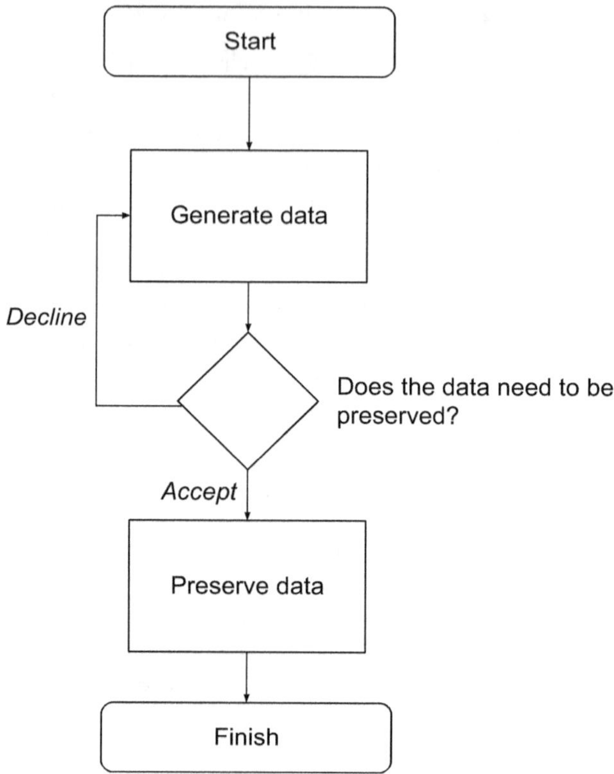

Figure 4.3 A workflow diagram (Activity Diagram) of a simple data generation and preservation workflow.

reproducible scientific workflows in Data Science, a web-based interactive computing platform like Jupyter Notebook (Figure 4.4) enables users to produce annotations by integrating live code, equations, text and media directly in a document that contains both the code and the documentation. It supports the use of various programming languages. The executable workflows of computer codes, with outputs and annotations as interactive documentation, allow data creators to efficiently create reproducible computational workflows. The system incorporates a prompt display of output and the capability to identify necessary documentation updates following alterations to the user interface or algorithms (Beg et al., 2021; Mendez et al., 2019). However, despite the advantages of using dedicated tools, the reproducibility rates sometimes remain low since the documentation and execution of tasks do not necessarily follow the existing guidelines and best practices (Pimentel et al., 2021).

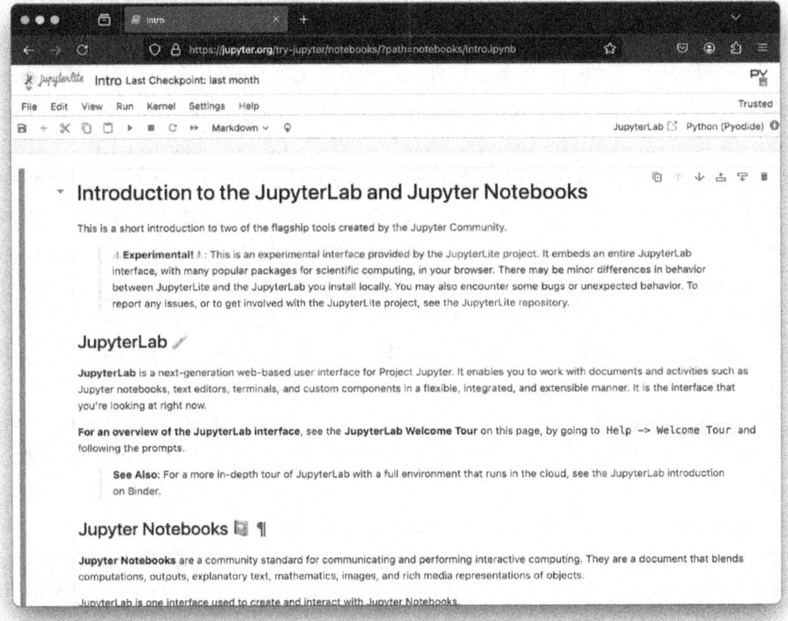

Figure 4.4 Jupyter Notebook (https://jupyter.org/try-jupyter/notebooks/? path = notebooks/Intro.ipynb).

To produce more usable and reproducible research data, Thomer et al. (2018) proposed a method of Research Process Modeling for documenting non-computational data provenance in geobiology fieldwork. This method consists of two inventories and two workflows: 1) an Activity Diagram (see above); 2) an artefact inventory documenting all digital and physical artefacts (including filenames, information on their creating and using processes, related artefacts, class and format); 3) a process inventory with information on involved processes (including title, description, agents, preconditions, inputs and outputs); and 4) a provenance graph modelled according to the PROV specification (PROV-Overview 2013). Research Process Modelling enables researchers to assess their work in relation to their planned activities, providing a means to prescribe and document research activities and artefacts to facilitate future reuse. Related workflow-based approaches to paradata generation have been targeted to specific tasks in other domains as well, including data harmonisation in survey research (Kołczyńska, 2022), life sciences (Cohen-Boulakia et al., 2017), and bioinformatics (Oinn et al., 2004).

Overall, workflow-based approaches offer a practical method for generating potential paradata in advance. This enhances the transparency of data creation processes before data is created, standardises data-related practices and processes, and facilitates data reuse. However, especially when applied to complicated practices and processes, workflows tend to become increasingly complex, and thus difficult to implement and manage. Even if the execution of an existing workflow intuitively might sound like a trivial task, capturing paradata relating to running a workflow for validating its correctness and performance remains a major concern. An illustrative context where this has become increasingly apparent are the GLAM (Galleries, Libraries, Archives and Museums) institutions that struggle with publishing their digital collections (Candela et al., 2023).

A related problem is the integrity of workflows and their associated paradata (Hoopes et al. 2022). For many data generation contexts, especially in social research, the relevance and even possibility of modelling tasks on a strict step-by-step basis remains an open question. However, even if the workflow remains an incomplete simplification, it can still be helpful in directing attention to key steps of practices and processes to document, even if the aim of paradata production is not to generate a comprehensive step-by-step model.

Key References and Further Reading

Kvale L. and Pharo N. (2020) Understanding the data management plan as a boundary object through a multi-stakeholder perspective. *International Journal of Digital Curation* 15(1), 16. https://doi.org/10.2218/ijdc.v15i1 .729. A journal article that provides insights into the perceived usefulness of data management plans (DMPs) from the perspectives of their different stakeholders.

Nosek B. A. and Lakens D. (2014) Registered reports: A method to increase the credibility of published results. *Social Psychology* 45(3), 137–141. https://doi.org/10.1027/1864-9335/a000192. An article that discusses rationales and the use of registered reports in experimental research.

International Clinical Trials Registry Platform (ICTRP) (https://www.who .int/clinical-trials-registry-platform) A knowledge base of trial studies across clinical trials registeries.

Thomer A. K., Wickett K. M., Baker K. S., Fouke B. W. and Palmer C. L. (2018) Documenting provenance in noncomputational workflows: Research process models based on geobiology fieldwork in Yellowstone National Park. *Journal of the Association for Information Science and Technology* 69(10), 1234–1245. https://doi.org/10.1002/asi.24039.

A research study that describes an approach to document provenance in non-computational workflows in geobiology fieldwork.

4.3 Discussion

An overview of a selection of potential approaches for generating and documenting paradata – that is, information on practices and processes – sourced from the literature reveals a plethora of usable methods. However, the overview also shows that since the methods introduced in this chapter are primarily designed for data creators, there is a tendency to stipulate the generation of paradata by following specific procedures and standardised formats.

Narrative descriptions represent a more *post hoc* approach that emphasises documenting practices and processes as they are experienced and observed. Recording and logging, on the other hand, generate paradata in the moment, at least in theory. In practice, however, both recording and logging are shaped by the technologies employed to capture paradata and the underlying concept of relevant information that guides what is documented.

A data management plan is designed with guidelines and templates for researchers to follow. Registered reports and computational workflow methods aim to provide comprehensive documentation of data creation processes by adhering to predefined procedures. Since the formal metadata-based methods are concerned with the standardisation of data for data sharing and exchange, their use requires systematicity and compliance to standards. Data creators need to be aware of relevant frameworks for data publishing, such as the 5 Star Linked Open Data (Berners-Lee 2009) model but also be aware of the limitations and consequences of formalising descriptions, the risk of data loss and the impact of their underlying assumptions and perspectives to data documentation.

One of the main drivers for working with paradata is to contribute significantly to the documentation of contextual information (Huvila, 2022). However, effective means to this end are not yet well developed or commonly used. It appears that as a research approach becomes sensitive to situation and context, it also becomes less structured either regarding the specifics of generated paradata, its structure or both.

Apart from narratives and recordings, there are some proposals for capturing contextual information, including paradata, about the data, using a template for data summary. Philips and Smit's guidelines for unstructured descriptions of datasets emphasise the importance of presenting the dataset as a research output and elucidating the context in which the data was generated (Philips and Smit, 2021). Koesten and colleagues' (2020) dataset summary template is another example of an approach that provides a structured framework for generating meaningful textual representations of data (Koesten et al., 2020).

There are also proposals of reporting standards and guidelines for experimental protocols and data analysis procedures in a checklist format (Considine and Salek, 2019; Giraldo et al., 2018). Such checklists also include the large set of reporting standards developed for enumerating various facets of various types of study designs, data collection and analysis methods in publication. The EQUATOR network[15] (2008-) guidelines in the health domain are a prominent example that are also partially applicable to other domains, although careful consideration must be applied to their suitability when applying them and appropriate tailoring may be necessary.

Collecting best practices across research contexts can be helpful. Proven methods for documenting practices and processes offer guidance to improve the transparency of data creation processes, though they may be difficult or impossible to integrate into the research process if the best practices emerge from far off domains. Another challenge, not to be taken lightly and necessary to solve on a domain to domain basis, requires data creators and users to work together with real data creation and use cases and scenarios to determine precisely what information needs to be documented.

Given the contextual and situational nature of paradata and paradata generation, rather than aiming at using a single approach for generating and documenting paradata, using a combination of the methods introduced in this chapter can be helpful in broadening the scope of generated documentation. However, this should be done thoughtfully, considering what kind of information-specific methods would optimally provide the relevant amount and breadth of documentation.

The diffusion of paradata across data and data documentation suggests that a promising approach to limiting the excess of paradata generation and simultaneously enabling and improving the use and usefulness of existing information is to move towards more integrated interlinking of data and diverse forms of data documentation and secondary information resources. The examples from using 3D documentation as a centrepiece that provides an interface to all relevant information relating to a physical object are taking steps to this direction. Also, Mosconi et al. (2022) who argue that the integration of a narrative layer in data curation can capture the contextual and cultural nuances necessary for qualitative research, are essentially suggesting to package data and method description

---

[15] www.equator-network.org.

together. This approach, even if developed for science education, has wider applicability, featuring the integration of the metadata standards and promoting ongoing curation activities within daily workflows.

A growing number of authors advocate for shifting paradata generation from retrospective documentation to planning and creating documentation during and, where possible, before practices or processes are enacted. The combined use of registered reports and a narrative description of the data creation processes can assist researchers with following a predetermined procedure, leading to more precise documentation of the processes compared to a retrospective account (Huvila and Sinnamon, 2022). The Research Process Modelling method (Thomer et al., 2018) takes this approach. However, it is important to weigh the benefits of advance planning against the risk of rigidifying practices and procedures, making them less agile and flexible to context and situation.

Broadening the scope of paradata generation also involves embracing multiple forms and formats of paradata. Text and visualisations are not merely different approaches to mapping knowledge of practices and processes but also produce it differently, ideally complementing each other (cf. Schwandt, 2022; Vancisin et al., 2023). Keenan and Walker (2017) provide an example of combining different modes of representation to document data which can be applicable to the processing of paradata. The documentation of a research dataset of seismic data collected during a survey project in 1970 preserved in the University of Montana institutional repository consisted of narrative descriptions, formal Dublin Core metadata, and primary datafiles. The librarians responsible for the work also considered how to organise the datafiles and documentation in the repository and how to make it accessible for its intended users, including how to address possible hindrances caused by individuals' functional variation, for example, lack of eyesight or hearing impairment. There are many benefits of planning ahead and producing narrative descriptions during processes of interpretation and meaning-making for capturing ongoing research activities, in combination with formal metadata-based methods, such as metadata standards and ontology, for more precise documentation of data provenance.

4.4 Conclusions

The methods discussed in this chapter provide guidance for data creators seeking to capture and document paradata effectively during data generation processes. The distinction between prospective and in-situ methods provides a framework for understanding when and how paradata is generated in relation to the activities being documented. These methods range from formal metadata schemas and structured planning approaches such as data management plans and registered reports, to workflow-based techniques and narrative descriptions.

Formal metadata methods, including metadata standards, label sets and controlled vocabularies, play a critical role in ensuring consistency, discoverability and interoperability of data across diverse domains. However, their implementation may pose challenges for researchers lacking specialised technical expertise and resources, due to their inflexibility and inherent assumptions.

Narrative descriptions serve as rich sources of paradata, capturing contextual details, insights and reflections throughout the data creation process. From field notes in qualitative research to laboratory protocols in life sciences, narratives provide opportunities for conveying a nuanced understanding of data generation practices and interpretations.

Recordings, including images, audio and video, offer tangible documentation of processes, enabling researchers to visualise and analyse activities in detail. Logging methods, such as log files and blockchain technology, automate the documentation of events and actions within computer systems, enhancing transparency and security in data collection and analysis processes. While log files offer detailed records of system activities, techniques like the blockchain can help to secure the immutability and integrity of data transactions, particularly in sensitive domains like medical research.

Rather than documenting on-going or past practices and processes, it is also possible to prospectively generate descriptions to guide forthcoming work. The major advantage of this approach is that a prospective protocol or plan guides the practice in advance, helping to increase the consistency of practices and processes and minimising problematic ad hoc measures that may not be adequately documented.

Another advantage of prospective paradata generation is that in-situ and retrospective documentation might overlook crucial steps and measures. If paradata generation on-the-fly might increase workload by being a secondary undertaking to the documented practice or process, the shortfall of retrospective documentation is the difficulty of remembering what actually happened. However, while such prospective methods as protocols or data management plans offer guidelines and templates for researchers to follow in processing and managing research data, their effectiveness can be limited by varying stakeholder interests and tensions.

As the results of a survey study conducted in the CAPTURE project indicate, both data creators and users find value in documenting closely related aspects of practices and processes. However, their perception of what constitutes informative data varies (Huvila et al., 2024; cf. Chapters 2 and 3). Similarly, while registered reports aim to improve transparency and credibility by registering detailed study plans before data collection, their practical implementation can be challenging to align with researchers' needs during the research process. A plan should not by default restrict the execution of the planned practice or process. In research, an even more important aspect of planning is that a plan should not constrain the thinking of the data creator, manager or user, leading them to assume that the planned practice or process is the only conceivable option.

This also applies to workflows. Workflow-based approaches, such as diagrams and information visualisation systems, offer systematic ways to document processes and facilitate reproducibility in data analysis tasks. At the same time, there is a risk that these approaches might impose rigid practices and processes that are less desirable in contexts where the goal is understanding rather than reproducibility.

Overall, the selection and application of methods for generating and documenting paradata should be tailored to the specific needs and constraints of individual research contexts. There is no universal method or approach that suits all domains and situations.

However, even if getting the right paradata might still be a wicked problem without apparent solution (cf. Huvila 2022), there are a lot of means to improve the transparency, reproducibility and credibility of the practices and processes of data generation, management and use. Rather than assuming that one approach or type of paradata would be enough, it is necessary to knit together an array of approaches that are contextually and situationally appropriate for the task and together provide enough information. A mindful paradata creator formulates a *paradata finding aid* (as discussed in Chapter 6) that incorporates a map of the methods and generated paradata to facilitate both paradata discovery and its future use.

As we will explore in the next chapter, incomplete documentation before and during a practice or process takes place is not necessarily fatal. A lot of paradata can also be identified and generated retroactively even if it is not explicitly documented as paradata by anyone when data was created, managed or previously used.

References

Abbott D. and Read C. (2017) Paradocumentation and NT Live's 'CumberHamlet'. In Sant, T. (ed.), Documenting Performance. London: Bloomsbury Methuen Drama, 165–187. http://radar.gsa.ac.uk/5068/.

Baird, J. (2023). Unclassified: Structured silences in the archaeological archive. In Raja, R. (ed.), *Shaping Archaeological Archives Dialogues between Fieldwork, Museum Collections, and Private Archives*, 19–32. Turnhout: Brepols.

Batchu S., Diaz M. J., Ladehoff L., Root K. and Lucke-Wold B. (2023) Utilizing the Ethereum blockchain for retrieving and archiving augmented reality surgical navigation data. *Exploration of Drug Science* 1(1), 55–63. https://doi.org/10 .37349/eds.2023.00005.

Beg M., Taka J., Kluyver T., Konovalov A., Ragan-Kelley M., Thiéry N. M. and Fangohr H. (2021) Using Jupyter for reproducible scientific workflows. *Computing in Science & Engineering* 23(2), 36–46. https://doi.org/10.1109/ MCSE.2021.3052101.

Bentkowska-Kafel A., Denard H. and Baker D. (2012) Paradata and Transparency in Virtual Heritage Paradata and Transparency in Virtual Heritage. Farnham: Ashgate.

Berners-Lee, T. (2009). Is your linked open data 5 star? Retrieved from www.w3.org/ DesignIssues/LinkedData.html.

Berners-Lee T. and Hendler J. (2001) Publishing on the semantic web. *Nature* 410(6832), 1023–1024. https://doi.org/10.1038/35074206.

Blaise, Jean-Yves and Dudek, Iwona (2023) Research workflows, paradata, and information visualisation: feedback on an exploratory integration of issues and practices: MEMORIA IS. *Peer Community in Archaeology.* https://doi.org/10.5281/ zenodo.8311129.

Börjesson, L., Huvila, I. and Sköld, O. (2022). Information needs on research data creation. *Information Research*, 27(Special Issue), https://doi.org/10.47989/ irisic2208.

Bruseker, G., Carboni, N. and Guillem, A. (2017). Cultural heritage data management: The role of formal ontology and CIDOC CRM. In Vincent, M. L., López-Menchero Bendicho, V. M., Ioannides, M. and Levy, T. E. (eds.), *Heritage and Archaeology in the Digital Age: Acquisition, Curation, and Dissemination of Spatial Cultural Heritage Data*, 93–131. Cham: Springer.

Canfield M. R (2011) Field Notes on Science and Nature. Harvard University Press.

Chao T. C., Cragin M. H. and Palmer C. L. (2015) Data practices and curation vocabulary (DPCVocab): An empirically derived framework of scientific data practices and curatorial processes. *Journal of the Association for Information Science and Technology* 66(3), 616–633. https://doi.org/10.1002/asi.23184.

Chatman E. A (1992) The Information World of Retired Women. Bloomsbury Academic.

Choumert-Nkolo J., Cust H. and Taylor C. (2019) Using paradata to collect better survey data: Evidence from a household survey in Tanzania. *Review of Development Economics* 23(2), 598–618. https://doi.org/10.1111/rode.12583.

Cohen-Boulakia, S., et al. (2017). Scientific workflows for computational reproducibility in the life sciences: Status, challenges and opportunities. *Future Generation Computer Systems*, 75, 284–298.

Cox S. J. D., Gonzalez-Beltran A. N., Magagna B. and Marinescu M.-C. (2021) Ten simple rules for making a vocabulary FAIR. *PLOS Computational Biology* 17(6), 1–15. https://doi.org/10.1371/journal.pcbi.1009041.

Dawson I. and Reilly P. (2019) Messy assemblages, residuality and recursion within a phygital nexus. *Epoiesen.* https://eprints.soton.ac.uk/439599/.

Demetrescu E., Fanini B. and Cocca E. (2023) An online dissemination workflow for the scientific process in CH through semantic 3D: EMtools and EMviq Open Source tools. *Heritage* 6(2), 1264–1276. https://doi.org/10.3390/heritage6020069.

Derudas P. (2021) Archaeological publication systems: Which route to take? A compass for addressing future development. In *The 26th International Conference on 3D Web Technology*, 1–6. Pisa Italy: ACM. https://doi.org/10.1145/3485444.3487648.

DeVito N. J., Morley J., Smith J. A., Drysdale H., Goldacre B. and Heneghan C. (2024) Availability of results of clinical trials registered on EU Clinical Trials Register: Cross sectional audit study. *BMJ Medicine* 3(1). https://doi.org/10.1136/bmjmed-2023-000738.

Doerr, M., Kritsotaki, A., Rousakis, Y., Hiebel, G. and Theodoridou, M. (2014). *CRMsci: The Scientific Observation Model an Extension of CIDOC-CRM to Support Scientific Observation*, Heraklion: FORTH.

Doerr, M., Stead, S. and Theodoridou, M. (2016). *Definition of the CRMdig: An Extension of CIDOC-CRM to Support Provenance Metadata*, Version 3.2.1, Heraklion: FORTH.

Dourish P. and Cruz E. G (2018) Datafication and data fiction: Narrating data and narrating with data. *Big Data & Society* 5(2), 1–10. https://doi.org/10.1177/2053951718784083.

Durrant G. and Kreuter F. (2013) Editorial: The use of paradata in social survey research. *Journal of the Royal Statistical Society. Series A (Statistics in Society)* 176(1), 1–3.

Dykes, B. (2019). *Effective Data Storytelling: How to Drive Change with Data, Narrative, and Visuals*, Hoboken, NJ: Wiley.

Edwards R., Goodwin J., O'Connor H. and Phoenix A. (2017) *Working with Paradata, Marginalia and Fieldnotes: The Centrality of By-Products of Social Research.* Edward Elgar Publishing.

Emerson R. M., Fretz R. I. and Shaw L. L. (2011) *Writing Ethnographic Fieldnotes, 2nd ed.* University of Chicago Press.

EQUATOR Network. (2008). Enhancing the QUAlity and Transparency Of health Research. Retrieved from www.equator-network.org.

Fani Sani, M., Sroka, M., and Burattin, A. (2024). LLMs and process mining: Challenges in RPA. In De Smedt, J. and Soffer, P. (eds.), *Process Mining Workshops*, 379–391. Cham: Springer Nature Switzerland.

Fernández-Fontelo A., Kieslich P. J., Henninger F., Kreuter F. and Greven S. (2023) Predicting question difficulty in web surveys: A machine learning approach based on mouse movement features. *Social Science Computer Review* 41(1), 141–162. https://doi.org/10.1177/08944393211032950.

Gajbe S. B., Tiwari A., Gopal ji and Singh R. K. (2021) Evaluation and analysis of Data Management Plan tools: A parametric approach. *Information Processing & Management* 58(3), 102480. https://doi.org/10.1016/j.ipm.2020.102480.

Geertz, C. (1973). *The Interpretation of Cultures : Selected Essays*, New York: Basic Books.

Giglitto D., Ciolfi L., Lockley E. and Kaldeli E. (2023) *Digital Approaches to Inclusion and Participation in Cultural Heritage: Insights from Research and Practice in Europe*, 1st ed. London: Routledge. https://doi.org/10.4324/9781003277606.

Giraldo O., Garcia A. and Corcho O. (2018) A guideline for reporting experimental protocols in life sciences. *Peer Journal* 6, e4795. https://doi.org/10.7717/peerj.4795.

Goldhammer F., Hahnel C. and Kroehne U. (2020) Analysing log file data from PIAAC. In Maehler, D. B. and Rammstedt, B. (eds.), *Large-Scale Cognitive Assessment: Analyzing PIACC Data*. Cham: Springer International Publishing, 239–269. https://doi.org/10.1007/978-3-030-47515-4_10.

Golub K. and Liu Y.-H. (2022) *Information and Knowledge Organisation in Digital Humanities: Global Perspectives*. United Kingdom: Routledge.

Goodwin J., O'Connor H., Phoenix A. and Edwards R. (2017) Introduction: Working with paradata, marginalia and fieldnotes. In Edwards, R., Goodwin, J., O'Connor, H. and Phoenix, A. (eds.), *Working with Paradata, Marginalia and Fieldnotes*. Edward Elgar Publishing. https://doi.org/10.4337/9781784715250.00007.

Hann, R. (2021). Modelling Kiesler's Endless Theatre: Approaches to paradata for heritage visualization. *Theatre and Performance Design*, 7(1–2), 96–115.

Holtorf, C. (2010). Meta-stories of archaeology. *World Archaeology*, 42(3), 381–393.

Hoopes, R., Hardy, H., Long, M., and Dagher, G. G. (2022). SciLedger: A Blockchain-based Scientific Workflow Provenance and Data Sharing Platform. In 2022 IEEE 8th International Conference on Collaboration and Internet Computing (CIC), 125–134.

Huck, J. (2022). Knowledge graphs, metadata practices, and Badiou's mathematical ontology. *KULA: Knowledge Creation, Dissemination, and Preservation Studies*, 6(3), 1–17.

Huvila, I. (2022). Improving the usefulness of research data with better paradata. *Open Information Science*, 6(1), 28–48.

Huvila, I., Andersson, L., Sköld, O., and Liu, Y.-H. (2025). Data makers' and users' views on useful paradata: Priorities in documenting data creation, curation, manipulation and use in archaeology. *International Journal of Digital Curation*. 19(1), https://doi.org/10.2218/ijdc.v19i1.892

Huvila I and Sinnamon L (2022) Sharing research design, methods and process information in and out of academia. *Proceedings of the Association for Information Science and Technology* 59(1), 132–144. https://doi.org/10.1002/pra2.611.

Hyvönen E. (2023) Digital humanities on the Semantic Web: Sampo model and portal series. *Semantic Web* 14(4), 729–744. https://doi.org/10.3233/SW-223034.

International Standard Classification of Education (ISCED 2011). (2011), Montreal: UNESCO Institute for Statistics.

ISO 18629-1. (2004) Industrial automation systems and integration: Process specification language Part 1: Overview and basic principles. (2004). (Version 1). Retrieved from https://www.iso.org/standard/35431.html.

Keenan, T., and Walker, W. (2017). Considerations and challenges for describing historical research data: A case study. *Journal of Library Metadata*, 17(3–4), 241–252.

Knaflic, C. N. (2020). Storytelling with Data: Let's Practice!, Hoboken, NJ: Wiley.

Koesten L., Simperl E., Blount T., Kacprzak E. and Tennison J. (2020) Everything you always wanted to know about a dataset: Studies in data summarization.

International Journal of Human-Computer Studies 135, 102367. https://doi.org/10.1016/j.ijhcs.2019.10.004.

Kunz T., Daikeler J. and Ackermann-Piek D. (2024) Interviewer-observed paradata in mixed-mode and innovative data collection. *International Journal of Market Research* 66(1), 14–26. https://doi.org/10.1177/14707853231184742.

Kvale L. and Pharo N. (2020) Understanding the Data Management Plan as a Boundary Object through a Multi-stakeholder perspective. *International Journal of Digital Curation* 15(1), 16. https://doi.org/10.2218/ijdc.v15i1.729.

Lee S., Li W., Zhang P. and Wang J. (2023) Characterizing data practices in research papers across four disciplines. In Sserwanga, I., Goulding, A., Moulaison-Sandy, H., Du, J. T., Soares, A. L., Hessami, V. and Frank, R. D. (eds.), *Information for a Better World: Normality, Virtuality, Physicality, Inclusivity*. Cham: Springer Nature Switzerland, 359–368.

Lemieux, V. L. (2019). Blockchain and public record keeping: Of temples, prisons, and the (Re)Configuration of power. *Frontiers in Blockchain*, 2. https://doi.org/10.3389/fbloc.2019.00005

Lemieux V. L. (2022) Searching for Trust: Blockchain Technology in an Age of Disinformation. Cambridge: Cambridge University Press.

Lin, Y.-T. (2021). Reusing design information: An investigation of the document creation process in service design projects. *Journal of Documentation*, 77(3), 703–721. https://doi.org/10.1108/JD-06-2020-0111

Liu Y.-H. and Wacholder N. (2017) Evaluating the impact of MeSH (Medical Subject Headings) terms on different types of searchers. *Information Processing & Management* 53(4), 851–870. https://doi.org/10.1016/j.ipm.2017.03.004.

Liu Y.-H., Wu M., Power M. and Burton A. (2023) *Elicitation of contexts for discovering clinical trials and related health data: An Interview Study*. Zenodo. Retrieved from https://zenodo.org/records/7839282

MacDonald L., Almeida V. M. de and Hess M. (2017) Three-dimensional reconstruction of Roman coins from photometric image sets. *Journal of Electronic Imaging* 26(1), 011017. https://doi.org/10.1117/1.JEI.26.1.011017.

Mai J.-E. (2008) Actors, domains, and constraints in the design and construction of controlled vocabularies. *Knowledge Organization* 35(1), 16–29.

Mason J. (2018) *Qualitative researching*, 3rd ed. Los Angeles: Sage Publications.

Matei, S. A., and Hunter, L. (2021). Data storytelling is not storytelling with data: A framework for storytelling in science communication and data journalism. *The Information Society*, 37(5). https://doi.org/10.1080/01972243.2021.1951415.

Mendez K. M., Pritchard L., Reinke S. N. and Broadhurst D. I. (2019) Toward collaborative open data science in metabolomics using Jupyter Notebooks and cloud computing. *Metabolomics* 15(10), 125. https://doi.org/10.1007/s11306-019-1588-0.

Miksa T., Oblasser S. and Rauber A. (2021) Automating research data management using machine-actionable data management plans. *ACM Transactions on Management Information Systems* 13(2), 18:1–18:22. https://doi.org/10.1145/3490396.

Nosek B. A. and Lakens D. (2014) Registered reports: A method to increase the credibility of published results. *Social Psychology* 45(3), 137–141. https://doi.org/10.1027/1864-9335/a000192.

Nurmikko-Fuller T. (2023) *Linked Open Data for Digital Humanities*, London: Routledge. https://doi.org/10.4324/9781003197898.

Obels P., Lakens D., Coles N. A., Gottfried J. and Green S. A. (2020) Analysis of open data and computational reproducibility in registered reports in psychology. *Advances in Methods and Practices in Psychological Science* 3(2), 229–237.

Oinn, T., et al. (2004). Taverna: A tool for the composition and enactment of bioinformatics workflows. *Bioinformatics*, 20(17), 3045–3054.

Oldman D. and Tanase D. (2018) Reshaping the Knowledge Graph by Connecting Researchers, Data and Practices in ResearchSpace. In Vrandečić, D., Bontcheva, K., Suárez-Figueroa, M. C., Presutti, V., Celino, I., Sabou, M., Kaffee, L.-A. and Simperl, E. (eds.), *The Semantic Web – ISWC 2018*. Cham: Springer International Publishing, 325–340. https://doi.org/10.1007/978-3-030-00668-6_20.

Opgenhaffen L. (2022) Archives in action. The impact of digital technology on archaeological recording strategies and ensuing open research archives. *Digital Applications in Archaeology and Cultural Heritage* 27, e00231. https://doi.org/10.1016/j.daach.2022.e00231.

Ortlipp, M. (2008). Keeping and using reflective journals in the qualitative research process. *The Qualitative Report*, 13(4), 695–705.

Phillips, D., and Smit, M. (2021). Toward best practices for unstructured descriptions of research data. *Proceedings of the Association for Information Science and Technology*, 58(1), 303–314. https://doi.org/10.1002/pra2.458

Pimentel J. F., Murta L., Braganholo V. and Freire J. (2021) Understanding and improving the quality and reproducibility of Jupyter notebooks. *Empirical Software Engineering* 26(4), 65. https://doi.org/10.1007/s10664-021-09961-9.

Poirier, L. (2021). Reading datasets: Strategies for interpreting the politics of data signification. *Big Data & Society*, 8(2), https://doi.org/10.1177/20539517211029322.

Poirier, L. (2022). Accountable data: The politics and pragmatics of disclosure datasets. In *Proceedings of the 2022 ACM Conference on Fairness, Accountability, and Transparency*, 1446–1456. New York: Association for Computing Machinery.

PROV-Overview: An Overview of the PROV Family of Documents. (2013). Retrieved from www.w3.org/TR/2013/NOTE-prov-overview-20130430/.

Rheinberger H.-J. (2023) *A Phenomenology of Experimentation*. Chicago: University of Chicago Press.

Rupp, F., Schnabel, B., and Eckert, K. (2024). Implementing data workflows and data model extensions with RDF-star. *The Electronic Library*, 42(3), 393–412.

Rytter, M., Andersen, A., Dalsgård, L., Kusk, M. L., Nielsen, M. and Rubow, C. (eds.) (2020) Anthropology Inside Out: Fieldworkers Taking Notes. Sean Kingston Publishing.

Sandoval G. (2020) In pursuit of a reflexive recording: An epistemic analysis of excavation diaries from the Çatalhöyük research project. *Norwegian Archaeological Review* 53(2), 135–153. https://doi.org/10.1080/00293652.2020.1854338.

Sant, T. (ed.) (2017) *Documenting Performance: The Context and Processes of Digital Curation and Archiving*. London ; New York: Bloomsbury Methuen Drama.

Schwandt, S. (2022). Opening the black box of interpretation: Digital history practices as models of knowledge. *History and Theory*, 61(4), 77–85.

Shortt, H., and Warren, S. (2020). Photography: Using Instagram in participant-led field studies. In Ward, J. and Shortt, H. (eds.), *Using Arts-based Research Methods: Creative Approaches for Researching Business*, 237–270. Organisation and Humanities, Cham: Springer International Publishing.

Smale N. A., Unsworth K., Denyer G., Magatova E. and Barr D. (2020) A review of the history, advocacy and efficacy of Data Management Plans. *International Journal of Digital Curation* 15(1), 30. https://doi.org/10.2218/ijdc.v15i1.525.

Smith, L. (2020). *Emotional Heritage: Visitor Engagement at Museums and Heritage Sites*, London: Routledge.

Stead, S., and Doerr, M. (2015). *CRMinf: The Argumentation Model: An Extension of CIDOC-CRM to Support Argumentation, Version 0.7*, Purley: Paveprime.

Sullivan E. A. (2020) *Constructing the Sacred: Visibility and Ritual Landscape at the Egyptian Necropolis of Saqqara*. Stanford University Press.

Sullivan E. A. (2023) The senses & the sacred: A multisensory and digital approach to examining an Ancient Egyptian funerary landscape. In Landeschi, G. and Betts, E. (eds.), *Capturing the Senses*, 37–61. Cham: Springer International Publishing. https://doi.org/10.1007/978-3-031-23133-9_3.

Svenonius E. (1986) Unanswered questions in the design of controlled vocabularies. *Journal of the American Society for Information Science* 37(5), 331–340.

Swan M. (2015) *Blockchain: Blueprint for a New Economy*. Sebastopol, CA: O'Reilly Media.

Theodoridou, M., Tzitzikas, Y., Doerr, M., Marketakis, Y., and Melessanakis, V. (2010). Modeling and querying provenance by extending CIDOC CRM. *Distributed and Parallel Databases*, 27(2), 169–210.

Thomer A. K., Wickett K. M., Baker K. S., Fouke B. W. and Palmer C. L. (2018) Documenting provenance in noncomputational workflows: Research process models based on geobiology fieldwork in Yellowstone National Park. *Journal of the Association for Information Science and Technology* 69(10), 1234–1245. https://doi.org/10.1002/asi.24039.

Trippas, J. R., Al Lawati, S. F. D., Mackenzie, J., and Gallagher, L. (2024). What do users really ask large language models? In *Proceedings of the SIGIR'24, July 14–18, 2024*, New York: ACM. https://doi.org/10.1145/3626772.3657914.

Vancisin, T., Clarke, L., Orr, M., and Hinrichs, U. (2023). Provenance visualization: Tracing people, processes, and practices through a data-driven approach to provenance. *Digital Scholarship in the Humanities*, 38(3), 1322–1339.

Weigel T., Schwardmann U., Klump J., Bendoukha S. and Quick R. (2020) Making data and workflows findable for machines. *Data Intelligence* 2(1–2), 40–46. https://doi.org/10.1162/dint_a_00026.

Wilkinson M. D., et al. (2016) The FAIR Guiding Principles for scientific data management and stewardship. *Scientific Data* 3(1), 160018. https://doi.org/10.1038/sdata.2016.18.

Williamson K. (2018) *Observation. In Research Methods: Information, Systems, and Contexts*. Elsevier, 405–427. https://doi.org/10.1016/B978-0-08-102220-7.00017-0.

Wu M., Richard S. M., Verhey C., Castro L. J., Cecconi B. and Juty N. (2023) An analysis of crosswalks from research data schemas to schema.org. *Data Intelligence* 5(1), 100–121. https://doi.org/10.1162/dint_a_00186.

Zeng M. and Qin J. (2022) *Metadata, 3rd ed.* Chicago: ALA Neal-Schuman.

5

Methods for Identifying Paradata for Data Reuse

Ying-Hsang Liu and Isto Huvila

5.1 Introduction

Identifying appropriate methods to pinpoint potential paradata in existing datasets and data documentation is essential for data reuse. These methods work as a complement to existing formal documentation of practices and processes that, as discussed earlier in this book, are never fully complete. Data reuse refers to secondary data analysis and use in which researchers or other stakeholders use the data collected by others to address new research questions or for other novel purposes.

Data reusers often aggregate multiple existing datasets to address broader questions. They can also approach previously collected data from a new perspective in an attempt to solve problems other than those previously addressed. While many data reusers are researchers, data is also reused for education, societal decision-making and development of new products and services. Additionally, data reuse is crucial for reproducing earlier research and the validation of its results.

Data reuse, in its various forms – including secondary data analysis, meta-analysis, and validation – plays an important role in advancing scientific knowledge, particularly in data-driven research. While explicit 'reuse of data' is less common outside of this paradigm, it can be broadly understood as a reuse of earlier collected resources. This includes the use and analysis of public documents, archival records and material from cultural collections. Data reuse enables researchers to build upon the foundations laid by previous studies, optimising resources and avoiding duplication of efforts (Faniel et al., 2019; Gregory et al., 2020; Liu et al., 2023). Further, data reuse enhances methodological transparency by allowing researchers to examine and understand past research practices and processes, thus ensuring the validity and reliability of research findings across studies (Edwards et al., 2017; Huvila and Sinnamon, 2022), and enhancing the reproducibility of findings by facilitating the replication and verification of results (Deeks et al., 2023).

Previous research suggests that one of the important factors affecting data reuse behaviour is the availability of contextual information about the data, including data description, data attributes and documentation of research methods (Faniel et al. 2019; Gregory and Koesten, 2022; Murillo, 2022). This applies to all data reuse, independent of field (e.g., Faniel et al., 2019, Pickering, 1995, Rheinberger, 2023; Zimmerman, 2008). Paradata in particular is a key facet of contextual information because it documents the practices and processes relating to the creation, management and use of the data.

Paradata, despite its critical role in data reuse, is frequently not explicitly documented or structured as such. As discussed in Chapters 2 and 3, this type of information is often interwoven with various forms of primary and secondary research documentation and embedded within the research data itself. Moreover, the perspectives of data creators and reusers may differ regarding what specific information is critical for understanding practices and processes (Huvila et al. 2025). Consequently, the most important paradata from the reusers' perspective does not necessarily find its way into the formal description of a particular procedure. Therefore, even when creators, managers and previous users do their best to provide comprehensive documentation of how they worked with a particular dataset, data reusers often need to seek additional information. To mitigate the risk of misinterpreting data, data reusers also need to be adept at identifying paradata, and to be able to grasp and mobilise the resources required to access and utilise it (cf. Chapter 3). This applies not only to researchers but to everyone working with data.

A recent analysis conducted in the CAPTURE project by Juneström and Huvila recognised several retrospective methods for identifying and using paradata in support of data reuse. These methods are concerned with identifying chains of activities described in the data, analysing data with qualitative and quantitative approaches to discern practices and processes used to produce and process the data, and assessing the trustworthiness of digital records to ensure their authenticity.

The methods introduced in this chapter aim to support researchers interested in secondary data analysis guidance in identifying and extracting paradata from datasets and secondary documentation. These methods are examples of approaches that can be applied to identifying and extracting paradata where it does not exist as formal 'core paradata' but can be derived from other information, discussed later in this volume as potential paradata (see Chapter 6).

5.2 Methods Descriptions

The methods described in this chapter were chosen based on a scoping review of paradata-related practices in research activities from various disciplines. A preliminary framework of paradata generation developed at the beginning of the CAPTURE project formed a baseline for identifying methods (Huvila, 2022). It was complemented by reviewing a large number of articles sourced from the project team members throughout the first four years of the project. Additional texts were identified in the reference lists of the material uncovered during the reviewing process, with the focus being to include relevant complementary and contrasting descriptions of the methods and how they have been used in practice. Major categories of methods (qualitative and quantitative backtracking, data forensics and diplomatics) for post hoc identification of paradata were developed through an iterative reviewing process. This was used to develop an understanding of how documentation and paradata can be identified in different settings and how different approaches might be applicable for identifying different types of information relevant to understanding data creation-, management- and use-related practices and processes.

The methods selected for this chapter include approaches that are relatively broad and thus potentially applicable across disciplines. Some techniques specific to particular disciplines and study contexts are briefly described to exemplify an approach with potential wider relevance but are otherwise omitted in the present chapter to keep its focus on general principles and widely applicable approaches. Disciplinary specificity does not, however, always mean that a method had no wider relevance. Some of the approaches stemming from specific disciplinary contexts, such as natural language processing for the quantitative processing of textual material in the health domain, have clear potential for guiding paradata practices far beyond their original context.

In the following, three categories of methods are introduced and discussed: 1) qualitative and 2) quantitative methods of backtracking, as well as 3) data forensics and diplomatics.

5.2.1 Qualitative Backtracking

Qualitative backtracking refers to a category of qualitative methods of analysing data for discerning practices and processes used to produce and process the data. Broadly, qualitative backtracking qualifies as an umbrella term to describe the use of any conceivable form of qualitative data analysis to identify and create paradata. There are, however, certain methods that are specifically focused on practices and processes rather than creating new knowledge on, for example, objects and their attributes.

Close Reading and Thematic Analysis

The CAPTURE project has conducted a series of qualitative studies to understand where and what types of paradata can already be found in diverse data-related artefacts and datasets (see also Chapter 3). A major difficulty of generating paradata 'by extraction' (Börjesson et al., 2022) is that datasets and accompanying documentation are often geared towards primary analysis and knowledge-making rather than secondary analysis or aggregation. This means that a lot of paradata is scattered around research documentation and formal documentation in metadata, readme and field documentation files is sparse or sometimes non-existent.

While an ideal approach for extracting as much paradata as possible would be to conduct a comprehensive walkthrough of all data and documentation, it is not always possible (Börjesson et al., 2022). In such cases, it is reasonable to focus on artefacts with the greatest likelihood of containing relevant practice or process information. Such pieces of documentation could extend from datasets (Börjesson et al. 2022) to research reports (Huvila et al., 2021b), citations (Huvila et al., 2022), instruction manuals and handbook literature (Huvila and Sköld, 2023).

A qualitative analysis based on iterative close reading (DuBois, 2003) of an archaeological fieldwork dataset conducted by Börjesson et al. (2022) showed that a structured datafile, especially if it is not heavily cleaned of all anomalies and preliminary observations and interpretations can provide a lot of information on how it was created and processed. The approach is based on careful analysis of the data from paradata perspective, that is, keeping in mind that all can eventually be informative of practices and processes relating to data, marking such information in the dataset, iteratively developing a structured understanding of them, and finally visualising them in diagrams or narratives. The study showed that conducting the analysis requires understanding of both knowledge organisation (how databases and metadata schemas work, and how people generally use them) and subject expertise (in this particular study, of archaeological fieldwork). Both are needed to understand where and how paradata can eventually be found and extracted and to comprehend what information qualifies as paradata and what eventual limitations they are likely to be. After the analysis, the authors found that an additional step, reaching out to original data creators to verify interpretations and filling in gaps is highly desirable, if possible. At the same time, the work also clearly showed that a dataset itself can contain a lot of information to an extent which allows the reader to gain a reasonably good understanding of its earlier life.

In other studies within the CAPTURE project, the same general approach of close reading and iterative coding combined with variants of thematic analysis inspired by the constant comparative method were applied to other research artefacts. These included research reports and instruction manuals that prescribe data generation practices and processes. The analysis started with repeated iterative reading of material, the generation of categories from the material, coding the material according to these categories, writing summaries, and developing narrative descriptions of the identified themes.

The categorisation was informed by (research) questions underpinning the analysis. For example, in a study of what paradata could be extracted from archaeological field reports (Huvila et al., 2021b), the categories related to different types of information (including narrative descriptions of practices and processes, photographs, information sources) proved potentially relevant as paradata. In the study that focused on the analysis of a dataset (Börjesson et al. 2022), the categories typified different types of paradata (including knowledge organisation and presentation paradata).

The general approach is applicable also to close reading of diagrams, drawings and photographs (Huvila et al., 2023). An overall observation of this work is that while data, secondary research documentation and diverse artefacts that are used in data creation, management and use – including data management infrastructures (Börjesson, 2021) – contain a lot of traces of practices and processes (cf. Chapter 3) that makes it possible to extract a lot of paradata. It requires a lot of work and the varying quality and level of detail between different artefacts affects considerably the effort of backtracking paradata. One dataset and research report might contain a lot of extractable paradata while others can be relatively spartan and too 'cleaned' to reveal much about what happened even if analysed in detail. Another limitation of the approach is that the generated understanding of practices and processes stemming from analysis of heterogeneous data are as diverse as the data itself. Different accounts can also be difficult to compare and they do not necessarily provide systematic enough descriptions for stepwise reproduction of practices or processes.

Key References and Further Reading

- Börjesson, L., Sköld, O., Friberg, Z., Löwenborg, D., Pálsson, G., and Huvila, I. (2022). Re-purposing excavation database content as paradata: An explorative analysis of paradata identification challenges and opportunities. *KULA: Knowledge Creation, Dissemination, and Preservation Studies*,

6(3), 1–18. The article describes a study of an archaeological fieldwork dataset and discusses the opportunities and limitations of generating paradata 'by extraction' from research data.

- Rainey J., Macfarlane S., Puussaar A., Vlachokyriakos V., Burrows R., Smeddinck J. D., Briggs P. and Montague K. (2022) Exploring the role of paradata in digitally supported qualitative co-research. In CHI Conference on Human Factors in Computing Systems. New York: ACM, 1–16. https://doi.org/10.1145/3491102.3502103. This article illustrates how coding processes of qualitative data can be studied using thematic analysis.

Narrative Inquiry and Object Biography

Narrative inquiry is a type of qualitative analysis method that uses stories to describe and understand human action (Polkinghorne, 1995). Narrative inquiry is different from other forms of narrative analysis in that it focuses on identifying or constructing narratives for analytical purposes instead of analysing existing narratives, for example, diverse types of stories found in the literature or narrated orally (Sharp et al., 2018). Its focus on human action makes it apposite for qualitative backtracking of paradata. Polkinghorne (1995) notes that 'narrative is the type of discourse composition that draws together diverse events, happenings, and actions of human lives into thematically unified goal-directed processes' (p.5). For narrative inquiry, actions, events and happenings form the building blocks from which narratives are generated and that make the individual steps of activities become meaningful.

Phoenix et al. (2017) have used narrative analysis to investigate marginal comments written on paper questionnaires (i.e. marginalia) to understand the practices of interviewers and their struggle with the multiplicity of possible interpretations of the data they generate, their obligations to senior researchers, and their own emotions regarding the interview process, the participants, and their role in the research project they were involved in.

Carpentieri et al.'s (2023) narrative analysis of the open-ended questions from the first British Birth Cohort Study aimed at reusing existing data to study social mobility in post-war Britain. At the same time, their study also shows how narrative analysis and the construction of 'pen portraits' of individual study participants also produced new knowledge on the data collection processes in a cohort study (Carpentieri et al., 2023). Gaps, anomalies and trends in data creation are sometimes difficult to discern unless individual pieces of information are put together in an attempt to form a coherent whole. These two examples illustrate how identifying paradata linked to survey studies can be repurposed to address research questions not initially proposed by the original dataset, providing insights into the interaction between data creators and study participants.

Object biography is a method that has affinities with narrative inquiry in how it can improve understanding of dynamic relations between people and artefacts. The idea of writing life stories of objects in the manner of biographies of human beings was introduced by Kopytoff in 1986 (Kopytoff, 1986). The approach has become popular especially in material culture studies and archaeology in the analysis of a large variety of different types of smaller and larger artefacts (Joy, 2009). Friberg and Huvila's (2019) object biographical study of an archaeological collection showcases how the approach can be applied to assemblages, and larger and more heterogeneous artefacts than individual material objects. While Joy (2009) speaks for keeping biographical analysis focused on individual objects, the key question is rather to define what is an object, the unit of analysis, than to limit inquiry on individual physical things. The use of the metaphorical notion of biography has also faced critique. An alternative metaphor of itinerary has been suggested as a possible more neutral substitute to a biography. Biographies have been criticised for a risk of leading to think of non-human matters as if they were human-beings. Biography also comes with a strong connotation that a trajectory is historical and not only has a beginning but also an ending, which seldom is fully applicable to material objects or in the context of paradata, for practices or processes (Bauer, 2019; Fontijn, 2013).

Object biography has obvious affinities with other biographical approaches to research, including the chaîne opératoire discussed later in this chapter. Another related technique is life history research that has tended to focus on both spatially and temporally larger scale interactions relating to technology and material objects (Joy 2009). Object biography and its underpinning concept of biography, by contrast, is premised by the idea of idiosyncracy and uniqueness of every individual lifestory (Dannehl, 2017).

Narratives on the other hand, open up more explicitly for their a priori multiplicity (Schofield et al., 2020). In contrast to narrative inquiry that focuses on narrativising human action, the common denominator of biographical approaches is the relationship between people and objects (Gosden and Marshall, 1999). Their common feature is a parallel focus on change that brings practices and processes into the frame. A major limitation with narrative inquiry and object biography is that there are not always enough ingredients available to construct complete narratives.

As with close reading and thematic analysis, narrative inquiry and biographical research are time-consuming. At the same time, however, their advantage lies in how they help to weave people and artefacts together and through narratives verbalise their intermingling across time. Object biographies can be compared to identify norms and standard procedures (cf. Joy 2009), as well as to describe the variety of practices and processes in a given context. A parallel benefit emphasised both in narrative inquiries of survey data and object biographies is how the very act of trying to construct a narrative reveals absences, invisibilities and breaks in what is known about practices and processes. A limitation of narrative inquiry and biographical approaches is that even if the narratives would be well grounded in the available evidence, they are subjective. Also, while narratives are useful for conveying an understanding of a particular practice or process for a human-being, they are difficult for computers limiting their usability as paradata in computational analysis and replication of practices and processes.

Key References and Further Reading
- Bauer, A. A. (2019). Itinerant objects. *Annual Review of Anthropology,* 48(1), 335–352. A review of recent theoretical discussion relating to object biographies and itineraries.
- Dannehl, K. (2017). Object biographies: From production to consumption. In *History and Material Culture,* 2nd ed, Routledge. The book chapter compares the object biography method with the life cycle model providing useful insights to inform the choice of specific methods for life historical inquiry.
- Edwards R. (2017) *Working with Paradata, Marginalia and Fieldnotes: The Centrality of By-products of Social Research.* Edward Elgar Publishing. The edited volume contains multiple chapters that illustrate not only how to analyse paradata, marginalia and fieldnotes in social science research through case studies but also provides insights into how the underpinning research processes can be backtracked in datasets and research documentation.
- Phoenix A., Boddy J., Edwards R. and Elliott H. (2017) 'Another long and involved story': Narrative themes in the marginalia of the Poverty in the UK survey. In Edwards R., Goodwin J., O'Connor H., and Phoenix A. (eds.), *Working with Paradata, Marginalia and Fieldnotes.* Edward Elgar Publishing. The book chapter exemplifies how narrative inquiry can be used to analyse marginal notes in research documentation.

Chaîne Opératoire

As well as methods focused on proximally close analysis – literally close reading – of data, there are multiple approaches applicable to qualitative backtracking of paradata in research materials that focus on larger scales of inquiry. Chaîne opératoire (operational chain or sequence) is 'a *method* of documenting technical activities in the field' (Coupaye, 2022, p. 45, emphasis in original) developed and extensively used in archaeology and anthropology (Audouze and Karlin, 2017). Its focus on explicating social practices and technical processes, especially chains of producing, using and discarding of artefacts has obvious affinities with the ambitions of generating paradata.

Coupaye (2022) illustrates the use of chaîne opératoire as a descriptive and interpretive tool to analyse and make visible the dynamics, elements and levels of detail in technical activities. He exemplifies the use of chaîne opératoire by contrasting the operational sequences of his morning activities and yam cultivation in Papua New Guinea showcasing the versatility of the approach to represent both contemporary and past practices of different, both large (agriculture) and small (morning routines) scales. Chaînes opératoire are typically visualised using flow diagrams to depict the sequential and structural dimensions of the portrayed activities (Figure 5.1 for an example). The level of detail and steps included in individual sequences vary and as Coupaye (2022) notes,

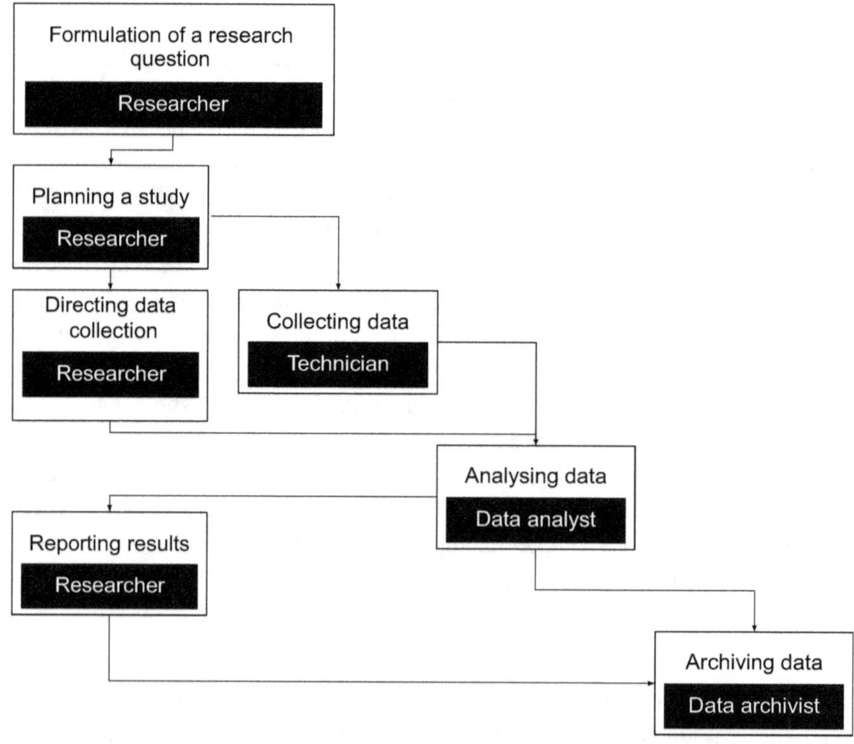

Figure 5.1 A simple chaîne opératoire representing a data collection, research and data archiving process with major operations and actors represented.

a specific chaîne opératoire is only a 'skeleton key' (p. 54) that cannot possibly incorporate everything about a specific process.

Instead of being complete representations, they are rather 'recordings of particular itineraries' as observed by particular individuals (p. 54). Rösch's (2021) analysis of an archaeological excavation process and Opgenhaffen's (2022) extensive work on analysing, modelling and documenting artefact production (Opgenhaffen, 2022) together with Coupaye's (2022) illustrative example of using chaîne opératoire in a contemporary everyday life context provide useful examples and templates for applying the concept for extracting and structuring information on past activities also in domains outside of archaeology.

The retroactive process modelling of constructing chaînes opératoire has obvious similarities with the prospective design of workflows (Chapter 4) but also fundamental differences. The gaze backwards and (re)construction of a past process on the basis of its diverse material and immaterial traces calls for particular caution in determining what steps to include in and exclude from the operational chain, and what remains invisible between them. Chaînes opératoire are not visible in the wild. They must be recognised as analytical constructs. Similarly for those working with data creation, managing and using it, hardly consider their undertakings being composed of a series of steps but rather to form a flow of practice.

From the perspective of qualitative backtracking, the method is primarily one of articulating and structuring observations of the key steps in a process, rather than modelling an operational chain as a whole. An operational chain should not be mixed with a recipe or a step-wise procedural code that allows rerunning a specific process. However, in spite of the evident incompleteness of the paradata that can find its way into a chaîne opératoire, it can still be highly useful in making elements of practices and steps of processes visible and by facilitating their critical reflection on them (Coupaye, 2022). What needs to be kept in mind is that the shape of every individual operational chain is dependent on what is observed and what questions guide the identification of its steps and of the sequence as a whole.

Key References and Further Reading
- Brysbaert A. (2012) People and their things: Integrating archaeological theory into prehistoric Aegean museum displays. In *Narrating Objects, Collecting Stories*. Routledge. This book chapter describes the use of the concept of the chaîne opératoire together with the notion of cross-craft interaction to provide insights in how people interact with material objects in the museum context.

- Coupaye L. (2022) Making 'Technology' visible: Technical activities and the Chaîne Opératoire. In Bruun M. H., Wahlberg A., Douglas-Jones R., Hasse C., Hoeyer K., Kristensen D. B., and Winthereik B. R. (eds.), *Palgrave Handbook of the Anthropology of Technology*. Basingstoke: Palgrave Macmillan, 37–60. A book chapter that provides an approachable introduction to the chaîne opératoire method.
- Rösch F. (2021) From drawing into digital: On the transformation of knowledge production in postexcavation processing. *Open Archaeology* 7(1), 1506–1528. https://doi.org/10.1515/opar-2020-0211. This article demonstrates how Chaînes Opératoire can be utilised to trace the steps of data transformation and interpretation in the context of archaeological work.

Conversation Analysis

In contrast to most of the methods discussed in this chapter so far, there are also more structured and formal approaches applicable to identifying and extracting paradata. Conversation Analysis (CA) is an approach for studying social interaction that focuses on the details of action. It originates from the work of Sacks, Schegloff and Jefferson in the 1960s on studying casual conversations in everyday-life situations (Goodwin and Heritage, 1990). As a naturalistic approach to study social interactions, CA focuses on analysing naturally occurring activities as they unfold in human interactions by recording and analysing actual situated activities (Mondada, 2012). In CA, recordings of naturally occurring activities, such as telephone calls, family dinner talks and doctor–patient communication are intensively analysed to shed light on the social rules underpinning communication.

Based on this premise, within CA several comprehensive data transcription schemes have been developed to capture the details of social interaction including nuances of speech, turn-taking and non-verbal actions. The following short conversation exemplifies some features of the popular Jefferson Transcription System (Jefferson, 2004):

A. Which one of the spectrometers did he use to take the measurements?
B. Did use what?
A. SPECTROMETERS?
B. I don't know, really. We probably have to check_
A. I'll go and see if there's something in the notebook_
B. O::k:, sounds good. We'll probably have to talk about it at the meeting tomorrow morning,
A. Alright (.) I can write it down on the agenda

To point attention to some of the features of the transcription system, CAPITAL LETTERS signify loudly spoken passages, _ unchanging pitch, comma (,) a slightly rising pitch, colons (:) prolonged sounds, and a full stop in parentheses (.) a noticeable pause.

Conversation analysts emphasise not only the content of what is said but also the manner in which it is said, including the visible verbal and non-verbal behaviours of the participants, such as the temporal and sequential relationships and aspects of speech delivery like changes in pitch, loudness and tempo (Hepburn and Bolden 2012). As such, CA research requires a deep engagement with recorded data, highlighting the importance of the researcher's participation in the manual transcription process and the close integration of transcription and analysis (Bolden, 2015). Nonetheless, the interactional details captured by CA transcription practices rely on the overhearer's perspective to piece together a plausible version of the participants' actual experiences (ten Have 2002).

As a qualitative backtracking approach, CA is a highly specific method for understanding practices and processes in naturalistic settings. When analysing the recorded data and transcripts, CA does not assume that such aspects of context as social categories (race, gender, power, class, etc.) have inherent relevance (Joyce et al., 2023). The starting point is to record the naturally occurring activities based on the specific aspects of practices or processes of interest and what in the analysed material indicates specific types of social interactions. For example, conversation analysts have examined turn-taking as a fundamental structure in everyday conversations, together with adjacency pairs as a basic element of sequence organisation. Adjacency pairs are sets of actions where if one speaker performs an initial action of a certain type, the recipient is expected to respond with a corresponding action (Drew 2004). The analysis of the organisation of sequences in conversations can facilitate our understanding of the social rules enacted in specific contexts of everyday interactions. As conversation analysts turn to the study of talks in specific institutional context, also known as institutional talk, one of the key objectives is to inquire into 'what kinds of institutional practices, actions, stances, ideologies and identities are being enacted in the talk, and to what ends?' (Heritage, 2004, p. 109).

When approached as a form of qualitative trace analysis, CA can be especially useful in identifying conversational practices related to data creation, management and use. The approach could be especially fruitful in the analysis of diverse types of recordings of practices and processes, including video and audio transcripts. Earlier CA-based studies have also examined, for example, responses in survey studies from conversational perspective. CA could be similarly utilised, for example, to analyse interviewers' conversational practices, or standardisation and deviations from standardised 'talk' with a database schema when data is input in a database system. Arminen and colleagues have investigated the practices of enacting and utilising practical know-how and institutionalised expertise in social interactions (Arminen, 2017; Arminen and Simonen 2021) showing an example that could be transposed to studying how they play out in data-related practices and processes.

Overall, CA provides a potentially powerful lens to understanding the specifics of human interactions in data creation and reuse processes and practices by meticulously analysing moment-to-moment interactions in conversations. Its apparent drawback is that it requires detailed recordings of actual conversations which are not always available. Another downside is that it is like the most qualitative methods, very time-consuming. CA comes also with specific theoretical and practical commitments that are different from many other approaches developed for analysing discourse and conversations (Ten Have, 2006). Such include its focus on individual conversations can limit its applicability to identify and account for the impact of broader societal discourses and sociocultural underpinnings of the conversations. It is also empathetically data-driven in a minute detail and its interest lies in explicating interaction and how it is organised rather than what drives the described practices or processes. However, as such it can – as the brief example above demonstrates – help to track minute details of practices and processes, and how they are talked about.

Key References and Further Reading

- Arminen I. and Simonen M. (2021) Expertise as a domain in interaction. *Discourse Studies* 23(5), 577–596. https://doi.org/10.1177/14614456211 016797. This journal article shows how CA can be used to analyse how know-how and expertise are enacted in social interactions.
- Hepburn A. and Bolden G. B. (2012) The conversation analytic approach to transcription. In *The Handbook of Conversation Analysis*. 57–76. https://doi.org/10.1002/9781118325001.ch4. This authoritative book chapter introduces the conventions of CA approach to transcribing conversations and discusses methodological issues of epistemological and practical concerns.
- McIlvenny P. and Davidsen J. (2023) Beyond video: Using practice-based VolCap analysis to understand analytical practices volumetrically. In Haddington P., Eilittä T., Kamunen A., Kohonen-Aho L., Oittinen T., Rautiainen I., and Vatanen A., *Ethnomethodological Conversation Analysis in Motion*. London: Routledge, 221–244. https://doi.org/10.4324/ 9781003424888-15. This book chapter demonstrates the use of the CA

method for enhancing transparency of analytical processes by examining how digital tools make sense for participants in a collaborative research setting.

5.2.2 Quantitative Backtracking

Quantitative backtracking refers to methods that can be used for quantitative analysis of data and diverse forms of secondary documentation and evidence for extracting paradata. Similarly to qualitative backtracking, we use the concept to describe a broad variety of approaches that apply quantitative analysis to identify, summarise and excerpt paradata, including both statistical and machine learning techniques.

Quantitative Trace Analysis

A variety of quantitative methods can be used to analyse datasets for identifying patterns in how they have come into being. The work of Börjesson et al. (2022) on close reading an archaeological fieldwork dataset provides multiple cues to how this can be done in practice with structured data. For example, using information of the point of time when specific data points have been entered in a database, it is possible to create a sequence of actions of how a dataset came into being. Depending on the routines of database creators, the sequence is likely to relate in one way or another to the procedures of creating, managing and using the data.

In cases where the data is entered directly at the moment of creation (cf. Huvila, 2012), the sequence extractable from databases corresponds well with the work process. However, in other cases when, for example data entry is done in batches after a certain amount of time has passed or a particular time of the day or week, the sequence is a less accurate and detailed representation of the data practice. In addition to identifying temporal sequences of actions, it is possible to identify patterns and follow changes in how vocabulary, descriptors or documentation of measurements evolve from the inception of a dataset to the point when it is finalised. If a dataset incorporates fields for preliminary and final interpretations like the one analysed by Börjesson et al. (2022), it is possible to trace the progress in the work of interpreting data points either as an individual or collaborative undertaking.

The surge of digital data collection both in social research and sciences has brought new opportunities to collect and backtrack trace data. Many devices used by data creators log a lot of data that can be purposefully collected as paradata as discussed in Chapter 4. However, as exemplified in Chapter 3, in cases where they have not been collected purposefully and remain as residues rather than as a part of formal documentation, they still provide opportunities for post hoc analyses and paradata generation.

Many digital cameras stamp photographs not only with information on the device and its technical characteristics and calibration but also the time when a photograph was taken and also the geographical coordinates of the place where the photo was taken. This information can be used for reconstructing the spatial and temporal sequences of data generation. Comparable information can also be extracted from other measurement devices, including 3D laser scanners and various types of laboratory equipment, and collected separately using a GPS device.

The automatic generation of potential paradata applies also to many software packages used in data collection and analysis. In social science survey research such trace data is explicitly termed paradata and occasionally collected and preserved on purpose for future use. Computer-assisted survey software programs collect a lot of secondary documentation, a part of which qualifies as formal, intentionally generated and collected paradata and is termed as such in the context of survey research (Durrant and Kreuter, 2013). Other parts may require more processing to explicate the understanding of data creation and management procedures. The latter applies especially to data embedded in the survey data itself.

In interview research, interviewers' movements in the field collected using a GPS device have been used to analyse to what degree sampling protocols have been followed and what has happened during the data collection process (Choumert-Nkolo et al., 2019). The analysis of response time from web-based surveys has been similarly used as an indication of whether respondents have difficulties understanding individual questions or to indicate the amount of effort they invest (Kunz et al., 2024). Much of the focus of the auxiliary data captured from survey and interview studies has been on enhancing the validity of collected data by addressing the issues of non-response biases in data sampling. However, diverse forms of (potential) paradata can also have many other uses in informing the understanding of data collection procedures. They can also facilitate the study of participant and researcher behaviour for greater understanding and more diverse transparency of data creation, management and use practices and processes.

Depending on the desired granularity and type of insights in practices and processes, different quantitative analysis methods can be applicable for making sense of quantitative trace data. Trend analyses, regression and straightforward correlation analyses can offer valuable insights into trace data, such as changes in vocabulary or patterns of documenting data points. Examining the terms used to describe observations or the frequency of measurements taken at different times during a field study can help identify changes in data collection practices and the types of decisions made throughout the process.

Visualisation of spatial or temporal movements and changes can also be helpful in the interpretation of trace data. To this end Ekström (2022) developed a tailored application to visualise the spatial and temporal aspects of citizen scientists' data collection practices on a map. In another study, Pentland et al. (2020) developed a method for extracting contextual information from the trace data of the audit trails of electronic medical records and used the open-source ThreadNet tool to visualise the process data. Visualisation can make especially quantitative paradata easier to understand, reveal patterns and help to obtain an overview of larger sets of traces.

Meta-analysis provides another potentially useful method for trace analysis, specifically as a framework for comparative analysis of practices or processes. It has been extensively used in the reuse of clinical trials data and involves defining the criteria for including studies, searching for and selecting studies, collecting data about a study (e.g., details of methods, participants, setting, context, interventions, outcomes and results), extracting data from reports, and then statistically combining findings from multiple distinct studies (Deeks et al., 2023). Techniques used in meta-analysis can be helpful in aggregating paradata from parallel practices and processes for comparison and broader understanding of wider constellations of how data is created, managed and used.

There are also other methods for revisiting and assessing earlier data that can be applied for quantitative backtracking. Evidence review, including integrity checks, data extraction, transformation and sense-making, has been used to identify the common outcome measures in data harmonisation (the process of integrating data from different sources for comparative purposes) tasks (Deeks et al., 2023; Liu et al., 2023). For example, similar to how Goldsmith and colleagues reviewed patient-reported and expert-identified scales of measuring pain using evidence mapping, identifying research gaps and multiple challenges in synthesising data (Goldsmith et al., 2018), the method can be utilised in comparing and synthesising parallel sets of quantitative traces of practices and processes.

Despite the increasing interest in collecting and analysing additional documentation on survey procedures, acquiring and integrating such data presents challenges (Sakshaug and Struminskaya, 2023), many of which are also relevant to other contexts and traces of data creation, management and use. Diverse behavioural cues, including temporal sequences and movements, are not always straightforward to link to a particular practice or process. Their meaning and implications to generated data can be difficult to interpret especially in secondary data analysis when the data was collected by other researchers.

In spite of the downsides of increased normalisation of paradata discussed earlier in this chapter, quantitative trace analysis would undoubtedly benefit from increased standardisation of trace data. Doing so might be feasible in such contexts as structured survey research but less so in other contexts of data generation, which lack standardised procedures and shared data structures. This applies to many branches of qualitative research but also elsewhere in domains where data practices are highly contextual and difficult to standardise due to local circumstances.

Many of the apparent problems and limitations can be mitigated by adjusting the procedures of how trace data is sourced following appropriate sampling strategies. Crucial steps to this direction is to try to ensure that the trace data is covering the relevant participants and aspects of the practice of interest. For example, if there are traces of the decisions made by only one member of a research team, the understanding of the work of the team as a whole remains limited. Some potential problems can also be managed by selecting robust analysis methods that work for the specific types of trace data with the potential to shed light on the specific data creation, management and use procedures in hand. To this end there are a plethora of statistical methods that help to mitigate problems, for example, with skewed distribution of samples and missing data points. The key point is that identifying and selecting trace data, as well as determining workable approaches, remains complex. This process requires a combination of methodological and domain expertise, which is essential for the successful quantitative analysis of trace data.

Key References and Further Reading

- Deeks J. J., Higgins J. P., Altman D. G. and Group CSM (2023) Chapter 10: Analysing data and undertaking meta-analyses. *Cochrane Handbook for Systematic Reviews of Interventions*. https://training.cochrane.org/handbook. An authoritative handbook that introduces the principles and methods of conducting meta-analysis in healthcare.
- Kocar S. and Biddle N. (2023) The power of online panel paradata to predict unit nonresponse and voluntary attrition in a longitudinal design. *Quality & Quantity* 57(2), 1055–1078. https://doi.org/10.1007/s11135-022-01385-x. This journal article demonstrates how to analyse trace data for identifying the predictors of panel participation in survey research.
- Venturini T., Bounegru L., Gray J. and Rogers R. (2018) A reality check(list) for digital methods. *New Media & Society* 20(11), 4195–4217. https://doi.org/10.1177/1461444818769236. This journal article reviews

conundrums relating to the use of online trace data for the analysis of collective action and provides a checklist of major issues to take into consideration.

Natural Language Processing

As a method of quantitative backtracking, natural language processing (NLP) techniques can be used to identify the process and practice information in human language data. NLP is a field of research that focuses on computational analysis and manipulation of human language.

Different types of NLP techniques exist. Symbolic NLP is based on processing textual or speech data using a set of rules. For example, an example of a rules-based approach to identify paradata in a research report is to generate a list of conditions where a particular phrase is interpreted as a description of a process. If the phrase 'was measured' appears in the section 'Methods' in a research report, it is considered as paradata on research data creation whereas, if the same sentence appears in the historical background it is supposed to be relating to a historical practice.

Statistical NLP is based on finding patterns in large masses of text. In the previous example, a statistical NLP approach could be used to find patterns in how methods sections in research reports are written and by searching for similar patterns in other texts, to figure out whether they contain methods descriptions, or at least passages that remind of methods descriptions.

Since the early 2000s, NLP has increasingly been based on the use of neural networks. In contrast to rules-based systems and statistical NLP that need to be trained by the researcher, neural networks can be trained automatically to learn features of human language provided large enough quantities of text are available as input. More recently, large language models (LLMs) have been applied to the task of process and procedure extraction for business process models beyond the existing rule-based approaches (e.g. Bellan et al., 2024; Neuberger et al., 2024). Nonetheless, to enhance the transparency and fairness of the developed systems, it is necessary to address language biases in the internal knowledge of LLMs (Salinas et al., 2023), as these biases can impact downstream applications, such as the task of process and procedure extraction for paradata generation.

Several commonly used NLP techniques are relevant to the extraction of process and procedure information. For example, Named Entity Recognition (NER) can be employed to detect all instances of the named entities (such as persons, organisations, locations, dates and times, and events) in the text as part of the information extraction task (Bird et al., 2009). Identifying, linking and tracing, for example, persons or organisations, in language data can provide insights into practices and processes they have been engaged in. Tracking dates, times, and events can help (re)construct temporal sequences and spatial locations.

Relation Extraction (RE) can be employed to identify and classify the relationships between entities within a text. In the sentence 'The committee approved the proposal,' Relation Extraction identifies the entities 'committee' and 'proposal' with the relationship 'approved'. In addition, Entity Resolution (ER) is able to identify semantically equivalent entities that refer to the same information object across different data sources. For instance, ER can identify that 'IBM' and 'International Business Machines Corporation' refer to the same company across different documents. To address the problem of rule-based method optimised for a specific domain, one approach involves extracting text and location of process elements (NER), resolving them into collections of unique entities (ER), and extracting entity arguments and relation types (RE) for extracting business process information (Neuberger et al., 2024). Extracting process elements and their interrelations can facilitate the automated generation of research process model.

For the application of NLP to paradata identification, a paradata extraction approach that involves close iterative reading can be assisted by NLP techniques (Börjesson et al. 2022). CAPTURE project tested this in a short pilot project with promising results (Huvila et al. 2022). To promote the semantic integration of datasets, different textual patterns for temporal expressions in archaeological datasets have been identified as part of a standardisation process, noting the importance of keeping the original context (and provenance) of the dating information (Binding and Tudhope 2023). As an application of NLP techniques to assess document similarity, Sakahira et al. (2023) analysed excavation report texts concerning buried cultural artefacts, demonstrating that the similarities of texts based on sentence embedding (transforming sentences into numerical vectors) of excavation reports can reflect the similarities among archaeological sites. However, the application of NLP techniques to large amounts of data, involving various steps of data standardisation and processing, requires a high level of technical skill.

For developing applications that perform simple NLP tasks, such as counting the number of words, creating a list of words, tracking the word position, and counting word frequencies in a text, it is possible to use an out-of-the-box toolkit. NLP Toolkit is an example of a popular programming library (www.nltk.org) that can be used directly to perform simple NLP work and to develop one's own complex NLP applications using the Python programming language (Bird et al., 2009). Many other toolkits exist for multiple programming languages and platforms for developing NLP applications.

Clinical Trial Risk Tool (https://app.clinicaltrialrisk.org) exemplifies how NLP toolkits can be used to develop user-friendly tools to extract process information from textual data. It takes as an input a clinical trial protocol in PDF format, extracts information on the key facets of the reported trial, compares it to quality norms, and produces a report with an assessment of the risk that the reported trial is uninformative.

The major drawback of NLP approaches to quantitative backtracking is that an NLP algorithm never understands its input as a human-being. The generated outputs are potential paradata rather than a definite list of all relevant information. Both false positives and false negatives results pose a risk, making the results only useful as an initial step towards more in-depth analysis.

Another obstacle to scaling up the application is the scarcity of extensive training datasets for extracting process information (Bellan et al. 2024; Neuberger et al., 2024). In spite of the shortcomings, NLP techniques can provide strong support for identifying potential paradata in text corpora that would otherwise be impractical to analyse by hand. Moreover, when combined with related techniques for analysing, for example, static and moving images (object analysis), NLP based backtracking can be extended from text and speech to trace data in other media formats and their combinations.

Key References and Further Reading

- Bach R. L., Kern C., Bonnay D. and Kalaora L. (2022) Understanding political news media consumption with digital trace data and natural language processing. *Journal of the Royal Statistical Society Series A: Statistics in Society* 185(Supplement_2), S246–S269. https://doi.org/10.1111/rssa .12846. An article that exemplifies how the NLP and statistical techniques can be used to elicit information on new media consumption practices from web browsing data.
- Bird S., Klein E. and Loper E. (2009) *Natural Language Processing with Python: Analyzing Text with the Natural Language Toolkit*. O'Reilly Media. An approachable book length hands-on introduction to NLP techniques, with detailed documentation available online at www.nltk.org.
- Neuberger J., Ackermann L. and Jablonski S. (2024) Beyond rule-based named entity recognition and relation extraction for process model generation from natural language text. In Sellami M., Vidal M.-E., van Dongen B., Gaaloul W., and Panetto H. (eds.), *Cooperative Information Systems*. Cham: Springer Nature Switzerland, 179–197. https://doi.org/10.1007/978-3-031-46846-9_10. This conference paper proposes an approach to process information extraction combining the tasks of named entity recognition, entity resolution and relation extraction.

Data Forensics and Diplomatics

In addition to discrete qualitative and quantitative data analysis methods that can be applied for backtracking practices and processes in primary and secondary material, there are also broader methodological frameworks developed for inquiring into data and its contexts, including paradata. In this section we briefly discuss the two parallel approaches of data forensics and diplomatics. They represent two distinct but prospectively complementary approaches to analysing documents and their characteristics (Duranti, 2009a). The focus of both forensic and diplomatic analysis is on assessing the authenticity, reliability and completeness of the records, and their 'ability to proof facts at issue' (Duranti, 2009a, p. 64), albeit from two different methodological outsets.

Data forensics refers to the analysis of digital data and how it is created and used (Pandey et al., 2020. It is sometimes categorised as a branch of digital forensics (sometimes computer forensics), that is, the forensic study of digital information and records. Its roots are in the study of digital information to support investigations of crimes committed with the help of computers (Pollitt, 2010). Much of the work in this area focuses on analysing digital data in legal contexts (Arshad et al., 2018), for example, collecting electronic evidence to support criminal investigations and law enforcement. It is also guided by principles derived from forensic science, including the crucial importance of not relying on a single source of evidence and corroborating and consolidating findings from multiple sources (Ries, 2018). Sub-branches of data forensics focus on forensic data analysis in specific contexts. For example, educational data forensics investigates what can be termed as potential paradata on test takers' response data to detect indications of test fraud (De Klerk et al., 2019).

Forensic techniques can be used in diverse digital contexts. Forensic analysis of media content shared via social media or web platforms has been used for verifying sources and integrity of media on social networks by analysing platform origins for shared content, and assessing the credibility of digital objects consisting of both text and audiovisual media (Pasquini et al., 2021). Content sharing on social networks leaves digital traces that enable the identification of processing platforms, reconstruction of sharing history, and extraction of upload system details (Pasquini et al., 2021), that is, information that effectively functions as paradata. Hodges (2021) demonstrates in a study of biomedical device maintenance work how forensic analysis can 'constitute a valuable approach to recovering knowledge about behaviors that have already taken place, or that have taken place in contexts where efforts at observation could encounter problems related to access, intellectual property, privacy, or safety' (Hodges, 2021, p. 1404).

Many tasks in digital forensics are based on the use of technical methods for recovering and scientific and computational, often quantitative, approaches to analysing data. The forensic analysis procedure consists of identifying and recovering digital evidence, prioritising the most promising data for closer inspection, analysis and finally evaluation and interpretation of the findings (Duranti, 2009a). Computational analysis can help especially in forensic analyses of large data resources in the context of what has been termed 'big data forensics' (Zawoad et al., 2015).

Hodges' (2021) work and forensic analyses in media studies (e.g., Kirschenbaum, 2008; 2014; Ries, 2018) and digital preservation exemplify how forensics also can benefit from the use of qualitative methods, including what can be described as the close reading of data files. Hodges applies an analysis method that draws on digital forensics and trace ethnography, a method developed for identifying and tracing actors and events that often remain invisible in digital data (Geiger, 2016; Geiger and Ribes, 2011). The approach follows the ethnographic logic of developing rich descriptions of activities, not necessarily by participating in them in the same physical location but rather through being present in the networks where activities take place, gathering and analysing documentary evidence.

The earlier use of qualitative forensic analysis exemplifies the use of the approach. Geiger and Ribes's (2011) study illustrates how the method can be used to inquire into the practices of vandals on Wikipedia by tracing their activities on the Mediawiki software platform running the encyclopaedia and external software tools. Hodges (2021) analyses traces of labour in a corpus of repair manual files in PDF format. While only a handful of analysed files contain formal metadata, the manuals contain handwritten page numbers indicating their users' need to refer and go back to specific pages in the document, evidence that that they have been from non-digital originals, wear of original documents before their digitisation, diverse marginalia (including underlining and circling of content), and added pages. All such traces evince of how the documents have been managed and used during their lifetime.

A typical problem for data forensics is that data is stored in a datafile of a format that is unknown or there are no readily available tools for opening them. Ries' (2018) study exemplifies how all, even unknown, types of binary data files (i.e. files coded not in plain text) can be read for close analysis and compared using generic hex-editors (a type of file editors capable of showing the contents of binary files). In the legal domain, data forensics is also complicated by diverse anti-forensic measures used by criminals to hinder forensic analyses.

Diplomatics is a methodology that was developed in the seventeenth century for verifying the authenticity of current and archival records (Duranti, 2014). Classic diplomatics is based heavily on the analysis of the physical characteristics of records, that is the form and format of documents written on, for example, parchment or paper. It aims to shed light into the contexts and reasons of record creation, persons and other agents involved in the process and the relation of records to other documents. Diplomatics of digital records or digital diplomatics refers to applying the approach in the digital realm utilising and benefitting from methods developed within digital forensic practice (Duranti, 2009a).

Duranti (2009a) has proposed that an amalgam of digital diplomatics and digital forensics could be termed digital record forensics. Contrary to the diplomatic analysis of human-readable aspects of physical documents, digital record forensics and computational digital forensics involve analysing trace data in machine-readable formats and documenting both the output data and the derivation method (Niu 2013).

A digital diplomatic analysis starts with description of the digital environment where the analysed data exist, their digital and logical structure and form. Applying the methodology for extracting paradata does not necessarily require that the analysed data or documents fulfil all the criteria of formal (digital) records (including identifiable context of creation, originator, action, links to other records, fixed form, stable content). However, many of these details are clearly informative of practices and processes relating to the record and, as such, are useful as paradata. Moreover, the focus of diplomatics on establishing the trustworthiness and authenticity of the evidence can provide direction to the work of identifying and extracting paradata. It allows the researcher to consider whether and to what extent the extracted paradata is authentic and trustworthy enough for the planned purposes.

The major difference between data forensics and diplomatics is in their underpinnings. Diplomatics builds on a long tradition of historical and linguistic research whereas many forensic techniques build on methods borrowed from sciences, medicine and engineering (Duranti, 2009a). Conducting digital forensic analysis requires some degree of technical skills whereas diplomatics requires in-depth understanding of the analysed materials, their context and mechanisms of creation and diplomatic criticism, a related method to historical sources criticism.

A comprehensive forensic or diplomatic analysis can be time consuming compared to many other approaches to paradata extraction. The focus of both data forensics and diplomatics is to assess the trustworthiness of digital records and ensure their authenticity rather than producing complete accounts of any particular practices or processes. Both methodologies, alone and combined, do provide, however, a practical framework to guide paradata extraction. Diplomatics offers a model and guidance to identifying how documents and records relate to their originating practices and processes whereas forensics offers a systematic framework for the technical work of identifying and recovering, prioritising and analysing, and evaluating and interpreting evidence.

Key References and Further Reading

- Duranti, L. (2009a). From digital diplomatics to digital records forensics. *Archivaria*, 68, 39–66. An approachable introduction to diplomatics, digital forensics and digital records forensics.
- Hamouda H. A. (2023) Authenticating citizen journalism videos by incorporating the view of archival diplomatics into the verification processes of open-source investigations (OSINT). In *2023 IEEE International Conference on Big Data (BigData)*. Sorrento, Italy: IEEE, 2036–2046. https://doi.org/10.1109/BigData59044.2023.10386935. This conference paper demonstrates how archival diplomatics can be applied to the analysis of citizen journalism videos and their authenticity through explicating their processual underpinnings.
- Pasquini C., Amerini I. and Boato G. (2021) Media forensics on social media platforms: A survey. *EURASIP Journal on Information Security* 2021(1), 4. https://doi.org/10.1186/s13635-021-00117-2. This journal article provides an extensive review of digital forensic methods for analysing media content shared via social networks.
- Rogers R. (2023) Tracker analysis: Detection techniques for data journalism research. In *Doing Digital Methods, 2nd ed.* SAGE, 239–258. This book chapter introduces digital forensics techniques for the media and social research projects, applicable as guidance for paradata extraction.

5.3 Discussion

Many types of methods can be useful for extracting paradata retrospectively from secondary information relating to practices and processes, although the data itself does not necessarily qualify as paradata. The approaches differ in the level of detail of the analysis, in their aims regarding what types of information and insights are produced and how practices and (or) processes are represented. They also have diverging theoretical underpinnings. Some, including formal metadata, are based on objectivist representation practices and processes whereas others, like close reading, are firmly based on interpretivist theorising.

The key practical difference between qualitative and quantitative approaches lies in their respective focus on close interpretative in-depth analysis of typically relatively small quantities of information and focus on developing explanations or predictions based on the analysis of relatively large amounts of data. Both general approaches require time and effort but the craft-like nature of qualitative analysis means that it does not scale as well as quantitative methods.

This means in practice that qualitative methods work better when the aim is to develop an in-depth understanding of particular practices or processes using a finite amount of material. Quantitative analysis is better suited for identifying broader patterns of activity based on larger quantities of data. This is not, however, the only difference between many of the methods discussed above and others applicable for extracting paradata.

The epistemological and ontological underpinnings of the approach used have implications as to what kind of information the method generates, and correspondingly, how the identified activity stands out, for example, as a practice, process, sequence of steps or flow of action. For example, using chaîne opératoire to understand practices or processes frames them as operational sequences with the ontological consequence that the described activity essentially becomes a sequence of discrete steps. Narrative inquiry leads to a very different outcome where a practice or process is both framed as and turned into a story.

Qualitative backtracking methods can be useful for discerning practices and processes used to produce and process data. One of the key steps in secondary data analysis involves data interpretation based on the contextual information about the data. There are guidelines available for writing and analysing fieldnotes in ethnographic studies (Copland, 2018; Emerson et al., 2011) that are useful for extracting information on both the practices and processes of generating the notes and those described in them.

In contrast, despite the long interest in paradata, there is still a lack of established traditions and consistent approaches in the social sciences for analysing comparative information relating to survey data (Goodwin et al., 2017). A part of the differences may be traced back to the epistemological debate around the relationship between the researcher and the data in survey research, and whether or to what degree the research process and data are separable from each other (Joyce et al., 2023). Specifically, since fieldnotes and findings are considered inseparable from observational process in ethnographic studies, ethnographic documentation and approaches to tracing practices and processes are based on the tenet that that documentation incorporates rich evidence of multiple, situational realities of fieldwork (cf. Emerson et al., 2011).

On the contrary, various branches of research, including survey studies, often treat research findings and evidence of the research process as distinct entities – a perspective frequently criticised by constructivist researchers and theorists. In such quantitative studies identifying and analysing evidence *linked to* rather than *embedded in* findings can comparably enrich the understanding of the research process (e.g. Fahmy and Bell, 2017; Phoenix et al., 2017). Such differences underline the importance of reflecting on one's own epistemological position and the significance of choosing and using different paradata creation methods in alignment with each other.

Pairing methods is also possible. Using a combination of methods can help to generate more comprehensive information on practices and processes. For instance, trace ethnography (as was discussed briefly in conjunction with data forensics and diplomatics) combines participant-observation with the analysis of extensive data found in computer logs to reconstruct user patterns and practices within online communities (Geiger and Ribes, 2011). A combination of computational analysis of digital traces in online ethnographic research and ethnographic observation can help to provide a more nuanced understanding of the investigated community (Barkhatova, 2023). Pairing methods can provide a more comprehensive and nuanced understanding of practices and processes.

Further, some of the prospective and in-situ methods of paradata generation discussed in Chapter 4 can be applied also to retrospective data on practices and processes. The presence of *core paradata* (cf. Chapter 6) is helpful not only for directly conveying an adequate understanding of practices and processes for data reuse but also as a starting point for closer examination of secondary sources. With a rudimentary core paradata in place, it becomes easier to start knitting diverse forms of secondary descriptions and traces together to form a richer account of how a dataset was created, and how it is managed and used. Moreover, it can also help to assess eventual constraints for secondary use of data as informative of practices and processes (Johns et al., 2023).

While formal metadata, data modelling and ontologies typically are used prospectively to prescribe data generation, they can also be used retroactively. The work of Thomer and colleagues on geobiology fieldwork (Thomer et al., 2018), discussed in Chapter 4 demonstrates some of these possibilities.

It is also possible to combine different prospective and retrospective methods. For example, the CIDOC CRM (formal ontology for the documentation of cultural heritage), PROV-DM (provenance standard for specific domain), and named graphs can be employed in combination to represent of objects and their related practices and processes (Shoilee et al., 2023).

All methods discussed in this chapter aim at what Lund (2024) calls a diachronic analysis of materials with a potential to function or be appropriated (cf. Chapter 7) as paradata. They aim at explicating and understanding, as for Lund, different phases of a particular process in a given situation, or if framed in terms of practices, the enactment of the unfolding of a practice. By using different methods, it is possible to extract not only different kinds of information on diverse practices and processes but in effect, extract different practices and processes out of the available primary and secondary traces.

In this sense, the choice of methods for identifying and extracting paradata goes beyond the simple question of choosing a method that is applicable to analysing a small or larger corpus of traces consisting of specific types of data. It is also, in a very fundamental sense, a question of choosing a method that is applicable for extracting, or more correctly constructing and enacting a specific kind of practice or process. A chaîne opératoire enacts an operational chain whereas narrative inquiry constructs a story similar to how following GPS coordinates enacts a journey in space rather than a rich description of a complex practice in its entirety.

Finally, the present brief review of a small sample of methods applicable for identifying and extracting paradata shows also how paradata not only adds to our understanding of data creation, management and use practices and processes to enable reuse (Goodwin et al., 2017) but can also generate new perspectives to the datasets and *how* they can be used (Carpentieri et al., 2023). When collecting data for meta-analysis in biomedical research, paradata associated with clinical trials data can be useful for ensuring the integrity of datasets (Li et al., 2023) and also reduce the publication bias effects of not including unpublished, difficult-to-find studies (Borenstein et al., 2009). Forensic analysis of digital footprints or traces from the activities on social networks can similarly help to establish the trustworthiness and authenticity of digital records in, for example, specific legal contexts (Duranti, 2009a; Pasquini et al., 2021). The multiple uses and usabilities of the different methods underline their diversity. It also demonstrates the malleability of paradata discussed throughout this volume and how it can be bent to diverse uses.

5.4 Conclusions

The effective identification of paradata during data creation processes is important for enabling and guiding data reuse. Retrospective methods of extracting paradata, including qualitative and quantitative backtracking, and data forensics and diplomatics, provide clues for discerning past activities but also for ensuring its integrity, authenticity and trustworthiness. Since contextual information about data (including data description, attributes and research methods) significantly influences data reuse across disciplines, data reusers can mitigate the risk of data misinterpretation by familiarising themselves with methods for identifying paradata related to data creation practices and processes.

The selection of methods introduced in this chapter provide researchers with guidance on effectively identifying and extracting paradata for secondary data analysis. Such analysis not only enriches our understanding of the research process but also generates new perspectives on datasets independent of research discipline and domain of practice. Qualitative backtracking methods enable the analysis of data to discern practices and processes, offering valuable insights, for example, into fieldwork dynamics, such as interviewers and participants' interaction in survey studies and data generation field sciences. Quantitative backtracking methods, including meta-analysis and natural language processing techniques, offer means to identify and extract practice and process information across large sets of data and secondary documentation. Data forensics and diplomatics are examples of methodologies that extend beyond individual methods. They both provide guidance in how to think and act regarding evidence on practices and processes and extraction of potential paradata. They also exemplify the benefits of systematicity in the work of identifying and extracting paradata-like information. Data forensics provide a tentative template on how to proceed with paradata analysis and extraction and digital diplomatics, a lens to direct attention into specific aspects of documentation as records, pertaining to practices and processes.

References

Arminen I. (2017). *Institutional Interaction: Studies of Talk at Work*. Routledge.

Arminen I. and Simonen M. (2021). Expertise as a domain in interaction. *Discourse Studies* 23(5), 577–596. https://doi.org/10.1177/14614456211016797.

Arshad H., Jantan, A. B. and Abiodun, O. I. (2018). Digital forensics: Review of issues in scientific validation of digital evidence. *Journal of Information Processing Systems*, 14(2), 346–376.

Audouze F. and Karlin, C. (2017). La chaîne opératoire a 70 ans : qu'en ont fait les préhistoriens français. *Journal of Lithic Studies*, 4(2), 5–73.

Bach R. L., Kern C., Bonnay D. and Kalaora L. (2022). Understanding political news media consumption with digital trace data and natural language processing. *Journal of the Royal Statistical Society Series A: Statistics in Society* 185(Supplement_2), S246–S269. https://doi.org/10.1111/rssa.12846.

Barkhatova L. A. (2023). The computational analysis of digital traces in ethnographic studies of online communities. *Bulletin of Sociological Methodology/Bulletin de Méthodologie Sociologique* 160(1), 30–56. https://doi.org/10.1177/0759106323 1196161.

Bauer A. A. (2019). Itinerant objects. *Annual Review of Anthropology*, 48(1), 335–352.

Bellan P., Dragoni M. and Ghidini C. (2024). Process knowledge extraction and knowledge graph construction through prompting: A quantitative analysis. In *Proceedings of the 39th ACM/SIGAPP Symposium on Applied Computing.* New York: Association for Computing Machinery, 1634–1641. https://doi.org/ 10.1145/3605098.3635957.

Binding C. and Tudhope D. (2023). Automatic normalization of temporal expressions. *Journal of Computer Applications in Archaeology* 6(1), 24–39. https://doi.org/10 .5334/jcaa.105.

Bird S.., Klein E. and Loper E. (2009). *Natural Language Processing with Python: Analyzing Text with the Natural Language Toolkit.* O'Reilly Media.

Bolden G. B. (2015). Transcribing as research: 'Manual' transcription and conversation analysis. *Research on Language and Social Interaction* 48(3), 276–280. https://doi .org/10.1080/08351813.2015.1058603.

Borenstein M., Hedges L. V., Higgins J. P. T. and Rothstein H. R. (2009). Publication bias. In *Introduction to Meta-Analysis.* Wiley. https://doi.org/10 .1002/9780470743386.

Börjesson L. (2021). Legacy in the making: A knowledge infrastructural perspective on systems for archeological information sharing. *Open Archaeology*, 7(1), 1636–1647.

Börjesson L., Sköld O., Friberg Z., Löwenborg D., Pálsson G. and Huvila I. (2022). Re-purposing excavation database content as paradata: An explorative analysis of paradata identification challenges and opportunities. *KULA: Knowledge Creation, Dissemination, and Preservation Studies*, 6(3), 1–18.

Brysbaert A. (2012). People and their things: Integrating archaeological theory into prehistoric Aegean museum displays. In *Narrating Objects, Collecting Stories.* Routledge.

Carpentieri J., Carter L. and Jeppesen C. (2023). Between life course research and social history: New approaches to qualitative data in the British birth cohort studies. *International Journal of Social Research Methodology* 1–28. https://doi .org/10.1080/13645579.2023.2218234.

Choumert-Nkolo J., Cust H. and Taylor C. (2019). Using paradata to collect better survey data: Evidence from a household survey in Tanzania. *Review of Development Economics* 23(2), 598–618. https://doi.org/10.1111/rode.12583.

Copland F. (2018). Observation and fieldnotes. In Phakiti A., De Costa P. Plonsky L. and Starfield S. (eds.), *The Palgrave Handbook of Applied Linguistics Research Methodology.* Palgrave Macmillan, 249–268.

Coupaye L. (2022). Making 'technology' visible: Technical activities and the chaîne opératoire. In Bruun M. H., Wahlberg A., Douglas-Jones R., Hasse C., Hoeyer K., Kristensen D. B. and Winthereik B. R. (eds.), *Palgrave Handbook of the Anthropology of Technology.* Basingstoke: Palgrave Macmillan, 37–60.

Dannehl K. (2017). Object biographies: From production to consumption. In *History and Material Culture,* 2nd ed, Routledge.

De Klerk S., Van Noord S., and Van Ommering C. J. (2019). The theory and practice of educational data forensics. In Veldkamp B. P. and Sluijter C. (eds.), *Theoretical and Practical Advances in Computer-based Educational Measurement*, Cham: Springer International Publishing, 381–399.

Deeks J. J., Higgins J. P., Altman D. G. and Group C. S. M. (2023). Analysing data and undertaking meta-analyses. In *Cochrane Handbook for Systematic Reviews of Interventions*. Wiley Online Library. https://training.cochrane.org/handbook/current/chapter-10

Drew P. (2004). Conversation analysis. In *Handbook of Language and Social Interaction*. Psychology Press, 71–102.

DuBois A. (2003). Close reading: An introduction. In Lentricchia F. and DuBois A. (eds.), *Close Reading: A Reader*, Durham, NC: Duke University Press, 1–40.

Duranti L. (2009a). From digital diplomatics to digital records forensics. *Archivaria*, 68, 39–66.

Duranti L. (2009b). Diplomatics. In Bates M. J. and Maack, M. N. (eds.), *Encyclopedia of Library and Information Sciences*, 3rd ed., CRC Press, 1593–1601.

Duranti L. (2014). The return of diplomatics as a forensic discipline. In Ambrosio A. Barret S. and Vogeler G. (eds.), *Digital Diplomatics: The Computer as a Tool for the Diplomatist?* Köln/Wien: Böhlau Verlag, 89–98.

Durrant G. and Kreuter F. (2013). Editorial: The use of paradata in social survey research. *Journal of the Royal Statistical Society. Series A (Statistics in Society)*, 176(1), 1–3.

Edwards R., Goodwin J., O'Connor H. and Phoenix A. (2017). *Working with Paradata, Marginalia and Fieldnotes: The Centrality of By-products of Social Research*. Edward Elgar Publishing.

Ekström, B. (2022). Trace data visualisation enquiry: A methodological coupling for studying information practices in relation to information systems. *Journal of Documentation*, 78(7), 141–159.

Emerson R. M., Fretz R. I. and Shaw L. L. (2011). *Writing Ethnographic Fieldnotes*, 2nd ed. University of Chicago press.

Fahmy E. and Bell K. (2017). Using paradata to evaluate survey quality: Behaviour coding the 2012 PSE-UK survey. In Edwards R., Goodwin J., O'Connor H., and Phoenix A. (eds.), *Working with Paradata, Marginalia and Fieldnotes*. Edward Elgar Publishing. https://doi.org/10.4337/9781784715250.00009.

Faniel I. M., Frank R. D. and Yakel E. (2019). Context from the data reuser's point of view. *Journal of Documentation*, 75(6), 1274–1297. https://doi.org/10.1108/JD-08-2018-0133.

Fontijn D. (2013). Epilogue: Cultural biographies and itineraries of things: Second thoughts. In Hahn H. P. and Weiss H. (eds.), *Mobility, Meaning and Transformations of Things*, Oxbow Books, 183–196.

Friberg Z., and Huvila I. (2019). Using object biographies to understand the curation crisis: Lessons learned from the museum life of an archaeological collection. *Museum Management and Curatorship*, 34(4), 362–382.

Geiger S. (2016). Trace ethnography: A retrospective. Ethnography Matters (Blog). Retrieved from http://ethnographymatters.net/blog/2016/03/23/trace-ethnography-a-retrospective/.

Geiger R. S. and Ribes D. (2011). Trace ethnography: Following coordination through documentary practices. In Sprague Ralph H. (ed.), *System Sciences (HICSS), 2011 44th Hawaii International Conference*, 1–10.

Goldsmith E. S,, Taylor B, C., Greer N., Murdoch M., MacDonald R., McKenzie L., Rosebush C. E. and Wilt T. J. (2018) Focused evidence review: Psychometric properties of patient-reported outcome measures for chronic musculoskeletal pain. *Journal of General Internal Medicine* 33(1), 61–70. https://doi.org/10.1007/s11606-018-4327-8.

Goodwin C. and Heritage J. (1990) Conversation Analysis. Annual Review of Anthropology, 283–307. https://doi.org/10.1146/annurev.an.19.100190.001435.

Goodwin J., O'Connor H., Phoenix A. and Edwards R. (2017). Introduction: Working with paradata, marginalia and fieldnotes. In Edwards, R., Goodwin, J., O'Connor H. and Phoenix A. (eds.), *Working with Paradata, Marginalia and Fieldnotes*. Edward Elgar Publishing, 1–19

Gosden C., and Marshall Y. (1999). The cultural biography of objects. *World Archaeology*, 31(2), 169–178.

Gregory K., Groth P., Scharnhorst A. and Wyatt S. (2020). Lost or found? Discovering data needed for research. *Harvard Data Science Review*. https://doi.org/10.1162/99608f92.e38165eb.

Gregory K. and Koesten L. (2022). Data needs. In *Human-Centered Data Discovery*. Cham: Springer International Publishing, 19–32. https://doi.org/10.1007/978-3-031-18223-5_3.

Haddington P., Eilittä T., Kamunen A., Kohonen-Aho L., Oittinen T., Rautiainen I. and Vatanen A. (eds.) (2023). *Ethnomethodological Conversation Analysis in Motion: Emerging Methods and New Technologies*. Oxford, UK: Taylor & Francis Group.

Hamouda H. A. (2023). Authenticating citizen journalism videos by incorporating the view of archival diplomatics into the verification processes of open-source investigations (OSINT). In *2023 IEEE International Conference on Big Data (BigData)*. Sorrento, Italy: IEEE, 2036–2046. https://doi.org/10.1109/BigData59044.2023.10386935.

Have P. ten (2002). Reflections on transcription. *Cahiers de Praxématique* (39), 21–43. https://doi.org/10.4000/praxematique.1833.

Have P. ten (2006). Review essay: Conversation analysis versus other approaches to discourse. Forum qualitative sozialforschung. *Forum: Qualitative Social Research*, 7(2). https://doi.org/10.17169/fqs-7.2.100

Hepburn A. and Bolden G. B. (2012). The conversation analytic approach to transcription. In *The Handbook of Conversation Analysis*, 57–76.

Heritage J. (2004). Conversation analysis and institutional talk. In *Handbook of Language and Social Interaction*. Psychology Press, 103–147.

Hodges J. A. (2021). Forensically reconstructing biomedical maintenance labor: PDF metadata under the epistemic conditions of COVID-19. *Journal of the Association for Information Science and Technology,* 72, 1400–1414. https://doi.org/10.1002/asi.24484.

Huvila I. (2012). Being formal and flexible: Semantic Wiki as an archaeological e-science infrastructure. In Zhou M., Romanowska I., Wu Z., Xu P. and Verhagen P. (eds.), *Revive the Past: Proceeding of the 39th Conference on*

Computer Applications and Quantitative Methods in Archaeology, Beijing, 12–16 April 2011, Amsterdam: Amsterdam University Press, 186–197.

Huvila I. (2022). Improving the usefulness of research data with better paradata. *Open Information Science*, 6(1), 28–48. https://doi.org/10.1515/opis-2022-0129

Huvila I., Andersson L., Sköld O. and Liu Y.-H. (2025). Data makers' and users' views on useful paradata: Priorities in documenting data creation, curation, manipulation and use in archaeology. *International Journal of Digital Curation*, 15(1), https://doi.org/10.2218/ijdc.v19i1.892

Huvila I., Börjesson L. and Sköld O. (2022). Citing methods literature: Citations to field manuals as paradata on archaeological fieldwork. *Information Research* 27(3). https://doi.org/10.47989/irpaper941

Huvila I. and Sinnamon L. (2022). Sharing research design, methods and process information in and out of academia. *Proceedings of the Association for Information Science and Technology*, 59(1), 132–144. https://doi.org/10.1002/pra2.611.

Huvila I., Sköld O. and Börjesson L. (2021b). Documenting information making in archaeological field reports. *Journal of Documentation*, 77(5), 1107–1127.

Huvila I. and Sköld O. (2023). A fieldwork manual as a regulatory device: Instructing, prescribing and describing documentation work. *Journal of Information Science*, https://doi.org/10.1177/01655515231203506.

Huvila I., Sköld O. and Andersson L. (2023). Knowing-in-practice, its traces and ingredients. In Cozza M. and Gherardi S. (eds.), *The Posthumanist Epistemology of Practice Theory: Re-imagining Method in Organization Studies and Beyond*, Cham: Palgrave MacMillan, 37–69.

Huvila I., Vats E., Friberg Z., Börjesson L., Kaiser J., and Sköld O. (2022). *Extracting process information from archival records. Digital archives, Big Data and Memory*, Springer: Copenhagen.

Jefferson G. (2004). Glossary of transcript symbols with an introduction. In Lerner G. H. (ed.), *Conversation Analysis: Studies from the First Generation*, Amsterdam: John Benjamins, 13–31. https://doi.org/10.1075/pbns.125.02jef

Johns M., Meurers T., Wirth F. N., Haber A. C., Müller A., Halilovic M., Balzer F. and Prasser F. (2023). Data provenance in biomedical research: Scoping review. *Journal of Medical Internet Research*, 25, e42289. https://doi.org/10.2196/42289.

Joy J. (2009). Reinvigorating object biography: Reproducing the drama of object lives. *World Archaeology*, 41(4), 540–556.

Joyce J. B., Douglass T., Benwell B., Rhys C. S., Parry R., Simmons R. and Kerrison A. (2023). Should we share qualitative data? Epistemological and practical insights from conversation analysis. *International Journal of Social Research Methodology*, 26(6), 645–659.

Kirschenbaum M. G. (2008). *Mechanisms: New Media and the Forensic Imagination*, Cambridge, MA: MIT Press.

Kirschenbaum M. G. (2014). Operating systems of the mind: Bibliography after word processing (the example of Updike). *Papers of the Bibliographical Society of America*, 108(4), 380–412.

Kocar S. and Biddle N. (2023). The power of online panel paradata to predict unit nonresponse and voluntary attrition in a longitudinal design. *Quality & Quantity* 57(2), 1055–1078. https://doi.org/10.1007/s11135-022-01385-x.

Kopytoff I. (1986). The cultural biography of things: Commodization as process. In Appadurai A. (ed.), *The Social Life of Things: Commodities in Cultural Perspective*, Cambridge: Cambridge University Press, 64–91.

Kunz T., Daikeler J.. and Ackermann-Piek D. (2024). Interviewer-observed paradata in mixed-mode and innovative data collection. *International Journal of Market Research* 66(1), 14–26. https://doi.org/10.1177/14707853231184742.

Li T., Higgins J., Deeks J., et al. (2023). Collecting data. In *Cochrane Handbook for Systematic Reviews of Interventions version 6.4* (updated August 2023). Cochrane. www.training.cochrane.org/handbook.

Liu Y.-H., Wu M., Power M. and Burton A. (2023). *Elicitation of Contexts for Discovering Clinical Trials and Related Health Data: An Interview Study*. Zenodo. Retrieved from https://zenodo.org/records/7839282

Lund N. W. (2024). *Introduction to Documentation Studies*, London: Facet.

McIlvenny P. and Davidsen J. (2023) Beyond video: Using practice-based VolCap analysis to understand analytical practices volumetrically. In Haddington P., Eilittä T., Kamunen A., Kohonen-Aho L., Oittinen T., Rautiainen I., and Vatanen A., (eds.), *Ethnomethodological Conversation Analysis in Motion*. London: Routledge, 221–244. https://doi.org/10.4324/9781003424888-15.

Mondada L. (2012) The conversation analytic approach to data collection. In *The Handbook of Conversation Analysis*, 32–56. https://doi.org/10.1002/9781118325001.ch3

Murillo A. P. (2022) Data matters: How earth and environmental scientists determine data relevance and reusability. *Collection and Curation,* 41(3), 77–86. https://doi.org/10.1108/CC-11-2018-0023.

Neuberger J., Ackermann L. and Jablonski S. (2024) Beyond rule-based named entity recognition and relation extraction for process model generation from natural language text. In Sellami M., Vidal M.-E., van Dongen B., Gaaloul W. and Panetto H. (eds.), *Cooperative Information Systems*. Cham: Springer Nature Switzerland, 179–197.

Niu J. (2013). Provenance: Crossing boundaries. *Archives and Manuscripts,* 41(2), 105–115. https://doi.org/10.1080/01576895.2013.811426.

Opgenhaffen L. (2022). Archives in action. The impact of digital technology on archaeological recording strategies and ensuing open research archives. *Digital Applications in Archaeology and Cultural Heritage* 27, e00231. https://doi.org/10.1016/j.daach.2022.e00231.

Pandey A. K. et al. (2020). Current challenges of digital forensics in cyber security: In Husain M. S. and Khan M. Z. (eds.), *Advances in Digital Crime, Forensics, and Cyber Terrorism*, IGI Global, 31–46.

Pasquini C. (2021). Amerini I and Boato G (2021) Media forensics on social media platforms: a survey. *EURASIP Journal on Information Security* (1), 4. https://doi.org/10.1186/s13635-021-00117-2.

Pentland B., Recker J., Wolf J. and Wyner G. (2020). Bringing context inside process research with digital trace data. *Journal of the Association for Information Systems*, 21(5).

Phoenix A, Boddy J, Edwards R and Elliott H (2017). 'Another long and involved story': Narrative themes in the marginalia of the Poverty in the UK survey. In Edwards R, Goodwin J, O'Connor H, and Phoenix A (eds.), *Working with*

Paradata, Marginalia and Fieldnotes. Edward Elgar Publishing. https://doi.org/10.4337/9781784715250.00010.

Pickering A. (1995). *The Mangle of Practice: Time, Agency, and Science*, Chicago: University of Chicago Press.

Polkinghorne D. E. (1995). Narrative configuration in qualitative analysis. *International Journal of Qualitative Studies in Education*, 8(1), 5–23.

Pollitt M. (2010). A History of Digital Forensics. In Chow K.-P. and Shenoi S. (eds.), *Advances in Digital Forensics VI*, Berlin, Heidelberg: Springer, 3–15.

Rheinberger H.-J. (2023). *Split and Splice: A Phenomenology of Experimentation*, Chicago, IL: University of Chicago Press.

Ries T. (2018). The rationale of the born-digital dossier génétique: Digital forensics and the writing process: With examples from the Thomas Kling Archive. *Digital Scholarship in the Humanities*, 33(2), 391–424.

Rogers R. (2023). Tracker analysis: Detection techniques for data journalism research. In *Doing Digital Methods,* 2nd ed. SAGE, 239–258.

Rösch F. (2021). From drawing into digital: On the transformation of knowledge production in postexcavation processing. *Open Archaeology,* 7(1), 1506–1528. https://doi.org/10.1515/opar-2020-0211.

Sakahira F., Yamaguchi Y. and Terano T. (2023). Understanding cultural similarities of archaeological sites from excavation reports using natural language processing technique. *Journal of Advanced Computational Intelligence and Intelligent Informatics,* 27(3), 394–403. https://doi.org/10.20965/jaciii.2023.p0394.

Sakshaug J. W. and Struminskaya B. (2023). Augmenting surveys with paradata, administrative data, and contextual data. *Public Opinion Quarterly*, 87(S1), 475–479. https://doi.org/10.1093/poq/nfad026.

Salinas A., Penafiel L., McCormack R. and Morstatter F. (2023). 'I'm not racist but. . .': Discovering bias in the internal knowledge of Large Language Models. *arXiv.* http://arxiv.org/abs/2310.08780 (accessed 18 June 2024)

Schofield J., Wyles K. J., Doherty S., Donnelly A., Jones J., and Porter A. (2020). Object narratives as a methodology for mitigating marine plastic pollution: Multidisciplinary investigations in Galápagos. *Antiquity*, 94(373), 228–244.

Sharp N. L., Bye R. A. and Cusick A. (2018). Narrative analysis. In Liamputtong P. (ed.), *Handbook of Research Methods in Health Social Sciences*, Singapore: Springer, 1–21.

Shoilee S. B. A., de Boer V. and van Ossenbruggen J. (2023). Polyvocal knowledge modelling for ethnographic heritage object provenance. In *Knowledge Graphs: Semantics, Machine Learning, and Languages*. IOS Press, 127–143.

Thomer A. K., Wickett K. M., Baker K. S., Fouke B. W. and Palmer C. L. (2018) Documenting provenance in noncomputational workflows: Research process models based on geobiology fieldwork in Yellowstone National Park. *Journal of the Association for Information Science and Technology*, 69(10), 1234–1245. https://doi.org/10.1002/asi.24039.

Venturini T, Bounegru L, Gray J and Rogers R (2018) A reality check(list) for digital methods. *New Media & Society,* 20(11), 4195–4217.

Zawoad S., and Hasan R. (2015). Digital forensics in the age of big data: Challenges, approaches, and opportunities. In 2015 IEEE 17th International Conference on High Performance Computing and Communications, 2015 IEEE 7th International

Symposium on Cyberspace Safety and Security, and 2015 IEEE 12th International Conference on Embedded Software and Systems, 1320–1325.

Zimmerman A. S. (2008) New knowledge from old data: The role of standards in the sharing and reuse of ecological data. *Science, Technology, & Human Values,* 33(5), 631–652. https://doi.org/10.1177/0162243907306704.

6

Methods for Managing Paradata

Zanna Friberg and Isto Huvila

6.1 Introduction

This chapter changes the perspective on paradata offered so far in this volume. It builds on the insights into the creation, use and reuse of paradata from the studies addressed in previous chapters and places the focus on management of paradata in repositories. The chapter draws on the studies conducted in the CAPTURE project, on paradata in the context of creation and use within the research process, to inform practices in a repository setting. As such, this chapter can be read as an exploratory outline of methods for paradata management on that basis, or as possible directions for further exploration of paradata curation.

So far, this volume has covered paradata in the research process both as it is created and used, but between creation and use may very well be a repository housing the dataset in question. This chapter turns the attention to this crucial context. Efforts of researchers to be more aware of paradata as a means of making research data more reusable will be greatly diminished if it is not compatible with the processes in repositories.

Data managers need understanding of paradata in theory and practice, how it can be approached and thought about in management settings, and what is its place as a part of the broader data landscape. If repositories are not equipped to manage paradata when these are recorded or have not established practices to preserve potential sources of paradata, there may be considerable paradata loss when data is deposited. Furthermore, for a holistic approach to paradata in research it would be beneficial if repositories were able to provide data creators with instructions on how best to record paradata in preparation for repository management.

Similarly, repositories can play an important role in directing data users to potential sources of paradata in datasets. In this chapter, we primarily report on an exploration of the types of paradata researchers need (Börjesson et al., 2022) and where paradata might be found (see Chapter 3 in this volume) and frame the insights from those studies in terms that can help increase paradata literacy for curators and researchers. The chapter also utilises some of the lessons learned from other studies in CAPTURE (e.g. Börjesson et al., 2021; Börjesson et al., 2022; Huvila, 2020; Huvila et al., 2025). In doing this, this chapter seeks to provide insights about paradata that can inform management of paradata in repositories.

A few key terms need further explanation. Paradata management in this context is understood as the identification, preservation and dissemination (i.e. management) of information about research processes and practices (i.e. paradata). As discussed earlier in Chapters 2 and 3 of this volume, paradata can exist in many forms and in many places and what is paradata for one person may not be paradata for another. While paradata management goes on throughout the research process, in this chapter the scope is on management in repositories. The term repository is used broadly in this chapter, encompassing data repositories but also other management collections, including museum and archival repositories.

An important caveat needs to be asserted here. It is worth bearing in mind that the broad scope and general character of this chapter comes at a cost. While the aim certainly is to provide actionable advice on methods for the management of paradata, we focus on general strategies rather than on detailed instructions. These general strategies may be more or less applicable depending on research domain, repository and national context. Furthermore, the methods outlined here are purposely not entirely newly developed or experimental approaches, since the chapter aims to build on and support existing infrastructures and practices. What this chapter does is to position paradata (as is understood in this volume) on the map of repository management for those interested in paradata and data curation. It also proposes a framework that can function as a point of reference for dialogue between researchers and data curators on the documentation of research processes and practices.

Proposed best practices for research data management have frequently addressed issues that are relevant in the paradata context even if their focus has not been specifically on managing practice and process information. There are also many texts that provide relevant guidance for both researchers and data managers working in general data repositories (e.g., Austin et al., 2016) and in specific fields, for example, in archaeology (Kansa and Kansa,

2021) and plant science (Leonelli et al., 2017), and with particular types of resources (Thomer et al., 2022; VandenBosch et al., 2023). Surveys of specific (e.g., quality assurance in Kindling and Strecker, 2022) and general data management policies and practices do also provide insights into applicable management methods (e.g., Cofield et al., 2024; Geser et al., 2022; Schöpfel and Rebouillat, 2022). A more in-depth exploration of the definition of paradata can be found in Chapter 2 of this volume and the insights about where paradata is found is expanded on in Chapter 3. Paradata management in creation and use scenarios outside of repositories are to an extent covered in Chapters 4 and 5.

Finally, a note on the structure of the chapter. This chapter comes in three parts. It begins by introducing a way to categorise paradata from a management perspective that is useful for developing appropriate management strategies. The two broad categories being *core paradata* and *potential paradata*. After providing that lens to conceptualise paradata in a management context, the following section of the chapter expands on selected examples of paradata needs that may require management and sources of paradata to be mindful of in managing for paradata preservation. The last part of the chapter brings the two previous parts together to discuss two broad strategies for paradata management, standardisation and embracing messiness, before rounding off the chapter with a discussion of paradata literacy as a framework within which to conceptualise and situate paradata management and use.

6.2 Core Paradata and Potential Paradata

The management of paradata, like its creation and use, is situational, and different paradata types and potential needs require different management approaches. The strategies proposed for paradata management in this chapter focus on identifying ways in which existing structures and methods for research documentation can be adjusted or informed to account for paradata, in its many forms. In this chapter, the methods explored can be boiled down to two complementary approaches to managing paradata, based on categorisations of paradata that need management into two types: core paradata and potential paradata.

Core paradata is documentation of processes where there is a general consensus of the documented information being paradata. Core paradata can be structured or narrative descriptions of 'how it was done' or versioning data generated by digital systems. Two fields where the concept of paradata has become more established is survey research and 3D visualisation in cultural heritage. In these fields core paradata is therfore easier to exemplify. In survey research, records of a survey or interview process, timing, locations, secondary observations and data processing is commonly documented as paradata (Schenk and Reuß, 2024). An example from 3D visualisation would be formal encoding of the decisions preceding the generation of digital 3D objects (e.g., Havemann, 2012; Rabinowitz, 2019).

Potential paradata refers to information that was not purposely created as paradata but may emerge or is extracted in a specific context for a specific use. It encompasses the vastness of auxiliary documentation that could be paradata depending on the user, the use and the context of that use. Work logs, emails and personal notes will be further discussed as such auxiliary documentation on the basis of the discussion in Chapter 3 of paradata in research documentation, drawing on interviews conducted in the CAPTURE project (Börjesson and Sköld, 2021). Other previously identified sources of potential paradata are different types of marginalia, marginal notes and remarks providing additional context to the main document or artefact. Marginalia have been identified as potentially rich sources of paradata about research processes (see e.g. Edwards et al., 2017). A source from which a researcher can forensically extract paradata (that is, they can analyse and interpret its content to find useful process information), that was not purposely documented as such. What paradata they seek and extract would differ depending on what their particular research required and thus be very hard to define beforehand by either the data creator or curator.

Separating paradata into these categories is not clear cut, since there can conceivably be secondary process information within core paradata that would potentially be useful as paradata for some other research endeavour down the line. However, the categorisation helps us see how metadata curation could be adjusted to include paradata and also, more importantly, that paradata curation would in many cases need to be differentiated from metadata curation. If we agree that paradata is useful and needed for data reuse and also that much paradata is situational, we need to think of ways to manage the potential for paradata accordingly.

For core paradata, existing structures (i.e. traditional research documentation such as reports and metadata schemas) are generally useful starting points, and only minor changes of perspective or granularity may be needed to better manage for paradata. When dealing with potential paradata, however, where the potential is at heart context-dependent, standardisation is not only very difficult but also possibly counterproductive. When managing the potential for paradata extraction in research documentation we are instead exploring other strategies to prevent paradata loss, strategies to guide wayfinding and paradata literacy. All these strategies for core paradata as well as potential paradata, are listed below:

Suggested strategies for paradata management

- Expanding on the standardising work that is already being done
- Adjusting for a level of documentation granularity that is more conducive to paradata
- Preventing loss of paradata potential in datasets due to excessive data cleaning
- Facilitating paradata discovery and wayfinding
- Improving mutual paradata literacy among data creators and data curators

These strategies are expanded on at the end of the chapter as broadly being methods based in standardisation work or methods based in 'embracing messiness' as a way to preserve potential paradata. The literacy strategy is thought of as a holistic and overarching perspective. A further discussion of paradata literacy as an overarching strategy makes up the final part of this chapter. That deeper discussion will build on some specific insights gained from the CAPTURE project's work on paradata, which is the subject of the following part of this chapter.

6.3 Paradata Needs and Sources

There are several ways to paint an overview of the insights on paradata provided through the findings of the CAPTURE project that would facilitate a discussion of paradata management. The focus here will be on some of the needs for paradata among researchers and examples of where and how they seek to meet this need. This section outlines examples of the paradata needed by researchers and maps them to repository management. It also includes examples of how researchers try to satisfy these needs for information on processes and practices. Together, these insights provide a framing for the proposed management strategies explored in this chapter.

The discussion in Chapter 3 of where paradata may be found in research documentation shows the range of sources data reusers actually consult to meet the need for comprehensive information about data and ultimately to better understand what was done and how. To assemble as clear a picture of the research process as possible, the initial source researchers consult is often method descriptions available across research documentation. That includes method descriptions in both published and unpublished scholarly outputs such as journal articles, monographs, reports, manuals and guides. Though such descriptions can range from highly standardised to more free-form, there is a degree to which they are genre-bound and narratively accessible descriptions of such things as research questions, framing, methods, material, analyses and results.

However, it is well established that datasets and the narratives of how they were created and processed are cleaned and structured to make the often complicated and perhaps messy research process neater (see e.g. Börjesson et al., 2022; Huvila et al., 2021; Kim et al., 2019; Leighton, 2015). These practices and how they are documented do not always correspond with each other (Button and Harper, 1996). In attempting to reuse someone else's data, such formal, tidy descriptions are rarely enough to get a sense of the reliability or suitability of the data (for a further discussion of important considerations in reuse scenarios see Börjesson, Sköld, et al., 2022). At the same time, there can be an expectation of the tidiness of descriptions as an often false measure of the quality of the described practices and processes (Wylie, 2019).

Börjesson et al. (2022) explored four paradata needs that exemplify how data reusers go beyond report documentation to try and gain better understanding of the dataset at hand. In the study, the authors build on and confirm the well-studied general information needs of researchers, while exploring paradata needs as a subset of such information needs. The types of information generally shown to be needed by researchers are, as noted, contextual and varied, but include for example, information for different phases of a research project from idea generation to analysis and dissemination (Toms and O'Brien, 2008).

The needs vary between disciplines and especially different research approaches (Huvila et al., 2021). Concerning needs, paradata is not a mere attachment to research data but rather a parallel output of study results and an integral part of the process of how research conveys knowledge and understanding, as discussed further in Chapter 7.

In their study, Börjesson et al. (2022) suggested four types of interconnected process-related information needs and these will serve as illustrations of needs to take into account in paradata management. The list is perhaps neither exhaustive nor equally applicable in all fields but is useful as a starting point to structure the exploration of methods for managing paradata in this chapter.

Four categories of paradata needs

• **Methods paradata**: process information related to how the data was generated

- **Scope paradata**: process information related to what the data cover
- **Provenance paradata**: process information related to where the data come from
- **Knowledge organisation and knowledge representation paradata**: process information related to how the data are structured and communicated.

Methods paradata is information about research methods, techniques and decision-making related to processes and practices of generating data. This kind of information is to an extent included in more traditional scholarly documentation and metadata schemas, but paradata needs are a need for more detailed process information than can usually be extracted from those. There is often a need for information about the methods used to generate the data on a different level of granularity or detail than traditionally offered. Particularly elusive among the methods paradata is decision-making related paradata, which is more likely to be informally documented and/or cleaned away when reporting on the research. An example of important decision-making paradata could be information about how data outliers or sample contamination were to be treated in the particular data set.

Another example of this type of paradata relevant in archaeology as well as several other field sciences is process information about coordinates. Method descriptions that include coordinates can fail to specify if coordinates were generated through a GPS device, measured using a total station or theodolite, or measured from a map. In a reuse scenario where a researcher wants to either find a specific site or perhaps aggregate field data, this piece of process information about data creation (i.e. methods paradata) may be crucial. The implication of coordinates being generated based on a map could, for example, be a higher likelihood of human error, or potential need to identify and look more closely into what specific map was used (see e.g. Ullah, 2015). In contrast, GPS measurements are susceptible to poor satellite coverage leading to lower accuracy and differences between specific types of GPS devices.

Coordinates are also good examples of how paradata needs are interconnected. Provenance paradata about when or by which actor particular parts of a data set were generated could help establish whether the coordinates at hand were likely to have been created using a GPS device or not, based on when they started to be widely used in a particular setting. Information about, for example, the existence of additional data related to the same coordinates, whether located in the same repository or elsewhere, could constitute scope paradata – a third type of paradata identified by Börjesson et al. (2022).

Scope paradata expands on the type of scope-related metadata that provides information about the extent and field of reference of the data. This could typically include such information as the time period (temporal scope) and geographical area (spatial scope) covered by the data but also information on social groups or communities covered. An example of scope paradata would be information about where other data related to the previously discussed coordinates exists, regardless of whether it would be stored in the same or another repository, or remain in the hands of private individuals or research teams. Scope paradata could also inform of such process-related information as changes in policies or practices in the course of the research, such changes that may have led to differences in scope of the units of data within the dataset. In archaeology for example, policy changes on reporting practices, like whether it is mandatory or voluntary to report certain types of archaeological finds, will be important to know to be able to understand the scope of a data set. This is equally true on a smaller scale, where changes of the sampling strategies at a field site may result in different scope across a data set (see e.g., Faniel et al., 2021). Both are examples of paradata that is crucial for judging the reliability and usability of the data in a reuse scenario. Information about the sampling processes may also qualify as potential scope paradata and potential decision-making related methods paradata. This again illustrates both the interrelatedness and the contextual nature of different paradata types. Moreover, the same information could also constitute the next type of paradata need, provenance paradata.

Provenance paradata goes beyond structured metadata about the whys, whens and whos of the data. The reuse needs discussed in Börjesson et al. (2022) as needs for provenance paradata concern primarily information about the disciplinary and timebound provenance of data, the epistemological under-pinnings of data generation, and the rationale behind the data creation (cf. the discussion of paradata and provenance in Chapter 2). Just as knowing about the effects of a new reporting policy or specific sampling policies is important for the understanding and evaluation of a dataset, the temporal and disciplinary context may significantly condition data. Methods for selecting, classifying and collecting data change over time, just as typologies, theories and tools develop (see e.g. Montoya and Morrison, 2019). Data generation and docu-mentation also differ between disciplines (e.g. between archaeology and biol-ogy), between different research environments (e.g. two different departments within the same discipline) and with different aims (e.g. aiming to create a reference database or a database of primary data). The disciplinary and time-bound provenance of data could also be very informative in a secondary capacity when trying to meet the fourth paradata need identified by Börjesson, Huvila and Sköld, the need for paradata on knowledge organisation and knowledge representation.

Paradata on knowledge representation concerns how data are structured and communicated, something that can be highly specific to specific disciplines or times. This paradata need entails an expressed requirement to know how gaps, subsets, relationships and data points are represented in the dataset. It also encompasses the need to know not merely which standards, if any, have been used to structure the data but also how strictly a standard has been applied. For example, the format of coordinate information discussed previously forms an example of the type of knowledge representation paradata that can make a significant difference when trying to reuse or aggregate field data collected by someone else. The accuracy of coordinates and which one of the dozens of possible coordinate systems used to represent the information is critical for being able to use coordinate data (Hansen and Fernie, 2010; Verhagen, 2023). Furthermore, knowledge representation paradata can be information about the meaning of non-standardised elements including descriptors and keywords, and other information central to understanding the structure of the data set. Empty cells are a typical recurring element in a data table with multiple possible meanings. Börjesson and colleagues point out the importance of knowing whether the absence signifies, for example, that 'no data was gathered', 'no data was available', 'data was gathered but did not meet the database creator's quality criteria' or any other of the possible alternatives (Börjesson et al. 2022).

Regardless of whether information on methods, scope, provenance and knowledge representation exists or not, an additional layer of difficulty is that finding paradata on decisions made in relation to data creation can require a great deal of work from researchers. This particular issue led to the formulation of the London Charter document instituting the notion of paradata in the field of 3D heritage visualisation after the turn of the millennium (Denard, 2012).

The discussion in Chapter 3 of paradata types shows that researchers engage in quite impressive detective work to leverage sources of process information to find this kind of decision-making paradata. In gathering paradata to help in their investigation, a conventional strategy used by researchers is to consult other, auxiliary, documentation originating from the research process. Such auxiliary documentation can take the form of, work logs where tasks and procedures are tracked, emails where research activities are discussed within the team of researchers, or personal notes made by individual researchers. These three examples represent a range of auxiliary documentation that can be interpersonal and written with an audience in mind or written with no expectation of them ever being seen by anyone else.

Whether or not the documentation is intended for others to read will also impact its accessibility as a source of paradata, with the prevalence of abbreviations and shorthand increasing the more personal the documentation is. Wylie (2019) notes, the tidied descriptions written for external audiences have a tendency to be very different from the personal working notes that can be a much more crucial source of information in making datasets reusable. Correspondingly, as observed in Chapter 3, while work logs may require more domain-specific knowledge to interpret than a scholarly publication, a personal note may be mostly unintelligible for someone other than the person who wrote it.

In response to these needs, and the types of paradata sources they are associated with, different methods could be applied in order to manage for paradata. The paradata needs may be met through already existing core para-data or through potential paradata that is suitable for being turned into core paradata through structuring and revising it according to relevant data documentation standards. Some needs, in turn, may be hard to meet for a repository, too difficult or time-consuming to demand of data producers and documenters, or are from the outset best met through keeping the potential paradata as such, that is, by managing the potential rather than the (para)data. In the following section, we turn back to the strategies outlined in the chapter introduction and discuss them in more depth with these insights, on what paradata researchers seek, in mind.

6.4 Paradata Management

At the beginning of this chapter, we pointed to a set of possible strategies for managing paradata that we can now start to map to the insights from the studies of paradata needs and practices in order to create a framework for informing paradata management. The framework (Figure 6.1) builds on cat-egorising practice and process information generated during research as core paradata or potential paradata combined with insights drawn from identified categories of paradata needs and findings on where paradata is likely to be found.

We proceed on the basis of this framework, to outline two broad categories of methods for managing paradata through standardisation work and adopting strategies for coping with and navigating the messiness of practice and process information. The strategies presented at the outset are best imagined on a sliding scale between these two broader extremes of core paradata and entirely contextually dependent potential paradata. The strategies have been placed along this scale according to their alignment with managing either core para-data or potential paradata, as delineated in the Figure 6.1.

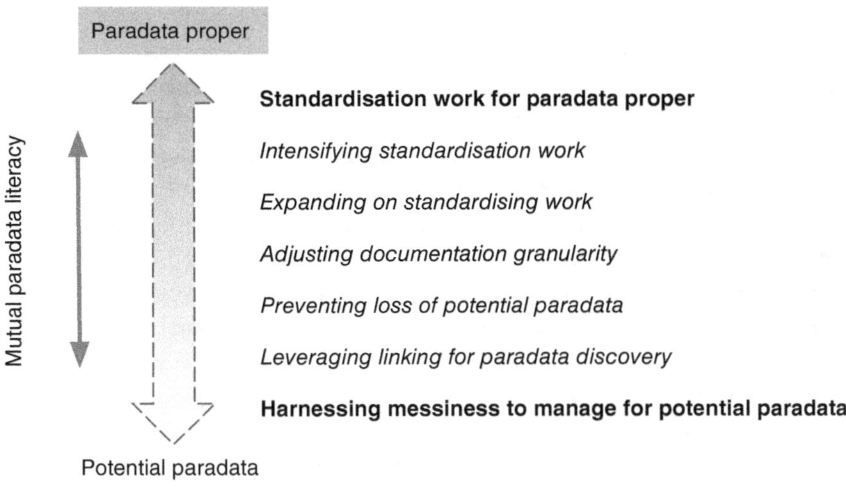

Figure 6.1 A framework for paradata management.

As suggested at the upper end of the spectrum (Figure 6.1), in most cases when a dataset ends up at a repository, there is a subset of information about processes that is already being documented as core paradata in conventional data documentation whenever even a very rudimentary description of a dataset is available. This includes available metadata elements and report documentation, whether the information is termed paradata or not. For this core of core paradata, the very elementary strategies for managing meta-information, that is, adjusting documentation guidelines and standards to include information about research processes and practices could to a larger extent help make the core paradata more visible and easily usable.

Standardisation work for core paradata (Figure 6.1), is a fundamental exercise towards this end. This would be an exercise to map the existing formal descriptors to the four previously described categories of paradata needs and to identify what information relating to the methods, scope, provenance and knowledge representation already is present, how it can be made searchable, and in specific contexts of research, complemented with critical missing elements.

On the far end of the spectrum, *intensifying standardisation work* (Figure 6.1) is the main suggested strategy. Methods paradata is represented to a varying degree in current data documentation standards and, even if the development of methods ontologies and taxonomies (e.g., Borek et al., 2016; Galliers, 1991; Sicilia, 2010; Xian and Fu, 2022) has started in certain fields, there is much variation in how methods are described and what terms and concepts are used. For some methods and data types, for example, measuring spatial coordinates, standards exist but they are not necessarily applied every-where. For scope paradata, spatial and temporal scope are covered in standards to a greater extent than, for instance, epistemic and practical issues, and for provenance, many standards put a lot of emphasis on curatorial provenance whereas other processes might be represented in a more cursory manner.

Beyond the core paradata, towards the middle of the spectrum, there is potential paradata that is likely to correspond to common enough paradata needs that it could be reasonable to consider standardising how it is docu-mented to make it core paradata. This kind of potential paradata might include various kinds of report documentation, metadata or reasonably genre-bound auxiliary documentation that has the potential to meet common and identifiable paradata needs. For this potential paradata, *expanding on standardisation work* and *adjusting documentation granularity* (Figure 6.1) are suggested.

Passing the middle of the spectrum going towards the opposite end (towards the bottom of the Figure 6.1), the potential of the paradata is imagined as more and more situational and thus less conducive to any standardisation. At this end of the spectrum of working with core paradata, there is immediate poten-tial to selectively expand standardisation to cover practice and process types according to appropriate taxonomies and ontologies, and standardise vocabu-lary use for knowledge representation paradata.

Harnessing messiness to manage potential paradata (Figure 6.1) is our suggested method for information that is less likely to be potential paradata in several use cases. This end of the spectrum recognises that in certain isolated cases, it is possible that even very unlikely information can convey crucial knowledge of practices and processes for knowledgeable data users. For this type of paradata, that is too context-dependent to be standardised with any foreseeable success, we are inclined to recommend focusing on the work of preserving messiness and providing wayfinding information. This is repre-sented by the strategies *preventing loss of potential paradata* and *facilitating paradata discovery* in Figure 6.1. Such paradata encompasses most qualitative and narrative descriptions of practice and processes and their elements relating to scope, provenance and how particular methods were applied and how their use deviated from standard practice. It is similarly pertinent when retaining the information inherent in the outputs of non-standard data practices and processes. Analyses of archaeological data (Börjesson et al., 2022) and research outputs (Huvila et al., 2023) provide illustrative examples of how the messiness of working documentation contains a lot of invaluable infor-mation on how it was conceived.

Paradata literacy (positioned to the left in Figure 6.1) is an overarching and necessary method for paradata management, valid along the whole scale.

There is evidently a pressing need for greater mutual paradata literacy between researchers creating and using data and curators caring for and disseminating data regarding all process information, regardless of it being deemed core paradata or potential paradata here. In the framework illustrated in Figure 6.1 the strategy presented at the outset as 'improving mutual paradata literacy among data creators and data curators' has thus been made such an overarching strategy. As a strategy, paradata literacy is crucial to making paradata work in stitching together measures covered by the other strategies. A working level of paradata literacy is necessary to identify what eventually is informative about diverse aspects of practices and processes and understand the vocabulary used to describe practices, processes and methods. In parallel, paradata literacy plays a key role in understanding how different forms of paradata link to each other, for example, how temporal and spatial scope can be informative about provenance and vice versa.

In the following final part of the chapter, we expand upon these in three sections devoted to discussions on standardisation work, ways to embrace messiness and paradata literacy respectively.

6.4.1 Standardisation

Standardisation is the accepted approach in the literature for facilitating data management and use. Better and more rigorous standardisation of data improves the efficiency (Ibanez et al., 2014; Santos et al., 2016), reliability and quality of research (Herres-Pawlis et al., 2022; Pétavy et al., 2019) and in general of data-based knowledge production (Gal and Rubinfeld, 2019), it helps to make data more manageable (Palaiologk et al., 2012; Pétavy et al., 2019), reusable (Faniel and Jacobsen, 2010; Herres-Pawlis et al., 2022), portable and interoperable (Blobel et al., 2022; Gal and Rubinfeld, 2019; de Mello et al., 2022; Ribes and Lee, 2010), and more easily integrated with other datasets (Ibanez et al., 2014). Standardisation improves the reproducibility of research (Ibanez et al., 2014), facilitates data discovery (Contaxis et al., 2022) and meta-analysis, that is, synthesising results from multiple studies (Laird et al., 2011). Data is also easier and more cost-efficient to preserve if it is well-standardised (Palaiologk et al., 2012). Finally, an often recited benefit is that standardised data is helpful in interdisciplinary collaborations where the different stakeholders lack common knowledge of each others' data practices (Ribes and Lee, 2010).

However, while standardisation has many evident benefits, it also has several drawbacks. Archaeological information management literature has for a long time debated the relative benefits of standardisation and allowing researchers to document their data as they find it relevant in their specific contexts of work (Huvila, 2012a). A major drawback of standardisation is that standards are always approximations and never entirely in line with local practices or understanding of the processes or knowledge that is being standardised (Ellingsen, 2004). Standards are not always easily scalable for larger or smaller use cases than was originally envisioned (Hanke et al., 2021). Also important to note here, as we indirectly discuss data reuse, is that even if retroactive standardisation and data wrangling is possible, standardisation works best when done upfront. Retroactive standardisation tends to be problematic not only because there are seldom resources for comprehensive retroactive working through large datasets but also because of the imminent risks of unintentional data loss, misinterpretations and misrepresentation of original data (Mandell, 2022).

Flexibility is often a practical necessity in highly context specific situations where standards are seldom comprehensive and nuanced enough to accommodate local variation, divergent epistemic perspectives and observations that are difficult to classify into predetermined categories. A study of archaeological heritage administrators' information work in Sweden provides evidence of how maintaining a fine balance between standardisation of both work processes and documentation, and what is described in the study as ambiguity, is crucial for the success of work (Huvila, 2021). Besides being cumbersome and costly, over-standardisation can become directly counterproductive and an obstacle to both data creation and use. This is an important perspective to hold on to in discussing something as contextual as paradata and one of the reasons for framing paradata management on a spectrum between standardisation and messiness. Keeping this in mind, the three strategies discussed in this section (i.e. intensifying, extending and adjusting granularity in standardisation from Figure 6.1) should be understood as strategies to complement and be complemented by strategies geared towards embracing messiness.

Intensifying standardisation work (Figure 6.1) is suggested in light of the fact that the standardisation of what we term in this chapter core paradata is still very much work in progress. Returning to survey studies and 3D visualisations (previously mentioned as a context where an emergence of core paradata as a documentation category is identifiable), we can say something about the state of paradata standardisation. Survey research has developed a robust corpus of metadata standards but standards for paradata are close to non-existent (Schenk and Reuß, 2024). A review of heritage visualisation standards shows that while many standards provide means to represent practice and process information, they have varying emphases and cover the full spectrum of practice and process information only partially. One of the most highly cited documents with direct relevance to paradata in that particular field are charters (including the London Charter, see Denard, 2013; and Seville Principles, or the International Guidelines for Virtual Archaeology, International Forum of Virtual Archaeology, 2011; Bendicho, 2013). The charters provide generic recommendations to document paradata rather than detailed advice on how to do it in practice. Existing metadata schemes and standards cover core paradata, but typically do not use the term paradata (exceptions e.g. CARARE metadata schema, see D'Andrea and Fernie, 2013). When they cover such paradata-like information, it is to varying degrees and often with a focus on historical processes and data curation.

A survey of major data documentation schemes conducted as a part of the CAPTURE project suggests that the situation is similar in many generic standards. At the same time, as Börjesson et al. (2020) suggest, even if there are few or no dedicated paradata standards, such generic conceptual models as the International Council of Museums (ICOM) International Committee for Documentation (CIDOC) Conceptual Reference Model (CIDOC CRM) provide means to represent practice and process information in detail to an extent that dedicated standards are perhaps not always necessary. Combining complete schemas and individual elements can help to achieve the required coverage of details. First and foremost, there is an urgent need to develop new and to adopt existing data documentation standards to cover paradata and devise guidelines for core paradata across data-producing and data-using communities. All of this work does not need to be exhaustive. For example, many fields have informal standards and vocabularies to describe phenomena interesting to them. Many of them have never been written down and the terms have not been explicitly described. As Huvila et al. (2022) remark, while such terms might be generally comprehensible, a systematic documentation of terminology and an effort to invite data producers to commit themselves to a better standardised use of concepts could provide significant benefits with relatively little overhead.

Expanding on standardisation work (Figure 6.1), not just intensifying the current work in progress, is also sorely needed. We particularly find it advisable to expand standardisation work on two fronts: generally to temporarily cover a larger part of the continuum (or life-cycle) of data; and, more specifically, to formalise the documentation of process information that corresponds to established paradata needs.

Along with the temporal extension, we are suggesting standardising critical elements of core paradata already as a part of routine research documentation. This would require, in practice, more structured advice in the methods literature (cf. Huvila et al., 2022b; Huvila and Sköld, 2023) about how to document key aspects of specific types of data creation and processing activities. In addition, there is a need for greater availability of hands-on advice on what specific paradata should be added to datasets that are produced for sharing and reuse at the planning stage of data collection or generation. This should cover not only what type of information should be added but also more specifically what it is expected to communicate.

As with all data documentation requirements, it should be adjusted to the plausible extent and types of uses relevant to particular datasets. For a lot of data, minimal paradata might be enough whereas datasets with high expectations of meticulous process documentation and high standardised reuse potential should be documented in more detail. With small-scale, highly contextual qualitative data collection with low likelihood of direct reuse of the generated data, a sufficient level of standardised documentation could be a brief narrative of data collection procedures and their underpinning rationale, especially if reusing the data can be expected to require a lot of interpretative work from secondary users. This type of data set and reuse scenario would, however, benefit from such strategies as presented further below, that would prevent the loss of potential paradata that could facilitate that interpretative reuse work. In contrast, there are datasets that require more formal and technical paradata to a much higher degree. This is true for cases such as longitudinal and cross-comparable survey datasets that are produced to be used broadly in both academic and societal knowledge production.

The parallel approach suggested here is equally necessary to starting the generation of core paradata earlier in the data creation process, that is, to formalise the documentation of practice and process information that corresponds to established and common paradata needs. In simple terms, this could mean verifying that the major categories of paradata needs (including those discussed previously in this chapter) are covered to a satisfactory degree in the existing and anticipated core paradata. While doing this it is crucial to consult data producing and using communities to establish what particular information corresponds with categories like methods paradata, scope paradata, provenance paradata and knowledge representation paradata in specific contexts. In such consultations, it is important to both include individuals with a relatively short working experience in the particular field, and those who are more reliable on formal explicit information. Huvila's study of archaeological heritage administrators suggested the experienced administrators could often compensate for missing explicit information due to their experience of working with the data on a daily basis. In contrast, other stakeholders could not be expected to be able to do that but must rely on the formal standardised documentation (Huvila, 2021). The categorisation presented in this chapter can, in consulting relevant communities, provide a starting point for discussion and a checklist for assessing whether conceivable types of needs have been covered in the documentation requirements.

Adjusting the granularity of documentation (Figure 6.1) is the last of the strategies that are conceptualised as standardisation work in this framework for managing paradata. However, as we shall see, it is placed in the middle of the spectrum for a reason. While determining the necessary level of granularity is certainly difficult, we suggest that it is possible to use the presence and expressed needs of auxiliary documentation as a working heuristic to assess the need of more or less core paradata. If a particular data-creating community is generating a lot of auxiliary documentation that qualifies as paradata, it is probably worth investigating whether some of it might be either replaced by or supplemented with core paradata. In some cases it might be possible if the additional documentation is kept due to the absence of adequate formal documentation standards, making it a question of standardisation work.

In other cases, as in ethnographic research, it is not feasible to replace a notebook with anything that qualifies as core paradata, rather the notebook might be kept or referenced as an identified source of potential paradata (more on this in Section 6.4.2). Correspondingly, repeated demand in data-using communities for either existing or missing auxiliary documentation might signal the need for additional core paradata. This could apply, for example, to the inconsistency identifying data creators or specific measurement instruments in the data documentation. The earlier discussed case of emails and personal information exchange being consulted for augmenting report documentation provides another example of a possible need for augmenting the scope of core paradata. It is seldom feasible to ask for a full email correspondence between researchers to be submitted alongside a dataset to a repository even if it would contain useful information for future reusers of the data. Nor is it reasonable to ask for testimonies or contact information for every single person involved in a research project to be included in report documentation.

However, leaning on our increasing knowledge of key actors and their correspondence being potential sources of paradata, the structures for documenting authors and contributors could be adjusted to increase the likelihood that a reuser can find the right person to talk to in order to better understand, for example, decision-making and contextual premises of making a specific dataset. Here, there are also important opportunities for synergies with the strategy of facilitating discovery and wayfinding, discussed Section 6.4.2 on embracing messiness.

6.4.2 Embracing Messiness

For potential paradata, the usefulness and, indeed, presence of anything deemed paradata will be particularly situational and the only course of action may be to embrace and cater to some level of messiness. It is apparent that cleaning a dataset too much obscures the research process behind it. Literal cleaning is unlikely to happen at a data repository due to the lack of time. Even researchers engage in cleaning proper only selectively. Instead, both data managers and producers alike make numerous decisions of requiring or depositing (only) structured data, leaving out parts of data, datasets or auxiliary information, converting and consolidating that all contribute to the resulting data being a little cleaner than before. It is a result of forcing systematisation of measurements, observations and interpretations, which might not be conclusive enough to be systematised to such an extent. Besides obscuring underlying processes, cleaning also challenges both reliability assessments and several reuse scenarios as discussed above. Of course, it is not possible to keep everything. Rather, as with documentation in general, the question is how to document (or keep) enough, and identify what is most likely to be useful. It is important to try to find a position comparable to what York (2022) terms 'reuse equilibrium' where there is sufficient information but not too much. Drawing on findings on where potential paradata is more or less likely to occur in a dataset in different contexts can facilitate the choice of what to leave messy, what to clean or not to keep. In this part of the chapter we explore how the resulting messiness can be managed and navigated. We propose starting by looking to traditional archiving practices for possible avenues for managing potential paradata. Guided by some of the fundamental principles of Western archiving practices we propose ways of embracing messiness that include a strategy to keep messes messy (i.e. preventing loss of potential paradata) and a strategy to navigate the messiness (i.e. levering linking for paradata discovery).

Preventing loss of potential paradata (Figure 6.1) is rather vague and not particularly actionable without further explicating by what means loss should be prevented. Unsurprisingly, the realisation that it is near impossible to predict what someone in the future will need to know in order to understand the context of some piece of information is far from new – nor is it born from paying attention to paradata. To some extent, a solution to this was proposed within Western archival practice more than a century ago. Having previously applied subject-based classification akin to classification in libraries, archivists in post-revolutionary France developed another principle for arranging and describing records that would be more efficient than the forbiddingly labour-intensive reorganisation of records.

The resulting system, which would be adopted gradually in the Western archival practice throughout the first part of the 1900s, is commonly referred to as *respect des fonds*. The general idea is that records should be maintained as they were originally accumulated, in their original *fonds*. A 'fonds' is all the records of, for example, an administrative authority, or a family, or a person (Trace, 2015, p. 21–24). Two important principles inform how records should be organised within fonds, that is, inform archival arrangement and description; these are the *principle of provenance* and *the principle of original order*. As discussed in Chapter 2, the principle of provenance puts emphasis on the importance of relationships between records and the context, functions and agents (e.g. organisations or individuals) involved in their creation, accumulation and use. The principle of original order promotes maintaining the ordering structure established by the records' creator in order to preserve important contextual information.

Inherent in the principle of original order is a view of the archival records as evidence of the activity of a particular organisation. The idea of *respect des fonds*, with its underlying principles, becomes rather more complicated when applied in practice, since the application of any standardised model of these principles, like Oliver Wendell Holmes's (1988) influential nested hierarchical model, will impose structure on the original order. However, the foundational idea of *respect des fonds* offers valuable insights that can be applied to the management of paradata, particularly for endeavours to preserve potential paradata.

The implication of *respect des fonds* and its parallel principles of original order and provenance for managing potential paradata is to keep the fonds of such information intact to an extent that is possible. From a repository perspective, potential paradata is essentially unmanageable when it falls outside the formal structure of how a data repository deals with datasets and metainformation, describes and preserves them, and works towards making and keep them formally FAIR or findable, accessible, interoperable and reusable (Wilkinson et al., 2016). Focusing efforts on keeping such information technically readable, and documenting it only superficially to maintain a rudimentary degree of findability is from a repository perspective obviously a question of managing resources. If keeping the information is useful enough, it is possible to avoid costs of turning it into core paradata.

However, as the previous discussion in this volume especially in Chapter 3 shows, it also has qualitative benefits. Turning potential paradata into core paradata is not only costly but it carries also a risk of losing information potentially available in the organic, unrefined messiness of such resources. For example, with methods paradata, looking into the terminology used to describe methods as a whole is informative not only of specific methods applied but also of how research practice and process is conceptualised as a whole. Moreover, as the work of Börjesson et al. (2022) shows, comparing earlier and later versions of interpretations in datasets can help to trace interpretative processes otherwise undocumented in the available research material.

Having established that some messiness may be beneficial for the preservation of potential paradata, the next question becomes how we might manage such a mess in a relatively systematic way. Again, we turn to the basic principles of archiving and, more specifically, how the idea of archival finding aids may be adapted to be useful tools for paradata management.

Facilitating paradata discovery (Figure 6.1) is a strategy that takes as its starting point archival finding aids. McNeil offers a useful definition of an archival finding aid as 'any tool that aims to provide users with intellectual and/or physical access to the holdings of archival institutions' (MacNeil, 2012, 486). This definition can easily be reframed in a data and paradata context, as a tool that aims to provide users intellectual access to the practices and processes underpinning a particular assemblage of data.

Taking directions from traditional archival practice in this way we can introduce some structure to how we can navigate the messes with paradata potential. There are obviously different means to implement a functioning paradata finding aid. Similarly to paradata itself, finding aids are also contextual. However, in contrast to paradata itself, considering the frame within which they are used, finding aids can be expected to be contextual first and foremost in relation to future data use rather than data creation. In parallel, rather than focusing on what such a finding aid should be, it is more fruitful to plan for what it should *do* (cf. MacNeil, 2012) for data creators, managers and users. It is important to consider earlier evidence of the advantages and affordances of traditional paper-based and digital finding aids when considering their potential adoption to paradata. A finding aid can facilitate paradata discovery through providing links between information resources, keeping traces of previous use of the data and the finding aid itself.

Perhaps the most significant function of a paradata finding aid would be to provide directions. Because all types of potential paradata require a lot of interpretative effort to use, it is superfluous to attempt to describe it beyond what is necessary to use the tool itself. Explicating the aboutness of datasets is crucial for understanding their processual context similarly to providing directions where to find information that helps to interpret it, including vocabularies and descriptions of colloquialisms. A finding aid should also provide an overview of the principles of how data was organised and made, and what standards were used and how un-FAIR as in unfindable, unaccessible, uninteroperable and unreusable the data is (Börjesson et al., 2022). In parallel, a good finding aid would provide directions across contextual and disciplinary boundaries. In many cases relevant data and paradata is not only disconnected in different logical units within one repository but literally scattered around the world. An illustrative example of this is historical and archaeological data that in many cases has been scattered to museums and research institutions located on different continents (e.g., Börjesson et al., 2022; Sobotkova 2018; Stilborg 2021). Remedying or at least bringing partial alleviation to the greatest obstacle in mediating practice and process information, namely its contextuality, is crucial for any tool proposed for the task. While a universalist ideal *a lieux* Otlet's Mundaneum or Bush's Memex would be a complete meta-level inter-institutional directory to (all) paradata, much more modest and context-specific directories could if not solve the paradata problem as a whole, at least alleviate it considerably.

However, rather than going entirely contextual, there would also be possibilities to develop standards for formats and contents of finding aids for potential paradata. Solving the problem of diverging expectations of data managers, creators and data reusers and what is feasible to achieve for paradata finding aids requires reaching a compromise between what (all) would be regarded as desirable. Such standardisation would be useful for potential reusers seeking potential paradata specific to their needs, but would also be helpful for data creators in providing rudimentary structure to data documentation efforts. Moreover, as Battley (2013) reminds us, archival findings aids are also records, or with paradata, another layer of paradata describing data management practices and processes (cf. Gant and Reilly, 2017). Generally, the standardisation of finding aids for paradata would also support paradata literacy, which is the topic we will now turn to in the final part of this chapter.

6.4.3 Paradata Literacy

There can be no doubt that solving the conundrum of generating or identifying paradata that is useful for its users, feasible to generate and keep for data creators, and manageable from a repository perspective is not merely an issue of selecting suitable technologies and particular types of resources to solve the problem. Paradata as a type of information, about processes and practices, is a moving target. The most comprehensive method for managing paradata may be simply to acknowledge that there is a need for process information not currently taken into account in documentation strategies and that information plays a much more critical role in the chain of knowledge-making and use than a mere footnote or an auxiliary attachment to data proper.

In contrast to finding aids that provide a map to existing paradata and guidance how to find and navigate it, we suggest looking to paradata literacies as a crucial step in making paradata (proper and potential) actionable in context and especially in working out the conundrums of identifying and making diverse forms of potential paradata. This discussion is both complementary to, and more overarching than, the discussion of paradata usefulness thresholds in Chapter 3. Finding aids and the notion of paradata literacy approach the paradata challenges from different angles. Finding aids can help make paradata and the practices and processes it documents better findable and accessible. Paradata literacies are needed to make data and data practices and processes work both on their own and in relation to each other. In practice, both have a much broader scope and in an ideal situation they would complement each other in a pursuit of increasingly relevant, resonant, ethical and sustainable paradata practices, practices that support corresponding, reflective and epistemically inclusive and sensitive data practices.

The argument for increased mutual paradata literacy is based on the insight that the discrepancy between available and desirable paradata is not simply an information problem. It is also, at least to an equal extent, a problem of disparity in paradata practices and competences, as observed in Chapter 3 where the issue is termed the 'epistemic usefulness threshold'. Researchers have been criticised in many studies for a lack of adequate competence in data management (e.g., Pálsdóttir, 2021). The same critique could be undoubtedly extended to paradata competences, although as our findings from a survey and interviews on researchers' paradata practices suggest, data creators, managers and users alike show a high degree of often tacit competence in sharing and acquiring practice and process knowledge. The trouble is that these competences, or literacies, do not necessarily converge.

Contemporary data repositories have structures in place to cater to many of the researchers' paradata needs, and data managers have skills and capacity to facilitate paradata practices but researchers are not always knowledgeable of what they are, how the existing structures and tools work, and how the available resources could be utilised for generating and preserving better paradata. Data managers are similarly struggling with securing a sufficient understanding of how data is created and used to be able to help researchers and other data users and producers. Therefore we want to underline the importance of improving *mutual paradata literacy* (Figure 6.1) instead of focusing on individual stakeholder groups.

Paradata literacy is a natural extension to what has been discussed in terms of data literacy or literacies (Huvila et al. 2024; 2025). It can unfold as something comparable to the competence and associated abilities that have been termed metadata literacy (Mitchell, 2013) and metadata literacy skills (Çakmak and Kurbanoğlu, 2015). It can also be seen as a complement to data literacy, essentially framing paradata literacy as a key facet of established data literacies. Paradata literacy, in the sense relevant here, would cover the competences of identifying, generating and keeping relevant and adequate core paradata and understanding what it does for data and data use.

The major implication of approaching the conundrum of managing paradata as a literacy question is that of acknowledging that making paradata work requires competence and effort and qualifies as a specific type of undertaking of its own. Data managers, creators and users all have specific roles and need to develop systematic competence to contribute to enacting paradata in practice. Acquiring and developing data management skills identified in the literature helps to develop that competence (e.g., Koltay, 2015; Schneider, 2013; Vilar and Zabukovec, 2019). However, considering the often indefinite boundaries of what paradata is and where to find it, paradata literacy extends beyond being a simple skill set. Paradata literacy is first and foremost a matter of understanding the complexities and challenges of working with paradata where theoretical, ethical and interpretative facets of practice cannot be detached from technical skills and practical doing (cf. the 'technical usefulness threshold' in Chapter 3 and Kansa and Kansa, 2020). It links to the broader field of data literacies (Verdi and Deuff, 2021) sharing many of the identified challenges but also opportunities and ways forward (cf. Koltay, 2021).

Like data literacies, paradata literacies are also never value-free. In their complexity and embeddedness in data practice, paradata literacies unfold rather as assemblages of ongoing processes and practices that need to evolve in time and across diverse contexts of data creation, management and use. Paradata literacies are also necessarily reciprocal in the sense that the making of paradata needs to be aligned with its management and use, and vice versa. being a competent paradata creator, manager or user, requires adeptness in the whole lifespan of paradata from its inception to management, use, reshaping and beyond.

Similarly to other literacies, paradata literacy is also about finding a balance between empowering users and providing them relevant services (cf. Huvila, 2012b). The analysis of Weber et al. (2023) points to a similar gap between archival users and archivists that is evident also in the broader sphere of data management. It is likely that much of future paradata use will not be mediated by data managers but rather by data creators and users themselves who are depositing and accessing datasets directly in online repositories.

However, even if this would be the case, there is still need for professional support, probably to a greater extent than is acknowledged in the contemporary management culture, which often downplays the significance and both qualitative and economic advantages of qualified professional service work. We are still to see a well-grounded division of labour between what users should be able to achieve independently and what types of services are necessary and appropriate to offer and when. Repositories and data managers occupy a position with a broad vista across diverse context-specific data practices. In doing so, they hold a unique position and responsibility to not only act as service-providers but to actively raise questions and act in dialogue with data creators and users to find virtuous paths forward.

References

Austin C. C., Brown S., Fong N., Humphrey C., Leahey A. and Webster P. (2016). Research data repositories: Review of current features, gap analysis, and recommendations for minimum requirements. *IASSIST Quarterly*, *39*(4), Article 4. https://doi.org/10.29173/iq904.

Battley B. (2013). Finding aids in context: Using Records Continuum and Diffusion of Innovations models to interpret descriptive choices. *Archives and Manuscripts*, *41*(2), 129–145. https://doi.org/10.1080/01576895.2013.793164

Bendicho V. M. L.-M. (2013). International guidelines for virtual archaeology: The seville principles. In *Good Practice in Archaeological Diagnostics. Natural Science in Archaeology*, 269–283. Springer. https://doi.org/10.1007/978-3-319-01784-6_16.

Blobel B., Ruotsalainen P. and Giacomini M. (2022). Standards and principles to enable interoperability and integration of 5P medicine ecosystems. In Blobel B., Yang B. and Giacomini M. (eds.), *Studies in Health Technology and Informatics*. IOS Press. https://doi.org/10.3233/SHTI220958.

Borek L., Dombrowski Q., Perkins J. and Schöch C. (2016). TaDiRAH: A case study in pragmatic classification. *DHQ*, *10*(1), a235.

Börjesson L., Huvila I. and Sköld O. (2022). Information needs on research data creation. *Information Research*, *27*(Special Issue), isic2208. https://doi.org/10.47989/irisic2208.

Börjesson L. and Sköld O. (2021). *The making and use of paradata: An interview study* [dataset]. https://urn.kb.se/resolve?urn = urn:nbn:se:uu:diva-455730

Börjesson L., Sköld O., Friberg Z., Löwenborg D., Pálsson G. and Huvila I. (2022). Repurposing excavation database content as paradata: An explorative analysis of paradata identification challenges and opportunities. *KULA: Knowledge Creation, Dissemination, and Preservation Studies*, *6*(3), Article 3. https://doi.org/10.18357/kula.221.

Börjesson L., Sköld O. and Huvila I. (2021). The politics of paradata in documentation standards and recommendations for digital archaeological visualisations. *Digital Culture and Society*, *6*(2), 1. https://doi.org/10.14361/dcs-2020-0210.

Button G. and Harper R. (1996). The relevance of work-practice for design. *Computer Supported Cooperative Work*, *4*(4), 263–280. http://dx.doi.org/10.1007/BF00749172.

Çakmak T. and Kurbanoğlu S. (2015). Metadata literacy skills: An analysis of LIS students. In Kurbanoglu S., Boustany J., Špiranec S., Grassian E., Mizrachi D. and Roy L. (eds.), *Information Literacy: Moving toward Sustainability* (262–269). Springer International Publishing. https://doi.org/10.1007/978-3-319-28197-1_27

Cofield S. R., Childs S. T. and Majewski T. (2024). A survey of how archaeological repositories are managing digital associated records and data: A byte of the reality sandwich. *Advances in Archaeological Practice, 12*(1), 20–33. https://doi.org/10.1017/aap.2023.29.

Contaxis N. et al. (2022). Ten simple rules for improving research data discovery. *PLOS Computational Biology, 18*(2), e1009768. https://doi.org/10.1371/journal.pcbi.1009768

D'Andrea A. and Fernie K. (2013). CARARE 2.0: A metadata schema for 3D cultural objects. *2013 Digital Heritage International Congress (DigitalHeritage),* 137–143. https://doi.org/10.1109/DigitalHeritage.2013.6744745

de Mello B. H. et al. (2022). Semantic interoperability in health records standards: A systematic literature review. *Health and Technology.* https://doi.org/10.1007/s12553-022-00639-w

Denard H. (2012). A new introduction to the London Charter. In Bentkowska-Kafel A., Denard H. and Baker D. (eds.), *Paradata and Transparency in Virtual Heritage* (57–71). Ashgate.

Denard H. (2013). Implementing best practice in cultural heritage visualisation: The London Charter. In *Good Practice in Archaeological Diagnostics: Non-invasive Survey of Complex Archaeological sites* (255–268). Springer. https://doi.org/10.1007/978-3-319-01784-6_15.

Edwards R., Goodwin J., O'Connor H. and Phoenix A. (2017). *Working with Paradata, Marginalia and Fieldnotes.* Edward Elgar Publishing.

Ellingsen G. (2004). Tightrope walking: Standardisation meets local work-practice in a hospital. *International Journal of IT Standards & Standardization Research, 2*(1), 1–22.

Faniel I., Austin A., Kansa S. W., Kansa E., Jacobs J. and France P. (2021). *Identifying Opportunities for Collective Curation during Archaeological Excavations.* OCLC. www.oclc.org/research/publications/2021/identifying-opportunities-collective-curation-during-archaeological-excavations.html.

Faniel I. M. and Jacobsen T. E. (2010). Reusing scientific data: How earthquake engineering researchers assess the reusability of colleagues' data. *Computer Supported Cooperative Work (CSCW), 19*(3), 355–375. https://doi.org/10.1007/s10606-010-9117-8.

Gal M. S. and Rubinfeld D. L. (2019). Data standardization. *New York University Law Review, 94*(4), 737–770.

Galliers R. D. (1991). Choosing appropriate information systems research methodologies; A revised taxonomy. In Nissen H.-E., Klein H. K. and Hirscheim R. A. (eds.), *Information Systems Research: Contemporary Approaches and Emergent Traditions* (327–345). Elsevier.

Gant S. and Reilly P. (2017). Different expressions of the same mode: A recent dialogue between archaeological and contemporary drawing practices. *Journal of Visual Art Practice, 17*(1), 100–120. https://doi.org/10.1080/14702029.2017.1384974.

Geser G., Richards J. D., Massara F. and Wright H. (2022). Data management policies and practices of digital archaeological repositories. *Internet Archaeology, 59,* Article 2. https://doi.org/10.11141/ia.59.2.

Hanke M., Pestilli F., Wagner A. S., Markiewicz C. J., Poline J.-B. and Halchenko Y. O. (2021). In defense of decentralized research data management. *Neuroforum, 27*(1), 17–25. https://doi.org/10.1515/nf-2020-0037.

Hansen H. J. and Fernie K. (2010). CARARE: Connecting archaeology and architecture in Europeana. *EuroMed 2010: Digital Heritage,* 450–462. https://doi.org/10.1007/ 978-3-642-16873-4_36.

Havemann S. (2012). Intricacies and potentials of gathering paradata in the 3D modelling workflow. In Bentkowska-Kafel A., Denard H. and Baker D. (eds.), *Paradata and Transparency in Virtual Heritage* (145–160). Ashgate.

Herres-Pawlis S. et al. (2022). Minimum information standards in chemistry: A call for better research data management practices. *Angewandte Chemie International Edition, 61*(51), e202203038. https://doi.org/10.1002/anie.202203038.

Holmes O. W. (1964). Archival arrangement: Five different operations at five different levels. *The American Archivist, 27*(1), 21–42.

Huvila I. (2012a). Being formal and flexible: Semantic Wiki as an archaeological e-science infrastructure. In Zhou M., Romanowska I., Wu Z., Xu P. and Verhagen P. (eds.), *Revive the Past: Proceeding of the 39th Conference on Computer Applications and Quantitative Methods in Archaeology, Beijing, 12-16 April 2011* (186–197). Amsterdam University Press. https://proceedings.caaconference .org/paper/21_huvila_caa2011/.

Huvila I. (2012b). *Information Services and Digital Literacy: In Search of the Boundaries of Knowing.* Chandos.

Huvila I. (2020). Information-making-related information needs and the credibility of information. *Information Research, 25*(4), paper isic2002. https://doi.org/10 .47989/irisic2002.

Huvila I. (2021). Ambiguity, standards and contextual distance: Archaeological heritage administrators and their information work. *Open Information Science, 5*(1), 190–214. https://doi.org/10.1515/opis-2020-0121

Huvila I., Sköld O. and Börjesson L. (2021). Documenting information making in archaeological field reports. *Journal of Documentation, 77*(5), 1107–1127. https:// doi.org/10.1108/JD-11-2020-0188.

Huvila I., Börjesson L. and Sköld O. (2022a). Archaeological information-making activities according to field reports. Library & Information Science Research, 44(3), 101171. https://doi.org/10.1016/j.lisr.2022.101171

Huvila I., Andersson L. and Sköld O. (2022b). Citing methods literature: Citations to field manuals as paradata on archaeological fieldwork. *Information Research: An International Electronic Journal, 27*(3). https://doi.org/10.47989/irpaper941

Huvila I., Kaiser J., Sköld O. and Andersson L. (2024). Paradata literacy and the challenges of research data management. *Informaatiotutkimus,* 43(3–4), 109–113. https://doi.org/10.23978/inf.148594

Huvila I., Olsson M., Sköld O., Kaiser J. and Andersson L. (2025). Being literate on data or practices: How paradata functions in the context of literacy. *Proceedings of the 2025 Conceptions of Library and Information Science Conference.*

Huvila I. and Sköld O. (2023). A fieldwork manual as a regulatory device: Instructing, prescribing and describing documentation work. *Journal of Information Science.* https://doi.org/10.1177/01655515231203506

Ibanez L., Schroeder W. J. and Hanwell M. D. (2014). Practicing open science. In *Implementing Reproducible Research.* Chapman and Hall/CRC.

International Forum of Virtual Archaeology. (2011). *The Seville Principles: International Principles of Virtual Archaeology.* http://smartheritage.com/seville-principles/seville-principles.

Kansa E. and Kansa S. W. (2021). Digital data and data literacy in archaeology now and in the new decade. *Advances in Archaeological Practice*, 9(1), 81–85. https://doi.org/10.1017/aap.2020.55

Kim J., Yakel E. and Faniel I. (2019). Exposing standardization and consistency issues in repository metadata requirements for data deposition. *College & Research Libraries*, 80(6), 843–875. https://doi.org/10.5860/crl.80.6.843.

Kindling M., and Strecker, D. (2022). Data quality assurance at research data repositories. *Data Science Journal, 21*, 18–18. https://doi.org/10.5334/dsj-2022-018.

Koltay T. (2015). Data literacy: In search of a name and identity. *Journal of Documentation, 71*(2), 401–415. https://doi.org/10.1108/JD-02-2014-0026.

Laird A. R. et al. (2011). The BrainMap strategy for standardization, sharing, and meta-analysis of neuroimaging data. *BMC Research Notes, 4*(1), 349. https://doi.org/10.1186/1756-0500-4-349.

Leighton M. (2015). Excavation methodologies and labour as epistemic concerns in the practice of archaeology: Comparing examples from British and Andean archaeology. *Archaeological Dialogues, 22*(1), 65–88. https://doi.org/10.1017/s1380203815000100.

Leonelli S., Davey R. P., Arnaud E., Parry G. and Bastow R. (2017). Data management and best practice for plant science. *Nature Plants, 3*, 17086. https://doi.org/10.1038/nplants.2017.86.

MacNeil H. (2012). What finding aids do: Archival description as rhetorical genre in traditional and web-based environments. *Archival Science, 12*(4), 485–500. https://doi.org/10.1007/s10502-012-9175-4.

Mandell R. (2022). Applying new standards to old data: Wrangling metadata in a sports archive. *Journal of Digital Media Management, 11*(1), 18–24.

Mitchell E. (2013). Trending tech services: Metadata use in everyday situations: What does it mean for libraries? *Technical Services Quarterly, 30*(4), 402–413. https://doi.org/10.1080/07317131.2013.819750.

Montoya R. D. and Morrison K. (2019). Document and data continuity at the Glenn A. Black Laboratory of Archaeology. *Journal of Documentation, 75*(5), 1035–1055. http://doi.org/10.1108/JD-12-2018-0216.

Palaiologk A. S., Economides A. A., Tjalsma H. D. and Sesink L. B. (2012). An activity-based costing model for long-term preservation and dissemination of digital research data: The case of DANS. *International Journal on Digital Libraries, 12*(4), 195–214.

Pálsdóttir Á. (2021). Data literacy and management of research data: A prerequisite for the sharing of research data. *Aslib Journal of Information Management, 73*(2), 322–341. https://doi.org/10.1108/AJIM-04-2020-0110.

Pétavy F. et al. (2019). *Global Standardization of Clinical Research Data. 28.* www.appliedclinicaltrialsonline.com/view/global-standardization-clinical-research-data

Rabinowitz A. (2019). Communicating in three dimensions: Questions of audience and reuse in 3D excavation documentation practice. *Studies in Digital Heritage*, *3*(1), Article 1. https://doi.org/10.14434/sdh.v3i1.25386.

Ribes D. and Lee C. P. (2010). Sociotechnical studies of cyberinfrastructure and e-research: Current themes and future trajectories. *Computer Supported Cooperative Work (CSCW)*, *19*(3), 231–244. https://doi.org/10.1007/s10606-010-9120-0.

Santos L. O. B. et al. (2016). FAIR Data Points Supporting Big Data Interoperability. *Enterprise Interoperability in the Digitized and Networked Factory of the Future.* 8th International Conference on Interoperability for Enterprise Systems and Applications, I-ESA 2016. https://research.utwente.nl/en/publications/fair-data-points-supporting-big-data-interoperability.

Schenk P. O. and Reuß S. (2024). Paradata in surveys. In Huvila I. Andersson L. and Sköld O. (eds.), *Perspectives on Paradata: Research and Practice of Documenting Data Processes.* Springer.

Schneider R. (2013). Research data literacy. In Kurbanoğlu S., Grassian E., Mizrachi D., Catts R. and Špiranec S. (eds.), *Worldwide Commonalities and Challenges in Information Literacy Research and Practice* (134–140). Springer. https://doi.org/ 10.1007/978-3-319-03919-0_16.

Schöpfel J. and Rebouillat V. (eds.). (2022). *Research Data Sharing and Valorization: Developments, Tendencies, Models*(1st ed.). Wiley. https://doi.org/10.1002/ 9781394163410.

Sicilia M.-Á. (2010). On modeling eesearch work for describing and filtering scientific information. In Sánchez-Alonso S. and Athanasiadis I. N. (eds.), *Metadata and Semantic Research* (247–254). Springer. https://doi.org/10.1007/978-3-642-16552-8_23.

Sobotkova A. (2018). Sociotechnical obstacles to archaeological data reuse. *Advances in Archaeological Practice*, *6*(2), 117–124. https://doi.org/10.1017/aap.2017.37.

Stilborg Ole. (2021). A study of the representativity of the Swedish ceramics analyses published in The Strategic Environmental Archaeology Database (SEAD). *Fornvännen, 116*(2), 89–100.

Thomer A. K., Starks J. R., Rayburn A. and Lenard M. C. (2022). Maintaining repositories, databases, and digital collections in memory institutions: An integrative review. *Proceedings of the Association for Information Science and Technology*, *59*(1), 310–323. https://doi.org/10.1002/pra2.755.

Toms E. G. and O'Brien H. L. (2008). Understanding the information and communication technology needs of the e-humanist. *Journal of Documentation*, *64*(1), 102–130. https://doi.org/10.1108/00220410810844178.

Trace Ciaran (2015) 'Archival arrangement' in Duranti L. and Franks P. C. (eds.) *Encyclopedia of Archival Science*, Rowman & Littlefield Publishers, Incorporated, Blue Ridge Summit.

Ullah I. I. T. (2015). Integrating older survey data into modern research paradigms. *Advances in Archaeological Practice*, *3*(4), 331–350. https://doi.org/10.7183/ 2326-3768.3.4.331.

VandenBosch A., Maull K. E. and Mayernik M. (2023). Jupyter Notebooks and institutional repositories: A landscape analysis of realities, opportunities and paths forward. *The Code4Lib Journal, 58.* https://journal.code4lib.org/articles/17751.

Verdi U. and Deuff O. L. (2021). La data literacy distribuée. Périmètres définitionnels, origines documentaire, perspectives réticulaires [Distributed data literacy. Definitional scope, documentary sources and reticular perspectives]. *Les Cahiers Du Numérique, 16*(2–4), 137–173.

Verhagen P. (2023). Spatial information in archaeology. In Pollard A. M., Armitage R. A. and Makarewicz C. A. (eds.), *Handbook of Archaeological Sciences* 1st ed., (1163–1181). Wiley. https://doi.org/10.1002/9781119592112.ch57.

Vilar P., and Zabukovec V. (2019). Research data management and research data literacy in Slovenian science. *Journal of Documentation, 75*(1), 24–43. https://doi.org/10.1108/jd-03-2018-0042.

Weber C. S., et al. (2023). *Summary of Research: Findings from the Building a National Finding Aid Network Project.* OCLC Research. https://doi.org/10.25333/7A4C-0R03.

Wilkinson M. D., et al. (2016). The FAIR Guiding Principles for scientific data management and stewardship. *Scientific Data, 3*, 160018. https://doi.org/10.1038/sdata.2016.18.

Wylie C. D. (2019). Overcoming the underdetermination of specimens. *Biology & Philosophy, 34*(2), 24. https://doi.org/10.1007/s10539-019-9674-2.

York J. (2022). *Seeking Equilibrium in Data Reuse: A Study of Knowledge Satisficing* [Thesis]. https://doi.org/10.7302/6170.

Xian C. and Fu M. (2022). *Towards a Taxonomy of Human-Computer Interaction (HCI) Methods Based on a Survey of Recent HCI Researches.* 2022 IEEE 2nd International Conference on Power, Electronics and Computer Applications (ICPECA), 1192–1196. https://doi.org/10.1109/ICPECA53709.2022.9718950.

7

A Paradata Reference Model

Isto Huvila

7.1 Introduction

In this volume we have traversed from exploring how paradata has been discussed in the literature to exploring where it can be found and how it can be practised by data creators, users and curators. What has not been touched upon so far is how these different strings can be tied together to advance a conceptual understanding of paradata: what paradata is and perhaps even more importantly, what it does and in what kind of a space it operates. The purpose of this chapter is to delve into these questions and, through assembling and disassembling a reference model, to work towards a proposed theoretical synthesis of paradata and its workings. Before proceeding any further, it is fair to note as a word of warning to any casual readers that the aim of this chapter is to question, problematise and theorise rather than to provide practical advice.

Our synthesis needs, however, to start with its opposite, an ἀνάλυσις (analysis) of what paradata allows us to do. Building on how paradata was characterised in the introduction of this volume as a form of information relating to informational – and other varieties of – doings, a fruitful starting point is to think more closely about the implications of thinking in terms of doings. To this end, Ingold (2022) makes a useful distinction between making and doing. If we imagine we approach a researcher, or a construction worker as Ingold did, and ask what you do, the answer is likely to be rather different from that to the question of what you make. Answers about doing are likely to refer to tasks at hand (what is happening right now) whereas answers about making are more likely to relate to the final output of the process. For a researcher it could be something tangible, like a research article or the planned outcomes of a research project, while for a construction worker it would relate to a building or a bridge depending on what they are building at the time.

Paradata strikes into this very distinction. In research work we are also often very much focused on what we are *making* and how to articulate and document it rather than what we are *doing* to achieve it. Rather than focusing on the outcome, we propose that paradata can help us to focus on doing. As '[d]oing . . . is hidden inside the box of making' (Ingold, 2022, p. 224). While paradata may not be able to take 'doing' out of the box, it does afford the opportunity to at least open the lid and provide a glimpse inside.

The difficulty with paradata and what we, in this chapter, term working knowledge is that there is no one obvious perfect approach to opening the box. Articulating something that is already outside of it is much easier. This is demonstrated vividly in studies of such colloquial impromptu forms of documentation as collaborative tagging systems (Golder and Huberman, 2006) where specific systematic modus operandi are not enforced.

The word paradata itself alludes to the possibility to understand practices and processes in (new) ways that make them more manageable and countable, turning them into what Latour (1987) would call immutable mobiles. The ideal of making processes comprehensible through documentation has multiple parallels in contemporary information cultures. It ties into what has been described as the explainability turn (Berry, 2023), an aspiration to mitigate the apparent opaqueness of algorithmic processes and increase their transparency through providing explanations.

More than a desire to satisfy curiosity, having an explanation is increasingly regarded as a legal right in modern legislation. An explanation becomes a product, a category of things, in the same way that the documentation and comprehensibility of data-related practices and processes are increasingly treated in the literature (cf. Chapter 2) as a manufactured product that reifies an obligation. However, as the previous chapters in this volume have demonstrated, paradata is also distinctly doing the opposite. There is no one way of capturing or generating paradata, or a single explanation it is capable of enacting. Attempting to use paradata to make practices and processes countable, makes visible their uncountability, precariousness and instability.

7.2 The Model

Instead of starting with an explanation of a set of premises, here the story begins with the model itself before delving into discussing its details. The paradata reference model (Figure 7.1) frames paradata as related to practices

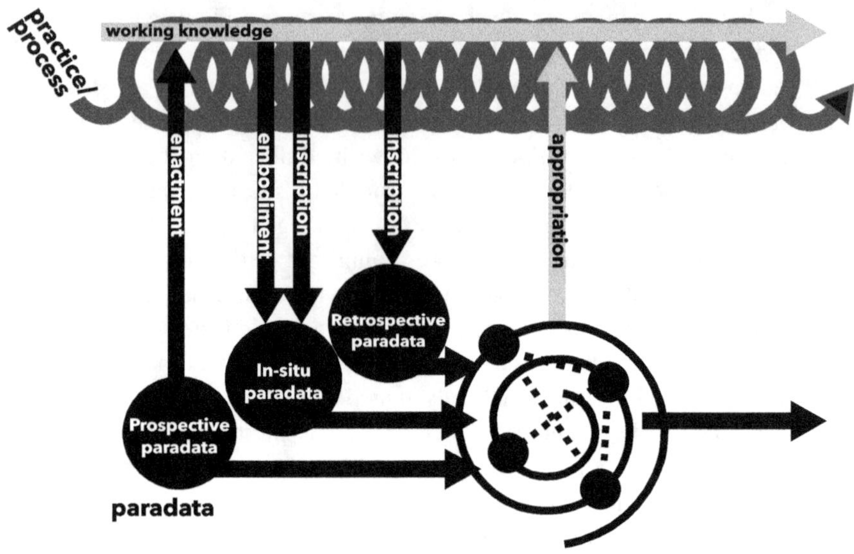

Figure 7.1 The paradata reference model.

and processes. *Working knowledge* on *practices and processes* (i.e. how practices and processes are known) and the practices and processes themselves engender paradata through *embodiment* and acts of *inscription*. Paradata turns back to working knowledge through *appropriation*. *Enactment* turns paradata to practices and processes. For *prospective paradata* engendered before its referent practice or process its enactment is also the very moment when it turns from a potential to actual paradata. Paradata is processual in the sense that it is perpetually *in the making* on a continuum and actualises as instances only through *temporal intersections* with the practices and processes it converges.

In parallel to being processual in time, consisting of interconnected types of information linked to each other, paradata forms a network. As the previous chapters have shown, while sometimes a single item might be enough to convey the necessary understanding of pertinent facets of a practice or process, the richness of paradata grows through assemblages where the different constituent parts come together to provide a richer understanding which goes beyond being simply the sum of its component pieces.

At this point, we turn our attention to the constituent parts of the model and return to discussing paradata as embodied or inscribed forms of working knowledge. We continue to explore what it means that paradata is created on a continuum where it is actualised through temporal intersections between practices and processes. This is followed by a closer look at the enactment of paradata in practices and processes; projected and unintended outcomes of working with paradata; and finally inquiring into how paradata resides in the borderlands between practices and processes; and embedded and explicable through ways of knowing.

7.3 Working Knowledge and Paradata

We start by zooming into the centre of the model to examine a section (Figure 7.2) where *working knowledge* intersects with paradata in the nexus of what belongs to the realm of practices and processes (upper part of Figure 7.1, marked in light grey) and the realm of paradata and documentation (lower part, in black).

The reason for starting with working knowledge is that much of the knowledge people act upon on a daily basis is incorporated into the processes and practices themselves. It is infrastructural: taken for granted, inherited background knowledge (Tsoukas, 2013; Wittgenstein, 1969). It is not knowledge

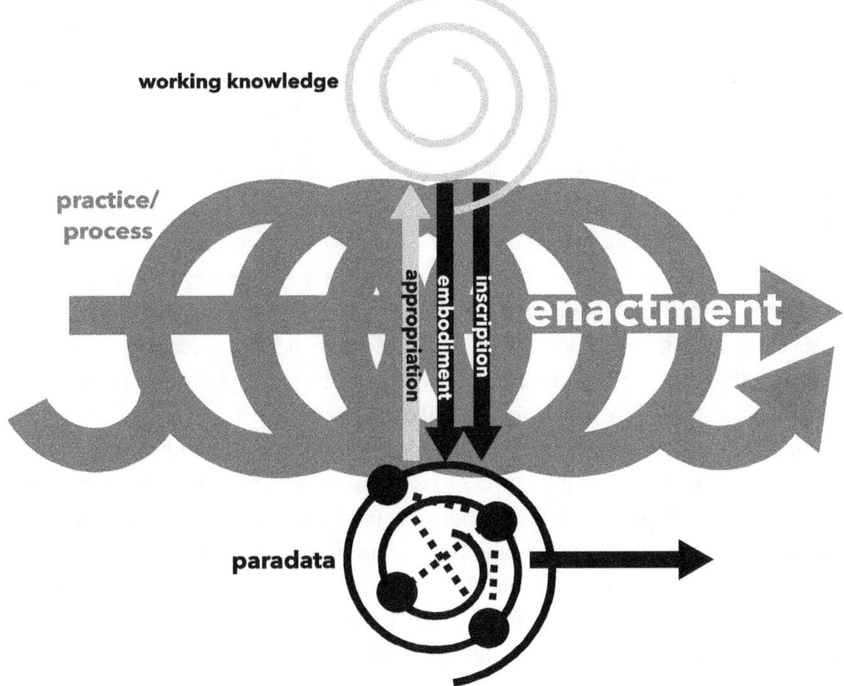

Figure 7.2 Working knowledge intersects with practices and processes.

about or even *of* but rather knowledge *in* the processes and practices themselves. The concept of working knowledge is akin to Polanyi's (1998) idea of personal knowledge – but rather than to a person, it is personal to a practice or process. Working knowledge is about how people know what they do in practice. The knowing is implicit in nature and craft-like, materially incorporated in the physicality of practices and processes. It is intrinsic, difficult to inscribe or even recognise as knowledge. Rather than being *about* a practice, working knowledge is a part of practice to an extent that distinguishing the two makes sense for analytical purposes but no more than that.

Understanding it becomes easier if we consider examples of how practices/processes and knowing are fused in practice. Researchers know how certain types of studies are conventionally expected to be done in their field. Comparably, a competent data archivist knows how data archiving is supposed to be done according to the existing guidelines, and data analysts know how they themselves and their colleagues do their work. Their knowledge incorporates both what happens in practice, including anything that can be conceptualised as steps, tasks or the workflows, but also the implicit and explicit contexts of processes and practices (Kowalczyk and Shankar, 2011), unarticulated decisions and their underpinning reasons. Essentially, working knowledge is a flow. It is about knowing rather than being.

In contrast to the working knowledge embedded in processes and practices, what we call in this volume paradata unfolds as a *category of things that can be appropriated as informative of processes and practices*. However, rather than embedded knowledge, it is a category of *process and practice information* which is to varying degrees externalised from its associated processes and practices. It is not necessarily *about* practices or processes but 'near' them (as metadata for Parry, 2023) to an extent that it has capacity to make them intelligible. In the context of this volume where the focus is on paradata describing activities pertaining to data, we have been particularly interested in things that are associated with and which can be appropriated as informative about data-related processes and practices.

This does not, however, mean that a general concept of paradata would need to apply only to data-related processes and practices when it is applied. Transparency of practices and processes is equally relevant when artificial intelligence technologies are applied to an increasing extent in decision-making, generation and summarisation of information (as per Davet et al., 2023). It has been a long-term concern in communicating the processes of making heritage visualisations (Bentkowska-Kafel et al., 2012) and a burning question with the processes underpinning and relating to generation and management of archival records (e.g., Jones and Bunn, 2024; Packalén and

Henttonen, 2024). The examples from the empirical research show how paradata can consist of physical and conceptual things including narratives and photographs in research reports (e.g., Huvila et al., 2021) or concepts used to describe observations in a dataset (Börjesson et al., 2022). It is always material to some degree through the materiality of the paradata-things and the materialities of its associated processes and practices.

There is no reason to limit potential paradata to intentional human-made documents (cf. Ferraris, 2014 and Chapter 2) even if humans perhaps have a particular appetite to develop and utilise accounts of doings – what Ferraris describes as human necessity to leave traces (Ferraris, 2014). In practical terms, paradata can be an individual narrative or visual depiction of a process or practice, or an assemblage or a sequence of such descriptions or prescriptions organised as a workflow. Many things appropriable as such are inscribable as metadata, textual descriptions or diagrams. They can be written out to provide (enough) information for an outsider to master (knowledge of) a process or practice. They can be made, captured, organised, managed and used as if paradata was a distinct entity. The malleability, durability and portability that paradata promises are major advantages. At the same time, it also comes with a potential risk of misrepresentation, incompleteness and over-simplification.

Unlike implicit and embedded working knowledge of processes and practices, when a knowledge is translated into paradata it is objectified in constellations of physical or conceptual things that span over both space and time. It forms a network (lower part in black in Figure 7.2) rather than a hierarchical structure or a monolithic entity. Rather than standing alone, paradata works together and links to a large variety of different types of information (e.g., Huvila et al., 2022). In a semiotic sense, a referent (practice or process) is encoded in a signans (paradata). The working knowledge is specified to a particular coordinate of reference and articulated either verbally or using some other means of expression (cf. Ingold, 2022).

However, rather than inherently being paradata, 'things' become paradata first when their particular kind of documentality (cf. Day, 2024; Ogden and Richards, 1930) as paradata is acknowledged. Equally, as formulated above, a thing becomes paradata when it is appropriated as such and becomes a part of a particular constructed totality (cf. Lund, 2024 on when a document becomes a document) where it functions as paradata.

As discussed in Chapters 3 and 6, the diversity of things potentially appropriable as paradata is so broad to an extent that even an absence of things, information gaps or non-information can occasionally become paradata, that is, informative of practices or processes (Huvila et al., 2023b). The idea of paradata becoming paradata through appropriation ties in with the idea of staying within and traversing boundaries discussed in Chapter 3 in terms of technical and epistemic thresholds. Such an understanding of paradata follows essentially the line of what Huvila (2022) describes as a middle-range approach to paradata, that is, whether a thing is paradata, data or metadata depends on perspective and how it is used. One person's data can be another's paradata and vice versa.

For example, while a researcher in physics uses lab notebooks as paradata on how experiments were conducted, a science studies scholar might use them as data when doing research on physicists' research practices. Sometimes, as with notebooks (Canfield et al., 2011) and protocols (Rheinberger, 2023) used to document both the subject and process of research, making such a distinction can be impossible. Data can be paradata at the same time as it is data.

7.4 Embodied and Inscribed

In the previous section, paradata was approached as things with informational potential. The origins of such things can vary and in much the same way that Mayernik observes of metadata: Paradata is performed 'differently in different social settings and situations' (Mayernik, 2020, p. 702). When considering what kind of information paradata is, there is a distinction to make between information or documents that are made-to-be (for Hauser 2024, facta) paradata in terms of that they are *inscribed* and given as such (for Hauser 2024, data) or *embodied* and merely taken as such (for Hauser 2024, capta). This characterises also the distinction between what is discussed in Chapter 6 in terms of made-to-be paradata proper and incidental, potential paradata.

A written document or drawing of a process or practice are typical examples of inscriptions that can be appropriated as paradata. They can be formal or informal, more or less structured, but typically at least to some extent they are products planned rather than outcomes of incidental information making (cf. Chapter 3 in this volume). As Mathieu (2023) suggests, inscriptions also vary in how they link to the practices and processes. As can be sensed in the different methods and approaches discussed in Chapters 4 and 5, it is possible to see inscriptions to (cf. Mathieu 2023):

- *describe* practices or processes by conveying an account of them;
- *prescribe* by instructing or stipulating them;
- *transcribe* by rearranging them;
- *proscribe* by forbidding access to them;
- *subscribe* by adhering to them;

- *circumscribe* by restricting access to them; or
- *ascribe* by explaining them.

Elements of practices and processes can, however, also be embodied in multiple things (Baker, 2017), for instance, in datasets of results created during a research project or physical artefacts crafted by artisans. As discussed in Chapter 2, paradata is often informal and unstructured, and of secondary nature.

Pagés ([1948] 2021) introduced the notion of auto-documents to discuss the documentary function of things not purposefully created as documents (see also Buckland, 2024; Day, 2024). Auto-documents are taken-to-be (*capta*) while documents are also given-to-be (*data*) information (Hauser, 2024) or paradata when used as such. While auto-documents are akin to natural information, documentary paradata is always either embodied or encoded (as information for Bates, 2006). Ingold makes a related distinction by emphasising that deposition and palimpsests are not inscriptions (Ingold, 2022, p. 186–190). In palimpsets, 'chalk marks are not inscribed. Rather than sinking into the surface … the chalk is deposited' (Ingold, 2022, p. 188).

The same distinction can be made between two types of paradata: inscriptions and embodiments. These roughly correspond to what has also been termed ingredients and traces (Huvila et al., 2023). Traces and embodiments follow the stratigraphic logic of hierarchy from the present to the past, whereas ingredients and inscriptions are rhizomatic by their nature, growing from below to the surface (cf. Ingold, 2022, p. 194). This means that embodied things may inform as paradata through going back in time to the moment when a process or practice took place. In contrast, with an inscription, the journey goes forward in time from the moment when the inscription was generated to the present where it is eventually appropriatable as paradata.

There are diverse mechanisms of how paradata comes into being as inscribed or embodied. Therefore, how things turn to paradata through appropriation and how things sometimes function as paradata and sometimes not means that there is no single moment when paradata happens. This is recognised in Figures 7.1 and 7.2 in the iterative, turbulent and irregular intertwined movement of processes, practices and paradata from left to right.

Being in the making is common to both working knowledge and paradata. Understanding the differences between the flow of working knowledge and the iterative remaking of paradata can help to overcome the gap between them. Working knowledge, like habits for Ingold (2022), 'resist explication' to a degree that paradata cannot be complete.

Thinking of paradata in an objectifying sense means to try to 'specify' or 'fix coordinates of reference' (Ingold, 2022, p. 231) of a practice or process and articulate them as being definite, essentially turning the practices and processes to aggregated models and sets of datapoints (cf. Hartley and Schjøtt, 2023). It has aspirations to be, in Vetter's (2016) terms, cosmopolitan across contexts and practices rather than strictly experiential. In contrast to assuming that paradata is according to the premises of systems-oriented knowledge management (Handzic, 2004) implicit process and practice knowledge made explicit, paradata is better understood as a verb (cf. Dervin, 1999; Latour, 2011) and being in-the-making. Such perspective recognises its incompleteness and fluidity in relation to working knowledge and the processes and practices themselves.

Being in the making means that paradata is potentially coming into being at multiple points of time. Rather than being determined only at and by the moment when a particular artefact may be paradata for someone, it is made again and again as paradata through embodiment, inscription and appropriations of things whenever they are (re)embodied, (re)inscribed or acted upon as paradata. Inscribed paradata is (re)made when it is conceived and whenever it is used.

Embodied paradata, if understood as paradata from the outset, may follow the same pattern. Sometimes things embodying working knowledge might be recognised and appropriated as paradata first at use, suggesting that it is crucial to distinguish the making of things appropriatable as paradata and paradata itself. This corresponds to how the authoring of documents and turning the documents to communicate, mediate or, for example, change practices are distinct acts (Huvila, 2019).

Approaching paradata from the perspective of being in-the-making does not mean that certain things might not be more widely recognised as paradata than others. Purposefully inscribed or recorded material (cf. Opgenhaffen, 2021) might generally be more obviously paradata than embodied practices but the dividing line is anything but clear. Earlier in this volume we have reviewed a plethora of categories of information that rather uncontroversially qualify as paradata for data creators, users and managers alike. Making a field diary or a workflow diagram to work as paradata often requires relatively little effort.

By contrast, we have seen how other artefacts like photographs of archaeologists working in the field (known as 'action shots') have potential to function as paradata, but making this eventually happen requires more work to render the artefact informative in terms of paradata, of practices and processes. The conundrum is comparable to what Sacks (1972) discusses in the context of children's stories: how something eventually can become recognisable as a possible description; how something may sound or look like a description; and how some of them unfold as recognisable descriptions. This work is likely to require both intellectual labour to reconceptualise a thing as (potential) paradata, as well as material labour to (re)work the thing in a form that makes it enactable as paradata. Rather than being a simple act of picking up paradata and using it, it requires active information filtration work (Nielsen, 2015) and 'taking' (Huvila, 2022b) it in use.

We can consider two examples of the multiplicity of the making of paradata: writing narrative descriptions of a work process and sketching a diagram representing the same process. Writing a narrative description of a work process and making it to become (regarded as) paradata can be expected to happen often simultaneously, either when the work is being done or retrospectively after it has been completed. This is, however, only the first iteration of paradata in the making. The narrative can obviously be revised and rewritten. Such actions correspond with different degrees of (re)making the written-narrative-as-paradata. The making of that particular narrative happens again every time it is enacted, or 'taken' (Huvila, 2022a), in use as paradata to inform of the specific process or practice it is describing. This might happen once or several times in the course of time with the paradata being performed as distinct instances of information depending on when, where, for what purposes and by whom it is taken into use.

Another example discussed earlier in this volume is when a workflow diagram is drawn to prescribe a work process. It is not necessarily conceived as paradata but rather as a plan or suggestion of a possible future way of working. At this time, a thing is made whereas it is first transformed into paradata when it is appropriated in use as such. Borrowing the term of Taylor (1971), paradata is not a 'brute' form of data: its referentiality and meaning are in the eyes of its beholder.

Besides putting emphasis on the reality that paradata is never finished, treating paradata as being in-the-making also shifts attention to the complexity of the circumstances of how paradata comes into being. Following Latour (2001), rather than being constructed by a constructor, paradata can be considered as being *instaurated* in something Pickering (1995) has described as a thick of things that spans over time between the moment when paradata is made and when it is enacted (or taken) in use.

As Mathieu (2023) notes of agency, also paradata and its agency is always to different degrees prospective and retrospective in time, introspective in how it is looking into itself, respective of the norms of the domain where it operates, and suspective of potential risks. Similarly, for Latour (2011), this process of instauration works backwards from the moment it is enacted to the practice or process it is linked to, and back to the present. Instauration involves making a turn (Strathern, 2005a) from looking forward to turning backward. Paradata, the processes or practices it describes and the actors (or actants) involved all participate in its making.

In identifying and understanding what might work as paradata, it is important – borrowing again from Pickering (1995) – to understand the mangle of practice within which the making takes place. Instead of merely asking what is paradata and who is making it, making one's way through the mangle requires raising a range of additional questions. Several scholars including Star and Ruhleder (1994) and Engeström (1990) have suggested asking *when* something is instead of *what* it is. Further, it is relevant to ask where and in what context something is turned into paradata, why and for what purpose, as well as how it is made. In the following sections, we are turning our attention to these heuristics by inquiring into the temporalities (when), enactment (how) and goals (why) of paradata.

7.4.1 In the Continuum

In the previous section we followed the movement of paradata between being made and appropriated as such. Another axis of movement in the model and the life of paradata, is the one that pertains to the temporalities of the making of different kinds of paradata. Even if the earlier literature has sometimes focused on paradata as created during and sometimes after a practice or process is taking or has taken place (e.g., in survey research, Kreuter, 2013; Schenk and Reuß, 2024), the potential temporalities of what can be termed paradata are broader. This has been touched upon already to some extent in the earlier conceptualisations of the term as discussed in Chapter 2 and goes beyond a dichotomy of past and future practices and corresponding records (cf. Duranti and Thibodeau, 2006).

As suggested in Chapters 4 and 5 of this volume, studies of paradata creation practices and information that qualifies as paradata occur on a temporal scale. Paradata can be extended to engender time before (*prospective*) and after (*retrospective*) but also during (*in situ*) a process or practice being performed (Chapters 2 and 3; see Figure 7.3). Plans, protocols, handbooks and guidelines are prospective in how they are created before the practice or process they are describing takes place. At the same time, many such artefacts tend also to be prescriptive in how they are generated in order to stipulate forthcoming practices and processes.

At the moment of creation, they emerge as a form of potential information that eventually can be appropriated as paradata of an actual process or practice when it has taken place. In addition to prospective paradata, much paradata making takes place in situ at the moment when a process or practice is happening.

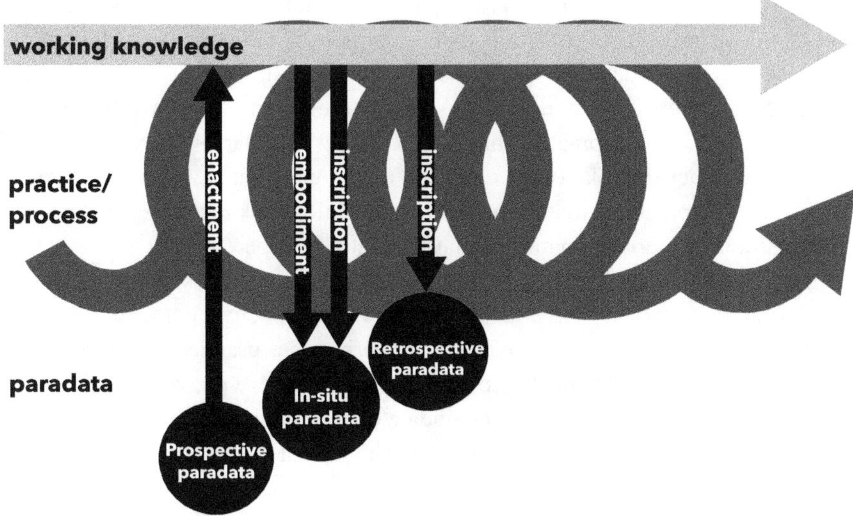

Figure 7.3 Prospective, in situ and retrospective paradata in the continuum.

As discussed earlier in this volume (Chapters 3 and 4), people write notes, keep diaries, take photos and record films – to mention only a few examples of how ongoing practices and processes can be documented. Finally, much paradata creation happens retrospectively. People write stories, draw diagrams and model previous practices and processes from memory. Sometimes paradata can be generated using various types of forensic methods (for possible methods cf. Duranti, 2009; Huvila, 2022a; Kirschenbaum et al., 2010), including metaphorically 'excavating' data, documentation and results (cf. Williams, 2011) of previous processes and practices to understand them better.

While paradata itself is not intrinsically prospective, in situ or retrospective, the moment of its making either before, during or after a particular process or practice is enacted will have implications for the resulting paradata and the limits to what it can be. This means that paradata, like a narrative (Tsoukas, 2013), is fundamentally asymmetrical. In situ observations differ from retrospective descriptions as clock time differs from narrative time (Ricoeur, 1980). An in situ account exhibits processes and practices differently than how they are remembered afterwards or conceived of beforehand.

While none of these types of accounts is necessarily better or worse than the others, the different conditions of envisioning future processes and practices (describing them while they are enacted versus attempting to recall them afterwards) mean that they differ in what they can achieve. As the methodological exposés in Chapters 4 and 5 show, documentation in situ might allow taking note of details that are impossible to remember afterwards. Retrospective paradata generation can, for its part, benefit from a richer contextual understanding unfolding through reflection and insights gained after the process or practice has taken place. Similarly to how Tsoukas (2013) describes the relation of rules and acting upon them, it is also conceivable that the paradata that is generated in situ as a practice is enacted or afterwards is richer than paradata that is created prospectively.

The fundamental difference between paradata that precedes action and those that parallel or follow it is that at the outset, prospective paradata becomes paradata first when it is enacted as a blueprint of a practice or process that actually takes place. Prospective paradata, for example, a prescriptive plan or a predetermined workflow, turns to paradata (proper) to an extent it corresponds with the practice that actually happened. The caveat is that the account might not be completely accurate as actions may have changed as the situation developed (cf. Huvila and Sköld, 2023). It may also not reflect current practices or be an accurate guide to future ones (cf. data management plans in Mannheimer, 2022). The part that is never followed becomes what can be termed a subjunctive description (cf. subjunctive provenance for Bettivia et al., 2023 cf. how they use the term of retrospectively identifying what could have been) of processes and practices that could have happened. It is paradata of a process or practice that never was.

The obvious merit of distinguishing prospective, in situ and retrospective paradata-making is in how the three categories correspond with the temporalities of the making of informative things. This has important implications for understanding the temporal limitations of their ability to act as paradata. Our judgement of their value as more or less accurate and sometimes subjunctive accounts, however, should not be judged solely in terms of temporality of their making, although this must inevitably influence our understanding of the potential utility as paradata. Therefore, rather than assuming that it is possible to say definitely that paradata should precede, parallel or follow practices, it is more fruitful to consider what different temporalities can contribute to our understanding of them.

7.5 Enactment of Paradata

Up to this point, this chapter has delved into the mechanisms of how paradata is generated and working knowledge turns to paradata through embodiment and inscription. Our understanding shifts when we view things from a different direction: one where paradata is *enacted* in practices and processes generating both action and working knowledge (Figure 7.2). In these enactments, paradata has agency. Comparably to how Duranti and Thibodeau (2006) distinguish instructive records from enabling ones, paradata can be *agentical* in how it provides agency to (re)enact processes and practices, learning, reuse of data and much more. It is *agentic* in how it itself has agency (cf. Hauser, 2024) to instruct, enable and influence processes and practices.

However, even if the idea of all paradata from the moment prospective paradata becomes actual paradata looks backward to a past practice, paradata functions forward (cf. Rheinberger, 2023). It should not be reified (Bachelard, 1949). Paradata cannot be used to exactly replicate the past. Paradata conveys something to someone in an unknown future from the perspective of the time when it was generated at the time when it is faced upon. It is not possible for paradata to explain or describe processes and practices from the perspective of the moment when they are put into practice in the future.

For the same reason, its quality can only be measured backwards. When it does what it is expected to do in the present in relation to a past process or practice, we can say that it is successful. This is impossible to determine in advance, neither in general nor in relation to a conceivable or unexpected future. The future-orientation means also that there are limits to what extent paradata can support what Ellingsen and Monteiro (2003) term 'rendering' both itself and practices comprehensible and actionable in an unknown future. Depending on the complexity of the processes and practices, enacting paradata might require varying amounts of repetition and experimentation (cf. Rheinberger, 2023) to succeed. Or it might fail. In addition to enacting versions of earlier practices and processes, its implementation is likely to create *collateral realities*, that is, practices and processes that are incidental and sometimes objectionable (Law, 2012).

The uncertain passage of prospective paradata from a potential account of what-is-to-be to a subjunctive or to a varying degree faithful and incomplete account of what happened in the past is illustrative not only of the fluid temporalities of paradata but also of how it informs of practices and processes in different situations. The shift of prospective paradata to a pre-scribed description shows how same artefacts can be enacted to prescribe and describe. Workflows and notebooks discussed in Chapter 4 illustrate the malleability of some approaches and genres of paradata.

The contextuality of paradata both in its making and its implementation means that it necessarily operates in and across multiple milieus that are in a constant state of flux. In terms of the Nonaka's notion of *ba* (Nonaka and Konno, 1998), a physical, virtual and mental place or space within which information becomes knowledge, paradata needs to operate in several *ba*s at the same time to function as their key constituent.

At the same time, different perspectives on how paradata is made and enacted are particular to these places or spaces, which are more than spaces or places where paradata operates but rather arrangements of everything involved in how paradata works. Following Stengers' (2005) theorising on *ecologies of practice*, they can be linked to broader constellations of sayings, doings and beings, sometimes termed *practice architectures* (Olsson et al., 2024) or *data cultures* in data practice-related research (Huvila and Sinnamon, 2025; Oliver et al., 2023). Each of the constellations comes with their respective ecologies of knowledge (Santos, 2016) – or perhaps, more aptly, of knowing – and 'styles of thinking and doing' (Hacking, 2012).

An ecology of practice, paradata comes with a potential to form a layer – a paradata practice – that compares to what Robichaud et al., (2004) have described as a meta-conversation. It is itself layered and forms a fractal (cf. Strathern, 2005b) of nested datasets of introspection. This is also reflected in Gant and Reilly's (2017) term 'peridata' and manifested in the many connected shapes and forms of provenance data involved in archival description models (Douglas, 2017).

Just as a meta-conversation does in a discursive sense, the layers of paradata practice generate and sustain an understanding of the practices and processes it informs about. The key relations in the paradata practice are the connections between paradata makers' and paradata users' practices and processes (cf. Robichaud et al., 2004).

Ideally, the continuum of practices and processes, paradata and paradata practice would be self-reproductive, autopoietic (cf. Maturana and Varela, 1980), without a need for additional explicit actions to sustain it. In practice, it is often far from being the case, as the frequent experience of a lack of process knowledge demonstrates. Rather than autopoietic, the continuum is sympoietic (as for Krippendorff, 2023), that is, dependent on its constituents, including paradata and its related practices and processes. It should also stay as an 'ecology of partial connections' (Stengers, 2018) in the sense that it remains open to critique and helps data making and use to change whenever data practices change.

As Hall (2007 [1973]) suggests of media production and consumption, paradata making and use also need to be studied in their own right. Knitting together a practice or process with paradata, whether it is a diagrammatic model or a narrative, requires curation in terms of discerning relevant readings of paradata and caring for it through repair and maintenance work (cf. Pink et al., 2018). Chapter 6 uncovers some of the intricacies of what keeping functioning paradata requires and how the management of paradata is intricately intertwined with how it is made to happen before, during and after its production.

7.6 Outcomes of Paradata

A relevant follow-up question to how paradata informs practices and processes is: what is paradata capable of achieving? The literature (e.g., Börjesson et al., 2022; Huvila and Sinnamon, 2022) and earlier chapters in this volume have described diverse practical desired outcomes of describing practices and processes. They include enabling and facilitating data-sharing, data reuse, reproducibility of research, verification of the outcomes and the quality of a particular process, and understanding a particular dataset and earlier interpretations based on the data. On a theoretical note, the question of paradata outcomes has somewhat different dimensions. Rather than being the outcome of what can be achieved *with* paradata, the fundamental question is what paradata itself might be capable of achieving.

With respect to what paradata is good for, independent of its context and domain, the common denominator is greater transparency (Sköld et al., 2022). What exactly is meant by transparency varies according to the ambitions of how much transparency is considered desirable or achievable. The introduction chapter of this book discusses some of the cultural and political underpinnings of the contemporary sense of urgency for particular kinds of transparencies, and how paradata stands out as a particularly opportune response to such aspirations.

The sometimes explicit but often unspoken ideal underpinning paradata discourse is an expectation of complete transparency. Entertaining the idea of what complete transparency and absolute opacity might entail in practice has obvious value as a thought experiment. It is also apparent that it is, as Bowker (2005) noted of raw data, both an oxymoron and a bad idea.

On one level, it is hardly desirable: both transparency and paradata are political and have a tendency to be unevenly beneficial to those it concerns. Actors with a lot of resources and uncontrolled power tend to prevail, and vulnerable and democratic systems lose (Adams, 2020). Even if limiting transparency is equally political and difficult, and has both positive and negative consequences, it is worth trying to imagine what Bates et al. (2023) term as meaningful and socially meaningful rather than total transparencies.

This is in part because total transparency is also hardly achievable in practice. Neither the continuum of working knowledge nor the circuit of generating and appropriating paradata can capture everything without any loss. The knowledge of practices is at best good enough and even as such, it is difficult to say how good it is and on what premises (cf. Huvila, 2012). Prospective forms of paradata might not correspond well with what eventually happens in the future, in situ generation of paradata cannot possibly capture everything, and retrospective paradata is subject both to amnesia and a false impression comparable to Bourdieu's (1986) biographical illusion, that is, representing the past as a deceptively coherent line of events leading to the present.

A parallel question to what type or level of transparency paradata might contribute is how paradata contributes to it. In this volume, we have rejected the objectivist aspiration of being able to turn implicit working knowledge to explicit paradata and back. Rather than achieving transparency by its presence (being), theorising paradata on a continuum (embodied, inscribed and enacted) suggests that it accomplishes transparency through a reciprocal enactment in the thick of things, incorporating not only paradata itself but also its makers and users.

As a form of prospective, contemporary or retrospective historical discourse (White, 1980) informative of processes and practices, paradata also both narrates by unfolding processes and practices, and narrativises by imposing on them a particular form either before, during, or afterwards. It has agency and capacity both to describe and create processes and practices. It does this through reification (Bachelard, 1949) or sedimentation (Husserl, 1989) of working knowledge on processes and practices (cf. Rheinberger, 2023).

As for design (cf. J. Bardzell and S. Bardzell, 2013; Dunne and Raby, 2001), forming a *lens*, paradata enables and facilitates critique and critical understanding of paradata generation practices as well as of the practices and processes themselves. For example, a description of a data collection episode can help to assess its validity, understand bias, and assess to what extent the generated data might be usable for addressing other research questions.

When operating as a form of data rather than a lens, paradata becomes a different type of a device: either affirmative of a particular process or practice, or a problem-solving one to address a certain predicament or obstacle. In this latter sense, as a form of data rather than a lens, the same description of the data collection episode operates as an *explanation*, either causal (description of a practice and/or process and evidence to support it) or teleological (what is the paradata's purpose). It does not *help* to understand as it does as a lens but it is expected to explain to an extent that conveys an understanding.

In practice, paradata can be mobilised as information to solve a problem but it can also serve an orientational purpose as a kind of domain information for a specific epistemic culture (cf. Korkeamäki et al., 2024). As an explanation (cf.

Berry, 2023), paradata faces a problem of how to represent practices and processes in such a way that make the explanations meaningful in relation to particular goals of both their producers and users.

As means to what Garfinkel has described as social groups' making of their activities 'visibly-rational-and-reportable-for-all-practical-purposes' (Garfinkel, 1967, p. vii) for themselves, paradata is meaningful in a very different sense than when its goal is to mitigate anxieties or to convey a comprehensive understanding of practices or processes. Explaining activities for insiders requires a different set of cues than explaining them to outsiders. If the goal of paradata is to mitigate external anxieties, explanation does not necessarily need to be complex, as providing a comprehensive understanding of a practice or process demands a lot of both the explanations and the sophistication of its intended 'user' (cf. Berry, 2023).

Further, while the usefulness of paradata as an explanation should not be underestimated, it might be an overtly unambitious aim to suggest that it suffices to make paradata helpful. It is reasonable to argue, as Berry (2023) demands of digital infrastructures, that the goal of comprehensive paradata should not be to function as mere explanations but rather to make processes and practices understandable. This is also what the paradata literature tends to insinuate. For example, heritage visualisation literature refers to 'intellectual transparency' as 'the provision of information, presented in any medium or format, to allow users to understand the nature and scope of a "knowledge claim" made by a computer-based visualization outcome.' (Bentkowska-Kafel et al., 2012, p. 262; also Forte and Pescarin, 2012). Paradata is expected to make it possible for users to understand instead of merely informing about the intellectual underpinnings of what is being described.

The multiplicity of the possible uses of paradata is, however, obviously also a part of the conundrum that makes it a wicked problem. Paradata might appear as a solvable problem as long as we only focus on either its makers or users but turns to a wicked one as soon as both communities' interests are brought in. A major challenge is to determine what is the 'information' (cf. Bentkowska-Kafel et al., 2012, p. 262) that 'allow[s] users to understand the nature and scope of a "knowledge claim"'.

While the general goals around what paradata is expected to achieve have a lot of similarities across domains, paradata research has made it apparent that the views on what exactly is needed to enable, reuse or verify the quality of outcomes differs between data creators and reusers and between different schools of data use. Research on data practices shows that from data creators' and users' perspectives, the aspects of data-related processes and practices that require explanation differ from each other (Lian et al., 2023; Thoegersen, 2018).

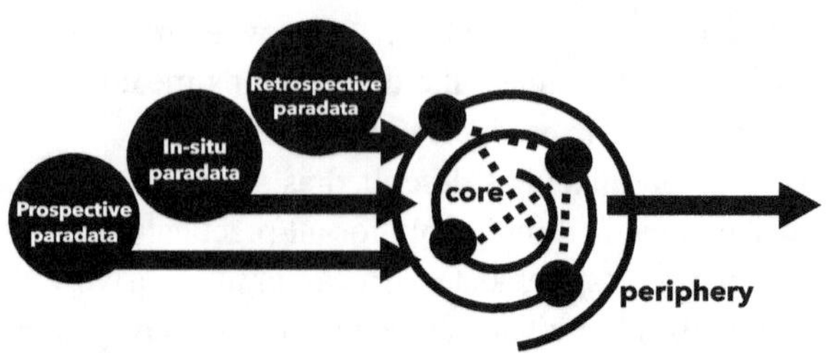

Figure 7.4 Paradata as a network.

Similarly, the requirements of paradata are different for a data user conducting statistical data analysis than for one engaged in ethnographic writing. In this respect, the key question is what kind of paradata is most useful and when.

However, as paradata does not merely exist but also does things, it can be meaningful even when it (invariably) fails to incorporate a complete understanding of a practice or process. There are other possibilities than everything or nothing. The network or meshwork-like nature of paradata (discussed earlier and illustrated in the Figures 7.1 and 7.4) means that paradata can indeed serve more than one purpose. The different things acting as such can open up parallel vistas to practices and processes and work in parallel tracks towards multiple goals instead of only one. Apart from simplifying and making something quantifiable, paradata can help to revive uncertainty and complexity.

However, while paradata may have no single goal, thinking of paradata as an explanation underlines the primacy of explaining and explanations rather than ensuring or even aiming at transparency, explaining or understanding. Explanations might not be able to make visible what Ingold (2022, p. 262) argues formal articulations fail to do, that is, to expose the *work* in practice or process, but they might still explain where and what the work is about.

Similarly crucial to making paradata meaningful is that it is clear what practices or processes paradata describes. The long temporal span from, multi-modality and broad contextual scope of paradata makes it difficult. In this respect, more important than worrying about the changes of vocabulary and connotations of individual descriptive terms is that the explanations in paradata remain clear in what they explain.

7.7 In the Borderlands: Implications for Paradata Practice

The diversity of the various things that can be appropriated as informative of processes and practices and the malleability of the ways they work means that the idea of paradata envisioned in this chapter and volume lends itself to multiple renditions. Even if the naive idea that paradata can act as a complete surrogate of a practice or process must be rejected, the concept of paradata still lends itself to be used in widely different epistemes. In a meticulously defined and parameterised context, a structured set of formally standardised paradata can operate as a script that holds together a perfect 'data supply chain' (cf. Spanaki et al., 2018). In an open world, practice and process information has a lot of friction, remains unfenced and refuses attempts to formalise it. Depending on the setting, paradata might take different forms and is interpreted differently. As a whole, it forms a network, or meshwork of practice. This meshwork operates from the outset of what Ettema and Glasser (1998) describe in the context of journalistic practices as *factual coherence*. Knowledge of a practice or process is formed through triangulating individual sources of information and looking at how they fit together and form a coherent whole, rather than relying on any one source.

Even if the meshwork of paradata lacks a definite form, it is radial and centred around an intersection of prototypical core elements in a given context and malleable non-prototypical periphery of elements at different conceptual distances from its nucleus (Figure 7.5). Core and peripheral elements and their value are interpreted according to the setting.

In laboratory research the core elements might consist of the documentation of instrumentation and formal steps of analyses whereas contextual information on those involved in the process and the laboratory itself could provide more peripheral but still valuable complements to the meshwork of paradata. In archaeological field documentation (Huvila et al., 2021), a textual, diagrammatic and photographic description of work process could form the core whereas citations to the literature might occupy a more peripheral position. In both cases, the formal core documentation might be considered as more authoritative as an account of laboratory or field practices for laboratory research and field archaeology. However, outside of such, to a varying extent

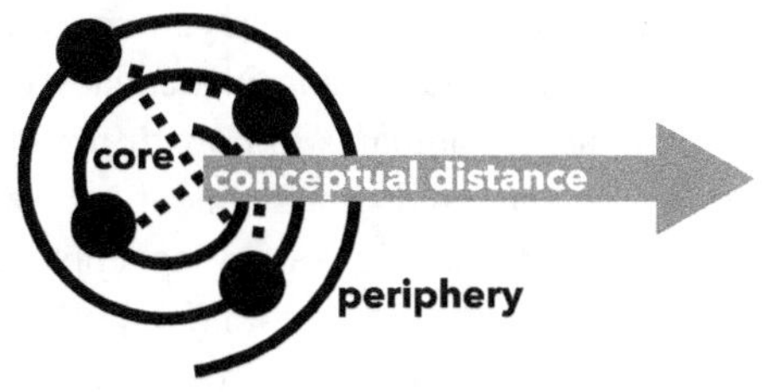

Figure 7.5 Core paradata forming a meshwork with peripheral elements at different conceptual distances from the core.

specific settings, the core and nucleus might shift radically. For a scholar of science and scholarship, the peripheral cues might form the core for understanding research practice and the formal accounts be much less interesting.

At the same time as being radial and centred, paradata exists somewhere between its makers and users, the situations where paradata emerges and is exploited, and ultimately between the practices and processes it refers to and within which it is used. Like the archaeological record according to Barrett (1988), paradata surfaces as a field of fragmentary traces of social practices and their relationships rather than as a clean narrative. In this space and state of in-betweenness, paradata engages in the boundary work of bringing people, practices and processes together and pushing them apart. Good paradata works as what Star (1988; 2010) terms as a boundary object.

Rather than forming an 'actuarial record' of a practice or process, paradata could do better acting – as Dallas has proposed of archaeological 3D visualisations building on Garfinkel (1967) – as an 'epistemic contract' between neighbouring contexts and communities. It needs to remain liminal and worked to stay as such, somewhere between tacit and explicable or specified (cf. Ingold, 2022, p. 231–232) to be effective across the contexts and communities where it can play a meaningful role.

Paradata is also characterised what Currie (2023) describes in his study of historiography as the difference between narratives and chronology. Currie (2023) notes that two parties might agree on chronology, that is, the sequence of certain historical events but at the same time find disagreement between narratives of what they mean and what is their significance and relation to other historical events. While the typical primary concern of knowledge organisation tends to be on achieving what might be compared to getting the chronology straight, paradata comes with an opportunity to focus on what can be likened to narratives, that is, providing context to an extent that makes it informative of complex practices and processes. The comparison to chronologies and narratives and Currie's (2023) observation that it is possible to find agreement between historical chronologies of events but simultaneously disagreement between historical narratives of them can be similarly transposed to elaborate on the paradoxical sufficiency and inadequacy of parallel forms of paradata in specific situations. It compares to how different forms of paradata can at the same time be adequate and in agreement on the level of technical details but at the same time inadequate in conveying a practice or process in its full complexity for different individuals or communities.

Thinking of paradata from the outset of the reference model residing in the borderlands helps also to explicate its impact in practice across the information field. Paradata has apparent value for advancing the *ideals of the open movement* including open science, open data and knowledge. However, it is equally obvious that the transparency and openness paradata generates is not unconditional and absolute in how it emanates from documentation or availability of information. Thinking back how paradata acts (cf. Mathieu, 2023), to mediate across the epistemic borderlines of practice architectures or data cultures in the time-space of practices and processes, paradata needs to look backwards and forwards, it needs be introspective and extrovert – or perhaps 'extrospective' – of itself and its context, respective of the norms of the domains where it operates, and conscious of potential risks. Accordingly, when working with paradata, it is vital to be serious about its potential desirable and undesirable consequences.

Paradata is a strong candidate to be one of the central keywords of the contemporary datafied experience. Data can hardly be called open if little or nothing is known about the processes and practices through which it came into being and through which it has been processed and used. The same also applies to 'data quality', which can be imagined to exist if the underpinning data remain concealed. The presence of paradata in the broad meaning of how the concept is used in this volume also forms a requisite to making data findable, accessible, interoperable and reusable (FAIR as for Wilkinson et al, 2016). This can only happen if it can accommodate the diversity of epistemes where data originates and is used. The crux of FAIRness and the necessary paradata to support is to acknowledge that FAIRness is not universal. If a dataset is FAIR for someone, it is probably MEAN, or miscellaneous, exceptional, arbitrary, and nonconformist, for many others (Huvila, 2017).

While paradata is indispensable both as a lens for dealing in practice with large data quantities, or big data, its most significant implication is to make and keep visible how big data really is an oxymoron. From this perspective, it has the potential to affect transformative change in *research practice* across disciplines.

For researchers using existing datasets, paradata opens up opportunities to better understand the processes and practices that data is a part of. It is not only a question of provenance (i.e. where data comes from) but also of a comprehensive understanding of the practices and processes as an element of what the data is. For researchers creating data for preservation, a major challenge and opportunity is to embrace the different means of making and keeping paradata to facilitate future enactment of practices.

Rather than thinking about paradata as an auxiliary attachment, paradata should rather be seen as a parallel to the results of a study, and a process of conveying knowledge and understanding rather than a mere output. It should not be generated and preserved only to assure others of the validity and relevance of the results but also to provide ingredients for generating a biography of the process itself for later use.

Being in the borderlands has both its advantages and its risks. A major advantage comes with being in the middle of complex circumstances. By being there, paradata both simplifies and complicates understanding practices and processes at the same time. Like all data in general (Mejias, 2023), it facilitates control by generating differences that are exploitable in both traversing and erecting boundaries.

However, working with paradata in the borderlands also leads to higher transaction costs (Williamson, 1981) compared to having the necessary working knowledge. Generating, capturing and keeping but also putting para-data to use requires time, effort and resources. This is especially true when working simultaneously with formal and informal paradata that operate on fundamentally different terms. One question is how to design paradata while keeping transaction costs acceptable. In this respect, paradata has implications for the *design of knowledge organisation systems*. Automation and techno-logical tools can mitigate some of the costs, for example, by providing and helping to maintain an overview of available information and keeping track of what a user has already consulted.

In contrast, information technologies generally struggle to support complex sociomaterial practices (Ellingsen and Monteiro, 2003). Formalisation can make paradata more manageable but it also makes it fixed, 'sanitized and re-represented' (Batist, 2023, p. 8) rendering invisible its instability and precar-iousness (Rheinberger, 2023) as was discussed in the Chapter 6. Formal paradata ascribes to the contradiction raised by Ingold that fixed and formally articulated working knowledge is that which is silent, static and inexplicable – in effect tacit – whereas working knowledge is 'turbulent and sometimes noisy' (Ingold, 2022, p. 232). While fixity of formal and structured paradata can help to overcome certain barriers to knowing, the translation from fluid to structured silences makes inexplicable many aspects of the practices and processes it documents.

Stories and other informal forms of paradata have different qualities. As Ingold argues, they 'allow experts to tell what they know *without* specify-ing it' (Ingold, 2022, p. 233) (emphasis in the original). Further on at the opposite end of the scale from structured standardised descriptions, like embodied craft, also processes and practices are themselves another 'a way of telling' (Ingold, 2022, p. 234) in how they convey and sustain working knowledge as a part of their existence.

As a result of the respective advantages and shortcomings of individual varieties of paradata, one form of paradata is seldom enough. Even seemingly complete 'recipes' and scripted workflows (Gupta, 2020) miss a lot of details. Both Duranti and Thibodeau (2006) and Ingold (2022) discuss the example of a music score and its relation to practice to illustrate the gap in between. Through a paradata lens, the score does rather uncontroversially qualify as paradata but what it does is that it 'specifies the elements of a completed work and shows how they articulate. Moreover it is silent' (Ingold, 2022, p. 250). A score is not enough to reproduce a performance. Both complementary inscriptions, embodiments and working knowledge is needed before a score can be enacted to music. They all are mobile in their particular ways.

Ingold contrasts 'computational' algorithms to 'ambulatory' practices (Ingold, 2022, p. 283) but it is easy to conceive a plethora of additional means in which the different forms of paradata discussed throughout the pages of this volume are mobile in their own terms. This poses an obvious challenge for *information systems design and information and knowledge management.* If all paradata is structured and standardised, much of the critical information is bound to disappear.

Rather than suggesting that the aim of thinking and working with paradata is to replace living practices and processes with embodiments and inscriptions, its aim should perhaps be seen as appreciating them as they are and keeping them apart but in correspondence with each other allowing us, as Feinberg suggests, to 'live with referential ambiguities' (Feinberg, 2022, p. 91). As she continues, data is too often thought of in terms of surrogates rather than 'networks, collectives, or other configurations of thingness' (Feinberg, 2022, p. 92). Information systems designed for paradata should not try to suppress one with the other but use formal means to provide access to and keep track of the miscellaneity of embodiments and inscriptions of practices and processes bringing together the human and systems-oriented approaches to information and knowledge management (cf. Huvila et al., 2023). Instead of transformative boundary crossings where practices and processes change shape, paradata is more likely to thrive when left meandering in the borderlands between the practices and processes inscribed or embodied and enacted. In a very fundamental sense, paradata should remain as much a question as an answer.

7.8 Conclusions

The purpose of this chapter has been to theorise and stage a reference model for paradata and how it is practised. Unlike in much of the earlier literature, the model presented here puts forward an understanding of paradata as a parallel mode of being where the practices and processes inscribe and embody. It goes side by side with working knowledge in practices and processes that themselves engender paradata through embodiment and acts of inscription. Paradata turns back to working knowledge through appropriation and through enactment to practices and processes. Paradata is perpetually in the making on a continuum, and actualises as instances only through temporal intersections with the practices and processes it causes to converge. In parallel to being processual, consisting of interlinked types of information connected to each other, paradata forms a network-like meshwork where the whole is larger than its individual constituents.

In contrast to how paradata is typically defined as a means to provide transparency, this chapter has problematised that idea, suggesting that it might instead be more fruitful to approach it in terms of explanations, acknowledging at the same time its spanning over the divide between practices and processes and knowledge thereof.

Rather than taking paradata as a script or comprehensive account of a practice or process, it can be more fruitful to leave it in the borderlands between doings and descriptions. Being there it can retain its malleability and continue to refer in both conceptual and practical sense to a much broader range of things (appropriable informative of practices and processes) than when essentialised as a specific category of information. Rather than using the concept of paradata to claim that knowing about practices and processes is a solvable, straightforward question, paradata does better by foregrounding the opposite: the unbearable complexity of knowing in practice.

References

Adams Rachel (2020). *Transparency*. London: Routledge.

Bachelard Gaston (1949). *Le Rationalisme Appliqué*. Paris: Presses Universitaires de France.

Baker Malcolm (2017). Epilogue: Making and knowing, then and now. In Smith Pamela H., Meyers Amy R. W. and Cook Harold John (eds.), *Ways of Making and Knowing: The Material Culture of Empirical Knowledge*. Ann Arbor: University of Michigan Press, 405–413.

Bardzell Jeffrey and Bardzell Shaowen (2013). What is 'critical' about critical design? In *Proceedings of the SIGCHI Conference on Human Factors in Computing Systems*. CHI 13. New York: ACM, 3297–3306.

Barrett John C. (1988). Fields of discourse: Reconstituting a social archaeology. *Critique of Anthropology* 7(3), 5–16.

Bates Jo et al. (2023). Socially meaningful transparency in data-based systems: Reflections and proposals from practice. *Journal of Documentation* 80(1), 54–72.

Bates Marcia J. (2006). Fundamental forms of information. *Journal of the American Society for Information Science and Technology* 57(8), 1033–1045.

Batist Zachary (2023). *Archaeological Data Work as Continuous and Collaborative Practice*. PhD thesis. Toronto: University of Toronto.

Bentkowska-Kafel Anna, Denard Hugh and Baker Drew (eds.), (2012). *Paradata and Transparency in Virtual Heritage*. Farnham: Ashgate.

Berry David M. (2023). The explainability turn. *Digital Humanities Quarterly* 017(2). ISSN: 1938-4122.

Bettivia Rhiannon, Cheng Yi-Yun and Gryk Michael (2023). What does provenance LACK: How retrospective and prospective met the subjunctive. In Sserwanga Isaac et al. (eds.), *Information for a Better World: Normality, Virtuality, Physicality, Inclusivity*. Vol. 13972. Cham: Springer Nature Switzerland, 74–82.

Börjesson Lisa, Huvila Isto and Sköld Olle (2022). Information needs on research data creation. *Information Research* 27. Special Issue, isic2208.

Börjesson Lisa, Sköld Olle et al. (2022). Re-purposing excavation database content as paradata: An explorative analysis of paradata identification challenges and opportunities. *KULA: Knowledge Creation, Dissemination, and Preservation Studies* 6(3), 1–18.

Bourdieu Pierre (1986). L'illusion biographique. *Actes de la Recherche en Sciences Sociales* 62(1), 69–72.

Bowker Geoffrey C. (2005). *Memory Practices in the Sciences*. Cambridge, MA: MIT Press.

Buckland Michael (2024). Revisiting Robert Pagès: Documents and culture. *Proceedings from the Document Academy* 10(2).

Canfield Michael R. et al. (2011). *Field Notes on Science and Nature*. Cambridge, MA: Harvard University Press.

Currie A. (2023). Narratives, events & monotremes: The philosophy of history in practice. *Journal of the Philosophy of History*, 17(2), 265–287.

Davet Jeremy, Hamidzadeh Babak and Franks Patricia (2023). Archivist in the machine: Paradata for AI-based automation in the archives. *Archival Science* 23(2), 275–295.

Day Ronald (2024). Powerful particulars as 'autodocuments' in documentality. *Proceedings from the Document Academy* 10(2).

Dervin Brenda (1999). On studying information seeking methodologically: The implications of connecting metatheory to method. *Information Processing and Management* 35(6), 727–750.

Douglas J. (2017). Origins and beyond: The ongoing evolution of archival ideas about provenance. In Macneil H. and Eastwood T. (eds.), *Currents of Archival Thinking*. Libraries Unlimited, 25–52.

Dunne Anthony and Raby Fiona (2001). *Design Noir: The Secret Life of Electronic Objects*. Basel, Switzerland : London: Birkhuser ; August Media Ltd.

Duranti Luciana (2009). From digital diplomatics to digital records forensics. *Archivaria* 68.Fall, 39–66.

Duranti Luciana and Thibodeau Kenneth (2006). The concept of record in interactive, experiential and dynamic environments: The view of InterPARES. *Archival Science* 6(1), 13–68.

Ellingsen G. and Monteiro E. (2003). Mechanisms for producing a working knowledge: Enacting, orchestrating and organizing. *Information and Organization* 13(3), 203–229.

Engeström Yrjö (1990). When is a tool? In *Learning, Working and Imagining, Twelve Studies in Activity Theory*. Helsinki: Orienta-Konsultit Oy, 171–195.

Ettema J. S. and Glasser T. L. (1998). *Custodians of Conscience: Investigative Journalism and Public Virtue*. Columbia University Press.

Feinberg Melanie (2022). *Everyday Adventures with Unruly Data*. Cambridge, MA: MIT Press.

Ferraris Maurizio (2014). *Documentalità: Perché è necessario lasciar tracce*. Gius: Laterza & Figli Spa.

Forte Maurizio and Pescarin Sofia (2012). Behaviours, interactions and affordances in virtual archaeology. In Bentkowska-Kafel Anna, Denard Hugh and Baker Drew. (eds.), *Paradata and Transparency in Virtual Heritage*. Farnham: Ashgate, 189–201.

Gant Stefan and Reilly Paul (2017). Different expressions of the same mode: A recent dialogue between archaeological and contemporary drawing practices. *Journal of Visual Art Practice* 17(1), 100–120.

Garfinkel Harold (1967). *Studies in Ethnomethodology*. Englewood Cliffs, N.J.: Prentice-Hall.

Golder Scott and Huberman Bernardo A. (2006). Usage patterns of collaborative tagging systems. *Journal of Information Science* 32(2), 198–208.

Gupta Neha (2020). Preparing archaeological data for spatial analysis. In Gillings Mark, Hacıgüzeller Piraye and Lock Gary. *Archaeological Spatial Analysis: A Methodological Guide*. 1st ed. Routledge, 17–40.

Hacking Ian (2012). 'Language, truth and reason' 30 years later. *Studies in History and Philosophy of Science Part A. Part Special Issue: Styles of Thinking* 43(4), 599–609.

Hall S. (2007 [1973]). Encoding and decoding in the television discourse. In Gray A., Campbell J., Erickson M., Hanson S. and Wood H. (eds.), *CCCS Selected Working Papers*. Routledge, 402–414.

Handzic Meliha (2004). *Knowledge Management: Through the Technology Glass*. Singapore: World Scientific.

Hartley Jannie Møller and Schjøtt Anna (2023). Imagining publics through emerging technologies. In Møller Hartley Jannie, Sørensen Jannick Kirk and Mathieu David (eds.), *DataPublics: The Construction of Publics in Datafied Democracies*. Bristol: Bristol University Press, 99–120.

Hauser Elliott (2024). Making-to-be: Documents, facta, and material-discursive agency. *Proceedings from the Document Academy* 10(2).

Husserl Edmund (1989). The origin of geometry. In Derrida Jacques (ed.), *Edmund Husserl's Origin of Geometry, an Introduction*. Lincoln: University of Nebraska Press, 157–180.

Huvila Isto (2012). *Information services and digital literacy: In Search of the Boundaries of Knowing*. Oxford: Chandos.

Huvila Isto (2017). Being FAIR When Archaeological Information Is MEAN: Miscellaneous, Exceptional, Arbitrary, Nonconformist. *Presentation at the Centre for Digital Heritage Conference 2017, Leiden June 14–16, 2017*.

Huvila Isto (2019). Authoring social reality with documents: From authorship of documents and documentary boundary objects to practical authorship. *Journal of Documentation* 75(1), 44–61.

Huvila Isto (2022a). Improving the usefulness of research data with better paradata. *Open Information Science* 6(1), 28–48.

Huvila Isto (2022b). Making and taking information. *JASIST* 73(4), 528–541.

Huvila I., Andersson L., Fulton C., Haider J. and Harviainen J. T. (2023b). Managing information gaps and non-information. *Proceedings of the Association for Information Science and Technology*, 60(1), 793–798. https://doi.org/10.1002/pra2.863

Huvila I., Börjesson L. and Sköld O. (2022). Archaeological information-making activities according to field reports. *Library & Information Science Research*, *44*(3), 101171. https://doi.org/10.1016/j.lisr.2022.101171

Huvila Isto and Sinnamon Luanne (2022). Sharing research design, methods and process information in and out of academia. *Proceedings of the Association for Information Science and Technology* 59(1), 132–144.

Huvila Isto and Sinnamon Luanne (2024). When data sharing is an answer and when (often) it is not: Acknowledging data-driven, non-data, and data-decentered cultures. *Journal of the Association for Information Science and Technology*, 75(13), 1515–1530.https://doi.org/10.1002/asi.24957

Huvila Isto and Sköld Olle (2023). A fieldwork manual as a regulatory device: Instructing, prescribing and describing documentation work. *Journal of Information Science*, p. 01655515231203506.

Huvila Isto, Sköld Olle and Andersson Lisa (2023a). Knowing-in-practice, its traces and ingredients. In Cozza Michela and Gherardi Silvia (eds.), *The Posthumanist Epistemology of Practice Theory: Re-imagining Method in Organization Studies and Beyond*. Cham: Palgrave MacMillan, 37–69.

Huvila Isto, Sköld Olle and Börjesson Lisa (2021). Documenting information making in archaeological field reports. *Journal of Documentation* 77(5), 1107–1127.

Ingold Tim (2022). *Imagining for Real: Essays on Creation, Attention and Correspondence*. Abingdon: Routledge.

Jones, Kevin and Bunn Jenny (2024). Mapping accessions to repositories data: A case study in paradata. In Huvila Isto, Andersson Lisa and Sköld Olle (eds.), *Perspectives on Paradata: Research and Practice of Documenting Data Processes. Knowledge Management and Organizational Learning*. Cham: Springer.

Kirschenbaum Matthew G., Ovenden Richard and Redwine Gabriela (2010). *Digital Forensics and Born-Digital Content in Cultural Heritage Collections*. Tech. rep. Washington, DC: CLIR.

Korkeamäki Laura, Keskustalo Heikki and Kumpulainen Sanna (2024). Types of Domain and Task-solving Information in Media Scholars' Data Interaction. *Journal of the Association for Information Science and Technology*, asi.24863.

Kowalczyk Stacy and Shankar Kalpana (2011). Data sharing in the sciences. *ARIST* 45(1), 247–294.

Kreuter Frauke (2013). Improving Surveys with Paradata: Introduction. In Kreuter Frauke (ed.), *Improving Surveys with Paradata Analytic Uses of Process Information*. Hoboken, NJ: Wiley, 1–9.

Krippendorff Klaus (2023). A critical cybernetics. *Constructivist Foundations* 19(1), 82–93.

Latour Bruno (1987). *Science in Action: How to Follow Scientists and Engineers through Society*. Cambridge, MA: Harvard University Press.

Latour Bruno (2009). *The Making of Law: An Ethnography of the Conseil d'Etat*. Oxford: Polity Press.

Latour Bruno (2011). Reflections on Etienne Souriau's Les différents modes d'existence. In Harman Graham, Bryant Levi and Srnicek Nick (eds.), *The Speculative Turn: Continental Materialism and Realism*. Melbourne: re.press, 304–333.

Law John (2012). Collateral realities. In Domínguez Rubio Fernando and Baert Patrick (eds.), *The Politics of Knowledge*. London: Routledge, 156–178.

Lian Zhiying, Oliver Gillian and Chen Yi (2023). Genres of online COVID-19 information and government information culture: A comparative case study. *Library & Information Science Research* 45(4), 101263.

Lund N. W. (2024). *Introduction to Documentation Studies*. Facet.

Mannheimer Sara (2022). Data Curation for Qualitative Data Reuse and Big Social Research. PhD Thesis. Humboldt-Universität zu Berlin.

Mathieu David (2023). Deconstructing the notion of algorithmic control over datapublics. In Møller Hartley Jannie, Sørensen Jannick Kirk and Mathieu David (eds.), *DataPublics: The Construction of Publics in Datafied Democracies*. Bristol: Bristol University Press, 27–48.

Maturana Humberto R. and Varela Francisco J. (1980). *Autopoiesis and Cognition : The Realization of the Living*. Dordrecht: Reidel.

Mayernik Matthew S. (2020). Metadata. *Knowledge Organization* 47(8), 696–713.

Mejias Ulises A. (2023). Notes on the Historiography of Data Colonialism. In Filimowicz Michael (ed.), *Decolonizing Data: Algorithms and Society*. London: Routledge, 1–14.

Nielsen Karen Dam (2015). Involving patients with e-health: The dialogic dynamics of information filtration work. *Science & Technology Studies* 28(2), 29–52.

Nonaka Ikujiro and Konno Noboru (1998). The concept of 'ba': Building a foundation for knowledge creation. *California Management Review* 40(3), 40–54.

Ogden C. K. and Richards I. A. (1930). *The Meaning Of Meaning*. London: Kegan Paul, Trench, Trubner.

Oliver Gillian et al. (2023). Understanding data culture/s: Influences, activities, and initiatives. *Annual Review of Information Science and Technology* 75(3), 201–214.

Olsson Michael, Sköld Olle and Andersson Lisa (2024). Layers Upon Layers: Data Reuse Challenges in Archaeological Contexts. In *Proceedings of the ISIC 2024*.

Opgenhaffen Loes (2021). Visualizing archaeologists: A reflexive history of visualization practice in archaeology. *Open Archaeology* 7(1), 353–377.

Packalén Saara and Henttonen Pekka (2024). Adding paradata about records processes via information control plans. In Huvila Isto, Andersson Lisa and Sköld Olle (eds.), *Perspectives on Paradata: Research and Practice of Documenting Data Processes. Knowledge Management and Organizational Learning*. Cham: Springer.

Pagès Robert ([1948] 2021). Transformations documentaires et milieu culturel. *Proceedings from the Document Academy* 8(1), Article 3.

Parry Kyle (2023). Metadata is not data about data. In Filimowicz Michael (ed.), *Decolonizing Data: Algorithms and Society*. London: Routledge, 15–33.

Pickering Andrew (1995). *The Mangle of Practice: Time, Agency, and Science.* Chicago: University of Chicago Press.

Pink Sarah et al. (2018). Broken data: Conceptualising data in an emerging world. *Big Data & Society* 5(1), p. 2053951717753228.

Polanyi Michael (1998). *Personal Knowledge.* London: Routledge.

Rheinberger Hans-Jörg (2023). *Split and Splice: A Phenomenology of Experimentation.* Chicago: University of Chicago Press.

Ricoeur Paul (1980). Narrative time. *Critical Inquiry* 7(1), 169–190.

Robichaud Daniel, Giroux Hélène and Taylor James R. (2004). The metaconversation: The recursive property of language as a key to organizing. *Academy of Management Review* 29(4), 617–634.

Sacks Harvey (1972). On the analyzability of stories by children. In Gumperz John J. and Hymes Dell (eds.), *Directions in Sociolinguistics: The Ethnography of Communication.* New York: Rinehart & Winston, 325–345.

Santos Boaventura de Sousa (2016). *Epistemologies of the South: Justice against Epistemicide.* London: Routledge.

Schenk Patrick Oliver and Reuß Simone (2024). Paradata in surveys. In Huvila Isto, Andersson Lisa and Sköld Olle (eds.), *Perspectives on Paradata: Research and Practice of Documenting Data Processes.* Knowledge Management and Organizational Learning. Cham: Springer.

Sköld O., Börjesson L. and Huvila I. (2022). Interrogating paradata. *Information Research. Proceedings of the 11th International Conference on Conceptions of Library and Information Science, Oslo Metropolitan University, May 29 - June 1, 2022*, 27(Special Issue), paper colis2206.

Spanaki Konstantina et al. (2018). Data supply chain (DSC): Research synthesis and future directions. *International Journal of Production Research* 56(3), 4447–4466.

Star Susan Leigh (1988). The Structure of Ill-Structured Solutions: Heterogeneous Problem-Solving, Boundary Objects and Distributed Artificial *Intelligence. In Proceedings of the 8th AAAI Workshop on Distributed Artificial Intelligence, Technical Report, Department of Computer Science, University of Southern California.* Los Angeles, CA, 37–54.

Star Susan Leigh (2010). This is not a boundary object: Reflections on the origin of a concept. *Science, Technology & Human Values* 35(5), 601–617.

Star Susan Leigh and Ruhleder Karen (1994). Steps towards an Ecology of Infrastructure: Complex Problems in Design and Access for Large-Scale Collaborative *Systems. In CSCW'94: Proceedings of the 1994 ACM Conference on Computer Supported Cooperative Work.* New York: ACM Press, 253–264.

Stengers Isabelle (2005). Introductory notes on an ecology of practices. *Cultural Studies Review* 11(1), 183–196.

Stengers Isabelle (2018). *Another Science Is Possible: A Manifesto for Slow Science.* Cambridge: Polity.

Strathern Marilyn (2005a). Experiments in interdisciplinarity. *Social Anthropology* 13(1), 75–90.

Strathern Marilyn (2005b). *Kinship, Law and the Unexpected: Relatives Are Always a Surprise.* New York: Cambridge University Press.

Taylor Charles (1971). Interpretation and the sciences of man. *The Review of Metaphysics* 25(1), 3–51.

Thoegersen Jennifer L. (2018). 'Yeah, I guess that's data': Data practices and conceptions among humanities faculty. *portal: Libraries and the Academy* 18(3), 491–504.

Tsoukas Haridimos (2013). Organization as chaosmos. In Robichaud Daniel (ed.), *Organization and Organizing*. London: Routledge, 52–65.

Vetter Jeremy (2016). *Field Life: Science in the American West during the Railroad Era*. Pittsburgh: University of Pittsburgh Press.

White Hayden (1980). The value of narrativity in the representation of reality. *Critical Inquiry* 7(1), 5–27.

Wilkinson M. D. et al. (2016). The FAIR guiding principles for scientific data management and stewardship. *Scientific Data*, *3*, 160018. https://doi.org/10.1038/sdata.2016.18

Williams Graham (2011). *Data Mining with Rattle and R: The Art of Excavating Data for Knowledge Discovery*. New York: Springer.

Williamson Oliver E. (1981). The economics of organization: The transaction cost approach. *American Journal of Sociology* 87(3), 548–577.

Wittgenstein Ludwig (1969). *On certainty*. Oxford: Blackwell.

8

Future Directions

Making Paradata Matter

Isto Huvila

8.1 Introduction

The starting point for this volume has been to demonstrate that paradata matters. At the same time, its aim has been to engage in a proper discussion on how and when it does so. However, as the previous chapters have demonstrated, the significance of paradata is not given and it can matter in different ways to different communities. In the final chapter of this volume, we are revisiting some of our original assumptions, considering conceptual and practical implications of paradata, and discussing directions for practical work with paradata, as well as future research on paradata, data-related practices and processes.

After a book-length examination, a fundamental question to ask is to what extent the concept of paradata really is meaningful and productive. Whilst not without its limitations, we see multiple theoretical and practical benefits in embracing it. In the earlier literature, paradata has often been portrayed as a new complementary data type and an artefact that solves the problems of understanding data-related decisions, practices, processes and their underpinnings. By contrast, our perspective on paradata has been less definite. Paradata is and remains a wicked problem in itself rather than an easy solution. It is not enough to acknowledge in passing that it is necessary to 'add paradata' to make data intelligible. Paradata deserves to be taken seriously.

In both theory and practice, we find that the concept of paradata and engaging with its applications is helpful in how it directs attention to practices and processes rather than attributes of data. As outlined in the first two chapters of this volume, engaging with paradata can benefit working with data in many ways, including:

- understandability
- accessibility
- interoperability
- trustworthiness
- reusability and reuse of data
- keeping track of its ownership
- improving the reproducibility of research

It can also help to open the black box of domain-specific practices and processes to transdisciplinary (Huvila, 2022) and non-specialist audiences (cf. Eichner et al., 2024) that are often excluded from the intricate working knowledge embedded in human practices.

At the same time, however, it also makes it increasingly evident that none of the anticipated outcomes of paradata are simple and straightforward to achieve, or uncontroversial in practice. Nothing is universally FAIR (Wilkinson et al., 2016) or MEAN (Huvila, 2017) and paradata cannot make them that. It can, however, function as a key ingredient in contributing to these goals while at the same time reminding and exposing in detail why, how, and to what extent they have been accomplished or remain out of reach.

8.2 Instrument of Knowledge Organisation

After stressing the limits and complexity of paradata and the need to take it seriously, we must ask how exactly it can take us closer to reaching the many expectations bestowed upon it. Even if the simplistic idea of paradata as a new form of auxiliary data is best abandoned, paradata is inherently a concept that belongs to the domain of knowledge organisation.

In a theoretical sense, rather than being a quick remedy, paradata can be helpful in directing attention to the diversity of means of how to inform and be informed about how data is created, managed and used, along with the underpinnings of these endeavours. As a concept, paradata has enough leeway to be complementary rather than an overlapping or a redundant notion. Compared to metadata, as conceptualised here, the object and objective of documentation are different with paradata. In a broad sense, both metadata and paradata are 'potentially informative' (Pomerantz, 2015, p. 26) and express 'ideas, feelings, emotions, and values' (Carbajal, 2021, p. 102). However, whereas metadata is typically, if not exclusively, conceptualised as being informative of resources, data or objects, the kernel of paradata is elsewhere. Its focal point of paradata is on shedding light on practices, processes and their underpinnings.

Paradata deserves to be saved from what Huggett criticises as a typical focus on technical aspect and 'digital background to digital data' (Huggett, 2022) rather than embracing it as a much broader and inclusive concept covering the whole entirety of practice and process information. Paradata engages primarily with other types of resources that are searched for and used in different ways. While metadata is conventionally, if not necessarily, expressed in words (cf. Carbajal, 2021), the brief overview of the diversity of expressions of paradata in Chapter 3 and the approaches to engage with paradata in Chapters 4–6 demonstrate how paradata is expressed and accessed in different terms than metadata. Even if a part of paradata might be structured and available for searching and retrieving like formal metadata and inscribed as metadata, much of what we conceive as paradata roams far beyond the scope of what is conventionally understood as metadata.

Rather than necessarily being created for the purpose, paradata is often discovered in existing material even if it is subsequently modified to fit its new purpose. While even informal metadata often retains a degree of formality, paradata is formal only occasionally and partially. Leveraging and combining the plethora of methods people use to find, access, use, make and manage paradata also presents a very different type of knowledge organisation challenge than those associated with using metadata. Their outcomes have differences, too. While both paradata and metadata are (potentially) informative, paradata is also very much performative, not only in theory but also in practice, in how it is enacted.

This multiplicity of paradata is critical to consider when it is put to work as an instrument of organising knowledge. Rather than assuming paradata to be a simple technique to organise knowledge, it warrants being approached as a form of *critical practice*. From this perspective (cf. Agre, 1997; Van Geenen et al., 2024), critique is not about disapproval or pessimism but about thinking and moving forward to make the most out of paradata both in theory and in practice.

While it can be tempting to suggest documenting everything, it is not feasible and most of the time it is impossible, as the examples in previous chapters have underlined. Trying to inscribe and collect too much can be highly detrimental in how it easily constructs a new facade very different from how the practices and processes unfolded in the first place. It both conceals and increases complexity, and takes time from other tasks. However, there are also sometimes small pieces of information that can truly make a difference and need to be inscribed to avoid losing them. Identifying them can be as difficult as determining where the fine line between enough and too much should be drawn. They both require a thorough understanding of the complex meshwork of paradata as a whole and how this meshwork links to the complex ecology of practices and processes it documents.

The flip-side of seeking to avoid increasing the complexity of documentation is that its opposite can be equally detrimental. Conscious and unconscious data cleaning through harmonisation, standardisation and selective preservation can be controversial. While it might make data more manageable, help to save resources (cf. Pasquetto et al., 2017), and cast an aura of reliability, professionalism and quality, it runs a major risk of depriving it of much of its richness. A better approach is to make the complexity of data, practices and processes visible and to provide strategies and tools for dealing with it.

With paradata, the most critical knowledge organisation task is not to document everything or to provide meticulous instructions on how to reconstruct practices in the future. Rather, it is to provide an overview of all available traces and ingredients to help to keep track of their intersections. The goal should not be to attempt to provide direct shortcuts and minimise paradata users' need to think but to provide them with maps and navigational aids. A crucial decision is to choose methods and approaches that are likely to be most helpful and possible to implement.

8.3 Mindset

The limits to which paradata can be operationalised in knowledge organisation point to another parallel perspective to paradata. We are inclined to see paradata as a lens or mindset that makes it possible to expand and refine our understanding of what can and needs to be known about practices and processes. When framed as a mindset, rather than being a question of finding an exact definition of what paradata is, paradata turns to a question of what data, or in a broader sense, things, can be appropriated to function as paradata.

Instead of claiming that there is too little paradata, thinking of it in terms of mindset directs attention to the question of whether there is indeed enough relevant information even if we might fail to make full use of it. The crisis of a lack of paradata turns to a 'crisis of definition' (cf. Escobar, 1999) of what is capable of functioning as paradata.

As a mindset, it reminds us of how many practices, processes and their underpinnings are never documented explicitly. There is always more to know about data and data-related practices than is ever inscribed in the formal record or embodied in traces of data practices. This evident fact does not mean, however, that having paradata would not matter, or that collecting it would be worthless. Rather it suggests that it is critical to reflect what such incompleteness means in practice and how it should be taken into account when pursuing a better understanding of practices and processes.

In this respect paradata is akin to archaeology, which also unfolds as an illustrative domain and has been remarkably successful in eliciting knowledge about past human practices on the basis of fragmented and incomplete (para) data. Archaeologists have developed methods to stitch together evidence, identifying marks of use in physical artefacts, using analogies, and experimentation to understand past practices and processes.

Fundamentally, thinking of paradata in terms of a mindset is a matter of developing a methods discourse for data reuse and practice in order to process knowledge in different research contexts. This is crucial everywhere but especially in domains where such discussion has so far remained unarticulated. Knowing how to discuss such matters entails a particular set of literacies and competencies, in a much broader sense than how data literacy is portrayed in a part of the literature (Koltay, 2015) as a straightforward skillset of being able to work with and understand a thing called data.

Rather it requires a comprehensive insight into the interrelation of data creation and reuse (Kansa and Kansa, 2021): a helix Mathieu and Pruulmann-Vengerfeldt (2020) describe in communication research as a data loop. It goes beyond the ability to collect and analyse data to master its effects, opportunities and constraints across domains and time. It incorporates both encoding and decoding of data and acknowledging that data users are also encoders (cf. Livingstone, 2019; Mathieu, 2023).

As a mindset paradata does also remind everyone engaged in working with data of the importance, to be '*involved* in the capturing, processing, and linking of any data they plan to use for their work' (Christen and Schnell, 2024, p. 7) (added emphasis). As discussed in Chapter 6, data literacies that incorporate a paradata mindset turn, like information literacies (Hicks et al., 2023; Lloyd, 2010; Tuominen et al., 2005), into meshworks of interlinked and overlapping practices of being with data.

Further, as suggested in Chapter 3, there are thresholds both in relation to how and when paradata is technically and epistemically useful and for whom. Such thresholds are built into data literacies but are also something data literacies can help to overcome. We have touched upon multiple aspects of such literacies in this volume from what types of things it applies to and where they can be found in Chapter 3, to methods, approaches and competences to master, to generate, identify and curate in Chapters 4–6.

8.4 Limits and Ethics of Paradata

Acknowledging that paradata materialises as a distinct form of mindset, literacy and practice obliges us to turn attention to where paradata ends and what might be its associated risks. We have already recognised that rather than assuming that paradata is a universal remedy, straightforward to achieve, and uncontroversial in practice, paradata should be approached as a form of critical practice.

Implementing paradata through standards and blanket expectation to produce comprehensive documentation leads easily to what Stengers (2018) describes, aptly considering the acronym of our project, in terms of a *capture*. Capture is for Stengers a situation in which the dominant institutions of research, or more broadly in case of paradata data work, lead to mediocrity and a sincere belief that a particular representation is genuinely consistent with a particular practice or process. A capture of practices and processes in the spirit of an 'ideology of information management' (Kamin, 2023, p. 191), substituting them with descriptions comes with a risk of an increasing sense of estrangement from the practices and processes themselves.

However, working with paradata does not need to follow dataism in its 'belief in the objective quantification and potential tracking of all kinds of human behaviour and sociality' (Van Dijck, 2014, p. 198). Embracing paradata as a form of critical practice and critique of itself, renders it capable of facilitating the opposite: to question and problematise itself and its premises, to learn and change. Doing so is hardly effortless and not a problem solvable with technology even at the time when the lightning fast development of artificial intelligence techniques has again put many old assumptions of the capabilities of technical systems to a question. At best, paradata is a partial solution. It is vital to be realistic with one's expectations of what and how it can be a useful tool. Otherwise it easily raises hopes of being capable of doing more than it can deliver.

A parallel question relating to the limits of paradata pertains to its social consequences. Just as transparency and openness are difficult to argue against in general terms, paradata also becomes easily shrouded in a veil of hard-to-criticise consensus. While much of the documenting and preservation of information on data-related practices and processes is beneficial, unveiling individuals and their practices can also have adverse effects. They can be used to harm people even beyond those individuals and groups who have participated in data practices and consented to be involved, documented and preserved. This applies both to living beings and non-living things and for example, in case of cultural and natural resources like archaeological sites or nature reserves, their combinations, all deserving protection and care.

In research with human subjects, paradata can expose study participants, individuals related to them and their activities, data collectors, and researchers in ways that can be difficult to anticipate. It does not require a sudden takeover of an oppressive regime to make paradata dangerous. Even something as seemingly uncontroversial as a new paradigm of measuring the effectiveness of data work can turn paradata into an instrument of exploitation and unjust treatment. Moreover, even if paradata would be harmless alone, when brought together and combined with other available information, the meshwork of paradata can have unintended consequences both at the present and in the future.

The fact that paradata can also cause damage should be taken as seriously as its possible benefits. Leonelli and Williamson (2023) advocate for data linkage that covers technical and legal infrastructures, guidelines and mechanisms for follow-up, and an open mindset for different perspectives to what constitutes good, bad and acceptable. There is critical need for a comparable 'responsible practice' in paradata.

Just as paradata as a whole is a complicated matter, its consequences are too complicated to anticipate and consequently, to be dismissed at the outset. While releasing paradata should not be restricted beyond reason, it is important to acknowledge that making and keeping paradata is a matter of trust and responsibility. Finding parallels to paradata, what it can achieve and where its limitations are is demanding. It can perhaps be compared to a certain extent to patents that ideally provide a mechanism to open information while retaining a necessary level of control of its particularly pertinent aspects and implications. As with the requirement of documenting practices and processes, the mechanisms to disclose them should be weighted against both imaginable and unimaginable risks and provide necessary protections to plausible social, political, epistemic and economic concerns in the particular contexts and situations. Only in carefully considered cases should they be made a non-negotiable requirement.

8.5 Conclusions

In the closing of this volume, it is evident that there are many loose threads to follow in the future. The question of (para)data literacy is only one of them. This book and our work in the CAPTURE project and the parallel work of colleagues elsewhere has obviously only started to provide insights into paradata and the broader questions of understanding and documenting, preserving and utilising information on data-related practices and processes.

Even if paradata is situated and deeply contextual, our aim with this volume has been to focus on issues that have resonance in multiple domains. However, as much of the empirical work conducted on paradata in the context of the CAPTURE project focused on archaeology, it is undoubtedly overrepresented here and in our conclusions. Therefore, even if we still believe that archaeology in its diversity and cross-disciplinarity provided us a useful starting point to inquire into paradata, we anticipate that future studies of paradata in specific domains will produce new knowledge that can further nuance the understanding of paradata and provide actionable insights in those contexts. Rather than helping to develop a blanket solution, archaeology has probably worked best as a healthy reminder of how such panaceas do not exist. Not only every field of research and practice but also diverse varieties of data making, management and use as particular types of undertakings have their own often contradicting priorities. They all deserve to be taken seriously from their very own premises.

In this volume we have shown how it can function both as a referent to a particular category of things that can be appropriated as informative about practices and processes but also as a mindset to aid thinking about practices, processes, their underpinnings and implications. For the time being, paradata is unquestionably a factish (Latour, 2011; Stengers, 2018), a preliminary term used to refer to a phenomenon but also perhaps a figuration (Braidotti, 2011; Haraway, 1992) in how it materialises an arrangement of ideas about practices and processes.

We are not sure if it is going to stick, if it will or should be replaced by something else, and (or) how it will evolve in the future. What we do think, however, is that the question of how to understand and document processes and practices of making, processing and using cultural artefacts is crucial to understanding how they are knitted and are knitting themselves into the social fabric. For doing so, we need appropriate concepts but also a lot of empirical work.

After investigating paradata with data creators and users, we have also observed that data management practices and data repositories are sites with a crucial impact to paradata. An earlier comprehensive body of work has developed means to document and preserve information on processes and transformations in the curatorial context, including curatorial provenance and management metadata. However, what remains less explored is how curatorial work and data governance and its underpinning political and normative ideals affects paradata in practice. The same applies to wider contexts of paradata in relation to how exactly it works in the intricate meshwork of social reality.

References

Agre Philip (1997). Toward a critical technical practice: Lessons learned in trying to reform AI. In Bowker Geoffrey et al. (eds.), *Social Science, Technical Systems, and Cooperative Work: Beyond the Great Divide.* Mahwah, NJ: Lawrence Erlbaum, 131–158.

Braidotti Rosi (2011). *Nomadic Subjects: Embodiment and Sexual Difference in Contemporary Feminist Theory,* 2nd ed. Columbia University Press.

Carbajal Itza A. (2021). Historical metadata debt: Confronting colonial and racist legacies through a post-custodial metadata praxis. *Across the Disciplines* 18(1-2), 91–107.

Christen Peter and Schnell Rainer (2024). When data science goes wrong: How misconceptions about data capture and processing causes wrong conclusions. Harvard Data Science Review 6(1).

Eichner Katrina C. L., Campbell Renae J. and Warner Mark S. (2024). Archaeological collections and the public: It isn't all about us. *Advances in Archaeological Practice* 12(1), 43–52.

Escobar Arturo (1999). After nature: Steps to an antiessentialist political ecology. *Current Anthropology* 40(1), 1–30.

Haraway Donna (1992). Ecce homo, ain't (ar'n't) I a woman, and inappropriate/d others: The human in a post-humanist landscape. In Butler J. and Wallach J (eds.), *Feminists Theorize the Political.* Routledge. 86–100.

Hicks Alison et al. (2023). Leveraging information literacy: Mapping the conceptual influence and appropriation of information literacy in other disciplinary landscapes. *Journal of Librarianship and Information Science* 55(3), 548–566.

Huggett Jeremy (2022). Digital Tools or Knowledge Devices? *Introspective Digital Archaeology.* https://introspectivedigitalarchaeology.com/2022/09/29/digital-tools-or-knowledge-devices/.

Huvila Isto (2017). *Being FAIR When Archaeological Information Is MEAN: Miscellaneous, Exceptional, Arbitrary, Nonconformist. In Presentation at the Centre for Digital Heritage Conference 2017,* Leiden June 14–16, 2017.

Huvila Isto (2022). Improving the usefulness of research data with better paradata. *Open Information Science* 6(1), 28–48.

Kamin D. (2023). *Picture-Work: How Libraries, Museums, and Stock Agencies Launched a New Image Economy.* The MIT Press.

Kansa Eric and Kansa Sarah Whitcher (2021). Digital data and data literacy in archaeology now and in the new decade. *Advances in Archaeological Practice* 9(1), 81–85.

Koltay Tibor (2015). Data literacy: In search of a name and identity. *Journal of Documentation* 71(2), 401–415.

Latour Bruno (2011). *On the Modern Cult of the Factish Gods.* Durham, NC: Duke University Press.

Leonelli Sabina and Williamson Hugh F. (2023). Introduction: Towards responsible plant data linkage. In Williamson Hugh F. and Leonelli Sabina (eds.), *Towards Responsible Plant Data Linkage: Data Challenges for Agricultural Research and Development.* Cham: Springer International Publishing, 1–24.

Livingstone Sonia (2019). Audiences in an age of datafication: Critical questions for media research. *Television & New Media* 20(2), 170–183.

Lloyd Annemaree (2010). Framing information literacy as information practice: site ontology and practice theory. *Journal of Documentation* 66(2), 245–258.

Mathieu David (2023). Deconstructing the notion of algorithmic control over datapublics. In Møller Hartley Jannie, Sørensen Jannick Kirk and Mathieu David (eds.), *DataPublics: The Construction of Publics in Datafied Democracies*. Bristol: Bristol University Press, 27–48.

Mathieu David and Pruulmann-Vengerfeldt Pille (2020). The data loop : How audiences and media actors make datafication work. *MedieKultur* 69, 116–138.

Pasquetto Irene V., Randles Bernadette M. and Borgman Christine L. (2017). On the reuse of scientific data. *Data Science Journal* 16(8), 1–9.

Pomerantz Jeffrey (2015). *Metadata*. Cambridge, MA: MIT Press.

Stengers Isabelle (2018). *Another Science Is Possible: A Manifesto for Slow Science*. Cambridge: Polity.

Tuominen K., Savolainen R. and Talja S. (2005). Information literacy as a socio-technical practice. *The Library Quarterly* 75(3), 329–345.

Van Dijck Jose (2014). Datafication, dataism and dataveillance: Big data between scientific paradigm and ideology. *Surveillance & Society* 12(2), 197–208.

Van Geenen Daniela, Van Es Karin and Gray Jonathan W. Y. (2024). Pluralising critical technical practice. *Convergence* 30(1), 7–28.

Wilkinson, Mark D. et al. (Mar. 2016). The FAIR guiding principles for scientific data management and stewardship. *Scientific Data* 3, 160018.

Index

9 781009 366618